BUSINESS STUDIES

Peter Fearns has wide experience in industry and teaching. As former chief examiner for A level Business Studies at the AEB, and an HMI in Business Studies, he helped to formulate the BTEC National module 'The Organisation in its Environment', and was consultant to the BBC/BTEC series *Business World*. He is currently Principal of Burton on Trent Technical College.

TEACH YOURSELF

BUSINESS STUDIES

Peter Fearns

Hodder & Stoughton

A MEMBER OF THE HODDER HEADLINE GROUP

British Library in Cataloguing in Publication Data
Fearns, Peter
Business Studies – 4 Rev. ed.
(Teach Yourself series)
I. Title   II. Series
650

ISBN 0 340 56825 9

First published 1980
Second edition 1984
Third edition 1987
Fourth edition 1992
Impression number   11 10 9 8 7 6 5 4
Year   1998 1997 1996 1995

Photoset by Rowland Phototypesetting Ltd, Bury St Edmunds, Suffolk.
Printed in Great Britain for Hodder & Stoughton Educational,
a division of Hodder Headline Plc, 338 Euston Road, London NW1 3BH
y Cox & Wyman Ltd, Reading, Berks.

CONTENTS

PREFACE

'Business Studies' deals with many different organisations and includes a wide variety of subjects. The key to understanding 'Business' activity is to learn how different organisations and the range of business disciplines are related and integrated. The aim of this book is to provide the foundations for such understanding.

The text links five disciplines: Economics, Accountancy, Law, Government and Administration. *Economics* is similar to Business Studies in that it draws upon a wide variety of concepts and topics such as public finance, inflation, unemployment and international trade, and all these are included in the text. In addition, the resources which are required by business, and the relationship between market forces are analysed. *Accountancy* is dealt with as a traditional business subject which provides the techniques for analysing and controlling business performance. Information on *Law and Government* covers the legal, political and constitutional framework of business activity. The text not only includes government intervention into private organisations, but also the business of Government itself: the provision of social services, the administration of government regulations and the commercial activity of public corporations are treated as subdivisions of Business Studies. The principles from the less well known disciplines of *Administration* and *Supervisory Studies* run through the text. Business functions such as personnel management, financial control, production and marketing, common to all public and private organisations, are also included.

Business organisations draw together the various disciplines which make up Business Studies and the book highlights how this is done. Similarly the text shows how organisations work together and are interrelated.

Integration of the subject matter is achieved by several features: firstly, by giving many examples which illustrate the relationship of the disciplines to all types of organisation; secondly, by providing cross-references which show the interrelationship of the chapters; and thirdly, by including a comprehensive index, to help further study of particular topics.

The book is a practical introduction to Business Studies; it is particularly appropriate for those who are studying for a BTEC qualification or GCE 'A' level in Business Studies. The text covers all of the course specifications of the BTEC National level core unit 'The Organisation in its Environment'; it includes some specifications of the core units 'People in Organisations' and 'Finance'. It also covers the syllabus of the AEB Business Studies 'A' level.

The book provides a sound basis for the evaluation of business problems and the analysis of the business environment. Students should use the book as a basic text but, in addition, should refer to textbooks of the various disciplines, as well as read newspapers and journals and obtain current ideas and information from television and radio. This requirement of wider reading applies particularly to the assignments which are included in the book. The assignments present ideas for developing and assessing the learning of Business Studies; it is hoped that they will be accepted and used in this spirit.

Business Studies is a dynamic subject which requires constant observation of current business activities. The book emphasises the nature of change, and at the same time gives students an insight into the spirit of modern society; it complements other social studies by attempting to provide a better understanding of the social and economic environment.

Preface to the Fourth Edition

Business Studies reflects the modern world, and so this revised edition incorporates many changes which have taken place in economics, politics and society over the past ten years. For example, the government's policies relating to privatisation in British industry, developments in the EEC and the Exchange Rate Mechanism are included in the text. Similarly the information on business practices in strategic planning, the management of quality and industrial training has been brought up to date.

When teaching yourself Business Studies it is important to find out how much you have learned and to relate your knowledge to previous chapters. To help you plan and develop your learning there are sets of questions and a project at the end of each chapter. The tasks are divided into three types.

The first type, **comprehension exercises**, test your knowledge and understanding of the main elements. After reading a chapter you should be able to answer these shorter questions; if you find this difficult then refer back to the information in the chapter.

The second set of tasks are **research exercises**, and before you attempt these you should look for information from different sources to support your work. The exercises test your skill in analysing and evaluating business issues and you will need to have read other textbooks, recent newspaper articles and business journals as well as watched and listened to appropriate programmes on television and radio.

Each chapter includes a **project** which is designed to bring together your knowledge and understanding of Business Studies from different aspects. For many of the projects you will need to collect information over a period of time and to use your skills in research: in finding out about business activities. These projects, together with the comprehension and research exercises, provide a foundation on which you can develop business skills and build your understanding of the business environment.

PART ONE

The Nature of Business Organisations

—— INTRODUCTION ——

The range of business organisations which exist today is extremely wide and includes public service institutions such as hospitals and local and central government as well as the regular business activities such as banking, farming and manufacturing.

Almost all organisations serve society in general or serve specific sectors of society. The food we eat, the clothes we wear, the form of transport we use and the type of house we live in have been provided by organisations. So, as customers or clients, we obtain benefits from organisations in the form of goods and services.

The relationship which most individuals have with organisations is two-way. Everyone is a consumer and most people are also engaged by organisations to work to produce either goods or services. Working people are producers as well as consumers.

The first part of this book examines the aims, formation, structure and obligations of organisations by looking at some of the main characteristics which organisations have in common. Not all characteristics are considered fully here (for example, the resources employed by organisations are examined in Part 2), but the list below provides an overview which is expanded in the following chapters.

1 Organisations have a purpose – aims. Organisations are established to meet a need in society. In meeting that need some organisations will set very definite and clear aims: for example, a manufacturing firm will want to stay in business and make a profit. Other organisations, such as hospitals or social services, will tend to react to changes in society rather than decide on specific aims (except the general aim of improving the effectiveness and efficiency of the services offered).

2 Organisations employ resources. All organisations employ people, they use consumables such as stationery and raw materials, and they have various types of plant and equipment as well as buildings.

3 Organisations have a formal structure. Each person in an organisation will be given a position in the organisational structure. The formal structure is often an hierarchical pyramid, as illustrated in Fig. 3.1, p. 27.

4 Organisations have to be directed and controlled. The function of managers and supervisors in an organisation is to acquire and control human and other resources in the organisation with the objective of implementing the policy of the business. Examples common to all organisations are the recruitment of staff and delegation of duties, financial control, and the purchase of equipment.

5 Organisations are accountable. Most organisations are responsible for their actions and decisions to some form of authority:

   public companies to shareholders
   civil servants to government ministers
   local authority officials to elected representatives
   governments to the electorate

6 Organisations have to meet legal requirements. All organisations which employ people have to comply with employment regulations dealing with recruitment, conditions of work and dismissal. Those organisations which sell goods have to meet legal requirements for consumer protection, and the actions of all private organisations are limited by company legislation.

Further characteristics of commercial organisations

Private organisations and nationalised industries in a mixed economy have some additional common characteristics:

7   Commercial organisations are subject to some form of competition.   The degree of competition varies from one industry to another.

8   The government intervenes in commercial organisations. The extent and nature of government intervention is influenced by the political party which is in power: a socialist government is much more inclined to intervene, but all governments will impose taxes and controls.

1

THE FORMATION AND
– CLASSIFICATION OF –
ORGANISATIONS

Organisations work within a legal framework. The nature and extent of the framework varies from the very formal, in which public limited liability companies operate, to the less formal rules which govern the operations of a social club.

—— The creation of organisations ——

Business organisations have their own legal identity which is separate from its members: an organisation is, in effect, an artificial 'person'. It can make contracts and can sue and be sued. This legal identity is acquired when businesses become incorporated associations; and 'incorporation' is the main method organisations use to establish themselves.

Private corporations

Registration under the Companies Act is the most common method whereby private firms become incorporated. The types of private company which can be created under company legislation are:

Public Limited Liability Company. Members of the general public can purchase shares in the company through the Stock Exchange.

Private Limited Liability Company. The shareholding of private companies is restricted: the public cannot subscribe for shares in private companies. The members of such companies tend to be families or small groups.

Both of these types of company have limited liability, which means that the personal liability of the owners is restricted. Unlimited liability would mean that in the event of loss all the members would be liable for all debts, and they might have to sell their private possessions (houses, cars, etc.) to repay the debts. Limited liability restricts a member's loss to the amount of money he or she has invested in the company.

The advantages of limited liability are that it:

(a) Limits the extent of an investor's risk and therefore encourages investment generally.
(b) Encourages institutions with funds such as insurance companies and trade unions to make investments.
(c) Attracts finance into high-risk ventures which under unlimited liability would not be considered.

Limitation on liability varies in the following ways:

1 Company limited by share. This is the most common type of limited liability and occurs when the extent of the members' risk is limited to the amount of their shareholdings. All companies quoted on the Stock Exchange are in this category.

2 Company limited by guarantee. In this instance shares are not purchased by members, but an incorporated association is formed and the members guarantee to provide a certain sum if the company is wound up at a loss. This type of formation is generally found in non-profit-making undertakings, such as trade associations.

3 Unlimited companies. Corporations can choose not to have the advantages of limited liability. This generally occurs in organisations where any liability would be small.

Public corporations

Public corporations are created either by Royal Charter or, more commonly, by special Act of Parliament (statute). The main public corporations are the nationalised industries and local authorities. The owners of public corporations are, in effect, the general public and the question of limiting liability does not arise: in the event of loss by a public corporation the State has unlimited liability.

Rules and relationships of companies

When a limited liability company is formed, the law requires the organisation to provide details of the nature of the association between its members, and information about its external relationships with other bodies. These details are contained in two documents: the Articles of Association and the Memorandum of Association.

The Articles of Association: internal rules of companies

The nature of the association between members can vary, but the Articles will always provide details of: *(a)* the nominal capital; *(b)* when and how shareholders' meetings are to be conducted, and the voting rights of members; *(c)* how profits and losses will be distributed; *(d)* the directors' names; and *(e)* how directors will be appointed and the nature of their authority.

The Articles of Association are a contract between the company and its members in respect of their ordinary rights as members.

The Memorandum of Association: external relationships of companies

The Memorandum of Association defines the constitution and powers of the company and the scope of its activities. It is the document which ensures that the stated aims of the company are legal and proper, and must include: *(a)* the name of the company, including the word 'Limited'; *(b)* the address of the registered office; *(c)* a statement of the company's aims; *(d)* the amount of capital the company wishes to raise; and *(e)* a statement that the shareholders' liability is limited.

Unincorporated associations

Unincorporated associations are the least formal type of association and they have far fewer legal obligations than corporations. The most common form of unincorporated association in business is a partnership, although employers' associations, trades unions and social clubs are also created in this way.

− The different types of organisation −

The legal framework in which organisations are formed, described above, has led to the establishment of many different types of organisations in both public and private sectors. The following provides brief details of the legal requirements each type of organisation faces in its creation and operation.

——— Private ownership ———

1 Sole traders

These are businesses which are owned by a private person who uses his own money to run the business. Consequently the sole trader is entitled to all the profits, but he must also bear any losses which are incurred. A sole trader has no legal obligation to make his accounts publicly available: and he is responsible for the day-to-day management of the business. Examples of sole traders are small shopkeepers, jobbing builders, plumbers and hairdressers.

2 Partnerships

These are unincorporated associations and the legal rules which govern them were established in the Partnership Act of 1890. A partnership does not have a separate existence from its members, the numbers of which can range from two to 20. The partners provide the finance for the organisation, and the profits and losses will normally be shared in an agreed proportion depending on the individual's contribution to the partnership. Partners have unlimited liability: each partner is jointly liable with the other partners for any debts. Like sole traders, there is no legal obligation for partners to publish their accounts.

Well-known examples of partnerships occur in the professions, such as solicitors, accountants and estate agents.

3 Private limited companies

This type of organisation is incorporated by the Companies Act 1948–85. The number of members can range from two to 50 and they provide the financial resources for the undertaking. Membership of the company is restricted to private individuals. The profits are distributed to the members as dividends on their shareholding. Losses are borne by the company. Private limited companies are often local family businesses and are common in the building, retailing and clothing industries.

4 Public limited companies

Public limited liability companies, despite their name, are the best known form of *private* company. They are corporations and obtain their share capital from members of the public. Profits are distributed as dividends to shareholders and the liability of members is restricted to their shareholdings.

Most industries include public limited liability companies and many of them, by developing a corporate image, have become household names: Barclays, Sainsbury, GEC, Ford and British Airways are public limited companies.

Some public limited companies have developed into massive organisations such that a few private corporations are as large as some sovereign states. In recent years two types of large private corporation have evolved, although the distinction between the two is not clear-cut:

(a) *Multi-national corporations.* A multi-national company is a private 'holding' company with shares in many overseas subsidiary companies. The head office of a multi-national is located in a host country and its operations will be carried out by different combinations of subsidiary companies located in different countries. Each company within the holding will be subject to the company law of the country where it is located. Companies within a multi-national are connected by share ownership and by managerial control. Examples of multi-nationals which operate in Britain are:
British – Cadbury-Schweppes, Hanson and Unilever.
European – VW, Nestles, Siemens, Philips and Shell.
United States – IBM, ITT, ESSO, Mars and Ford.

(b) *Conglomerate companies.* These can have extensive overseas operations and may therefore be multi-national, but a conglomerate is strictly a company which deals with a wide range of different products. In practice the normal conglomerate is a holding company which is the major shareholder in a series of non-complementary subsidiary firms. An example of a British conglomerate is the Rank Organisation, which owns subsidiary companies trading separately in films, bread, hotels, dance halls and office copiers.

Public ownership

1 Public corporations – nationalised industries

Public corporations are created by Parliament and owned by the State, although loan stock can be issued to the general public to raise capital. Any surpluses which are obtained on trading belong to the State, but for the most part such 'profits' are mainly used to finance capital investment projects or to keep down prices. In the event of any losses the State bears unlimited liability. The government minister whose department is responsible for the industry appoints the board and its chairman, and the day-to-day running of the corporation is in the hands of these appointees.

Some key industries in Britain, such as coal and railways, are publicly owned. However, in the 1980s the Conservative Government pursued a policy of privatisation of the public sector, and sold the Government's shareholdings in several nationalised industries including British Telecom, British Aerospace, the National Freight Company, British Gas and other public utilities.

2 Public corporations – local authorities

Before 1986, there were four principal types of local authority: District Councils, Shire Counties, Metropolitan Counties and Metropolitan Boroughs. In 1986 the Government abolished the Greater London Council and the Metropolitan Counties and their functions were transferred to the existing Borough Councils or to a system of Joint Boards.

The County Councils are the major providers of local government services. On average they have budgets which are fifty times bigger than

District Councils and are responsible for 85% to 90% of local government expenditure.

3 Central government departments

Public corporations do not employ civil servants. The Civil Service administers central government departments. Central government, like local government, provides a range of services in such areas as trade, employment, education, social services, defence and foreign affairs. New departments are frequently formed and old departments merged or even abolished to meet new problems and new pressures. For example, in recent years departments have been formed to deal with prices, energy, social security and the environment.

The income of central government is obtained through taxation and government borrowing, and the level of public expenditure is decided by the Government. Profits and losses do not occur: departments under-spend or overspend.

4 QUA(N)GOs

These are quasi-autonomous (non- or national-) governmental organisations such as the Medical Research Council, the Commission for Racial Equality or the Commonwealth Development Corporation. There are three kinds of QUANGO: executive bodies, advisory bodies and tribunals. Executive bodies, such as the Civil Aviation Authority, generally employ their own staff and control their own finances. Advisory bodies and tribunals do not normally employ full-time staff, and their expenditure is paid for by the relevant government department.

—— Dissolution of organisations ——

Private companies which fail to achieve their aims and objectives and make successive losses are eventually wound up. This is a legal process which can take three forms:

1 **Compulsory liquidation.** Winding-up by order of the Court usually occurs when the company is unable to pay its debts when required by its creditors. It can also occur if statutory requirements such as the

holding of a shareholders' meeting are not met, or when the company fails to begin business within one year of incorporation.

2   Voluntary liquidation.   In this instance, the members pass a 'special resolution' agreeing to dissolve the Association. If the company is unable to continue in business, then dissolution will occur when the members pass an 'extraordinary resolution'.

3   Winding-up under the supervision of the Court.   Even when members have passed a resolution to wind up voluntarily, the Court may still order that dissolution shall take place under the supervision of the Court and in this instance the Court may appoint a liquidator in addition to the liquidator appointed by the company.

Exercises

Comprehension

1   What is the difference between a public limited liability company and a private limited liability company?

2   List the items which are included in a Memorandum of Association.

3   Find five examples of partnerships which operate in your locality.

4   Find five examples of multi-national companies which operate in your area.

5   Define and give examples of a QUANGO.

Research

1   Explain why different types of organisation exist.

2   Examine the difference between Articles of Association and a Memorandum of Association.

3   Evaluate the role of sole traders in the retail sector of the economy.

Project

Collect newspaper cuttings relating to companies which have recently gone into liquidation and compile a report analysing the reasons for the failure of these businesses.

2

THE AIMS AND
——— POLICIES OF ———
ORGANISATIONS

——— Different contributions ———
by organisations

Private organisations are formed mainly to provide for material wants and commercial needs in society, and so manufacturing and commerce dominate the private sector of British industry. Government organisations, on the other hand, tend to satisfy society's need for defence, law and order, management of the economy, education and social welfare. Organisations can only exist if they respond to needs and wants, and therefore their aims are primarily to satisfy the needs and wants of people, either directly or indirectly, or through meeting the needs of other organisations.

There is a distinction between an aim and an objective. *Aims* tend to be long-term, they indicate intentions rather than specific goals. *Objectives*, however, are more specific, and generally they can be measured. The attainment of profit illustrates this difference. The best-known aim of a private organisation is its desire to obtain, and possibly maximise, its profits. But this is not a clear-cut goal because *(a)* profitability is sometimes difficult to assess; and *(b)* short-term losses are sometimes incurred to bring about long-term profitability (for example price reductions which can undercut and eventually eliminate a competitor).

A company will convert the *aim* of profitability into a more specific *objective* such as to obtain a 15% return on capital during twelve months' trading.

The aims of an organisation are normally decided by the board of directors. The policies of an organisation clarify the aims and establish long-term plans. The conversion or implementation of an organisation's policy into specific objectives and tasks is the role of administrators and managers, and the process gives rise to the sequence shown in Fig. 2.1.

Set Aims ⟶ *Decide* **Policy** ⟶ *Organise* **Tactical Action**
Long-term plans   Set short-term
                                     departmental
                                     objectives

Fig. 2.1   The administrative process

—— Aims of private organisations ——

Shareholders and owners ensure that profitability is a main aim of private organisations, but the profit motive can obscure the fact that businesses are groups of people and each person in an organisation may have a desire to get prestige from the growth and size of the firm as well as satisfy a basic need for job security. The influence of employees on an organisation's aims is very strong. This point is most important because evidence in the published literature of companies shows that most companies have several different aims which may become clear long-term goals in themselves, with profitability being a measure of success rather than an ultimate goal. Examples of these other aims are:

1 **Survival.** A desire to remain in business almost at all costs is frequently illustrated by workers taking over insolvent organisations. Job security also dominates the activities of managers who, when a firm is in financial difficulties, will appeal to the Government for help and at the same time declare a belief in private enterprise.

2 **Increasing the share of the market.** Expansion of the company's activities is often good for the morale of employees and share-

holders, although it can lead to problems of administration and lower profitability.

3   Prestige – improving the company image.   Many companies will develop customer and public relations in the hope of creating a 'status' image. The desire to obtain a Queen's Award for Industry illustrates this aim.

4   Cash flow.   Some firms will aim to maintain a constant flow of cash into the company so that working capital is always available. Working capital is often more important than profitability, although the two are obviously interlinked.

The wide range of personal goals, expectations and decisions which exist in a firm make it very likely that the most significant aims of a private organisation will be influenced by the people within the organisations.

__ Aims of government departments __ and local authorities

The aims of government departments and local authorities are laid down by statute, and each organisation within the public sector has legal obligations to provide certain services. For example, the Department for Education, through the Local Education Authorities, provides compulsory education for children between the ages of five and 16 years. The provision is the responsibility of the LEAs, and the maintenance of educational standards is the responsibility of the DE.

Government departments and local authorities thus have their aims much more clearly defined than private companies. They are not in business to make a profit; they acquire their funds primarily through taxation and so do not have the yardstick of profitability with which to measure success. However, techniques have been developed in recent years which enable government bodies to clarify the aims of a particular project or service.

Policy formulation

Policy provides a definition of what people in organisations must or must not do. For example, the pricing policy of the nationalised industries is defined by the Government. The investment policy of a public limited liability company will be decided by the board of directors. The policies of government departments are established by the Cabinet.

Policy decisions affect all aspects of an organisation. They provide a guide for further decision-making and are a framework for organisational activity. In private organisations the policy decisions will be written in the Memorandum and Articles of Association, and they will also be contained in previous decisions of the Board. In government organisations policy is mainly laid down by statute, but guidelines are also given through rules and regulations which are composed by ministers with the help of senior civil servants.

Policy decisions in organisations

There is a relationship between the aims and objectives of an organisation and its policy decisions. Similarly there is a relationship between the long-term plans of a firm and its policy framework. The formulation of policy will be integrated into strategic plans.

Many firms will design corporate plans for the organisation based on a systematic study of the company's long-term objectives. In such a study the company is considered as a whole rather than as a collection of departments. Policy may be redefined to meet aims and long-term objectives.

This corporate approach can be summarised as shown in Fig. 2.2.

Set Aims ⟶ *Decide* Policy ⟶ *Organise* ⟶ *Appraise* the
Long-term   Strategic   **Tactical Action**   **Process**
corporate   planning   Set short-term   Evaluate the
objectives   objectives   success of plan

Fig. 2.2 The planning process

Policy decisions: strategic planning areas

The range of policy decisions is extremely wide since, by definition, policy provides a framework for all organisational activity. The following examples illustrate this wide range:

1 **Human resources policy.** People are the most important asset in an organisation, and many institutions will have a policy on people which will be designed to meet the long-term needs of the organisation while also meeting the requirements of employment legislation. Manpower policies deal with the selection and recruitment of people, training and promotion programmes, and dismissal procedures. For example, the policy will indicate whether the promotion of employees will primarily be from within the organisation or by recruitment from outside. Similarly, policy decisions will be made as to where the education and training of staff will take place: it could be within the firm or provided by outside agencies. The main features of the policy will be the estimates of the numbers of people the organisation will need, and the type of experience and qualifications future employees will require.

2 **Investment policy.** In private companies, the board of directors will make policy decisions on investment programmes. The Cabinet and ministers will make similar decisions for public organisations. Investment programmes provide new buildings or new plant and equipment, and the extent of an organisation's investment often illustrates the success or failure of previous policy decisions.

3 **Marketing policy.** In private corporations, the Memorandum of Association will provide a guide to the range of a company's activities, and the board of directors will make policy decisions on the mix of products which are to be marketed. For example, a firm might decide to diversify its interests into other fields, just as the Rank Organisation, which in the 1950s was a film distributor, made a policy decision to enter the office copying market with the Xerox Corporation of America and started to produce the market Rank-Xerox machines.

4 **Pricing policy.** Commercial organisations in the public sector are given guidelines by the Government with regard to their pricing policies. Nationalised industries are monopolistic and are given some discretion over the prices they charge. Their monopolistic power gives them greater freedom than private firms which face competition: the more

competitive the market, the less influence an organisation will have on its own prices. There are legal restrictions in the UK on price agreements between firms, but some international producers such as the Organisation of Petroleum Exporting Countries (OPEC) make unified pricing policy decisions.

5 Distribution policy. Organisations have a choice of distributive outlets for their products as well as a choice of transport. Their distribution policy will say whether agencies should be used, where depots should be located, whether the firm should use its own fleet of lorries or subcontract to British Rail or private road hauliers.

Communication of policy decisions

During the establishment of an organisation many policy decisions will be made, but as the organisation grows further policies will be formulated. Very often these on-going policy decisions will not be written into one single document but will be scattered around in various publications. Established policy will be found in: the Memorandum of Association, the Articles of Association, Annual Reports and Company manuals. New policy guidelines will be communicated through: internal memoranda, newsletters, notice boards and external publications.

—— Policy decisions in government ——

Organisations in the public sector which have commercial obligations will adopt very similar policy decisions to firms in the private sector. Non-commercial organisations in the public sector are subject to changes in society and in politics, and they must have policies which enable them to react to change, but generally they do not control their own policies: these are decided for them.

The main function of a government is to formulate policy. Ministers are assisted in this function by the Civil Service, which provides the administrative experience as well as information and research services to help governments decide on policy. The focus of policy formulation is the Cabinet, which is subject to control by Parliament and ultimately the electorate. It is Parliament which enacts the laws in which most public policy is embodied.

Sources of public policy

The policies of a government influence all individuals and all organisations. The nature of parliamentary legislation and its effect on business will vary according to the political party in power, and as far as business is concerned will provide a framework of control with regard to employment, taxes, prices and consumer protection. These controls are implemented by government departments and are in effect their policies.

The main sources for government policy are:

1   The political manifesto.   All political parties have a philosophy which gives rise to principles and theories as to how society and therefore business should be governed. As a general rule in Britain the Conservatives prefer less legislation and interference than the Labour Party.

The philosophy of a political party is influenced by public opinion as well as by members of the party. Political parties which want power must temper their philosophy to meet the wishes of the general public. Thus the pre-election policy statements which parties publish in their manifestos are frequently a compromise between their political philosophy and public opinion.

2   Pressure groups exist inside and outside political parties and all governments find that pressure on policy decisions comes from many sources: trade unions, the CBI, the large banks, professional bodies and other governments are the main sources of such pressure. The objective of a pressure group is to ensure that their interests, and the interests of their members, are considered in policy decisions.

3   The Civil Service.   The degree of influence on public policy formulation by the Permanent Civil Service is open to argument. The British Civil Service does attempt to provide impartial advice to ministers, but past experience as well as the nature of the information provided will have some influence on ministerial decisions.

4   Unforeseen circumstances.   Governments have to react to events. Society has become more complex and more interdependent and this has forced governments to be practical rather than philosophical in their policy decisions. Unforeseen circumstances mean that governments and organisations have to be flexible in policy decisions. The framework of organisational activity can never be static.

Exercises

Comprehension

1 Describe briefly the planning process in organisations.

2 Distinguish between aims and objectives in a business setting.

3 Give examples of the activities of pressure groups which have been in the news recently.

4 Define 'policy formulation'.

5 List the sources of public policy.

Research

1 Compare the aims of private organisations with government organisations.

2 Explain why organisations need to formulate policies.

3 Do you consider that 'survival' is the most important aim of any organisation? Explain your answer.

Project

Obtain a copy of the annual report from three different organisations and compile a list of the differences in aims, policies and reporting methods between the organisations.

3

THE STRUCTURE AND MANAGEMENT OF — ORGANISATIONS: — POLICY IMPLEMENTATION

The purpose of a formal organisation structure is to enable the firm to define objectives for each section or department which will help the organisation achieve its corporate aims; to define the responsibilities in each department in order to ensure that tasks are not duplicated between functions and to coordinate the functions within the organisation so that each department blends its activities with those of other departments to form a corporate strategy.

The functions which are found in organisations vary according to the type of organisation. Government organisations tend to have few functions, such as finance, administration and research. In business generally there are more functions, particularly in those companies which are producing products rather than providing a service. The four functions which are described below are the main ones which exist in most organisations.

The main functions in organisations

1 Production

The creation of a good or service is the most basic function within any organisation, and obviously the type of good or service determines the nature of the production process: coal can only be obtained direct from nature; cereals can only be grown on arable land. It is relatively easy to define the production function in firms which are engaged in primary production or manufacturing, but for those organisations which provide a service the definition of production becomes more complex. This is because the relationship between the producer and the client is part of the production function.

The following are examples of the operation of the production function in some service industries: a doctor examining a patient, a solicitor advising a client, a shopkeeper serving a customer.

2 Marketing

In the above examples, the marketing function is so strongly interrelated with the production function that the two are almost identical: the nature of the shopkeeper's service is both producing and selling, and his technique will influence his customers.

In the primary industries, the marketing function is quite separate from production. The relationship between the marketing department and the production department in manufacturing is closer. The two departments are normally independent within the organisation but will liaise on product design (R&D) and market research, production control and sales forecasts, production costs and selling price, quality control and after-sales service, despatch/transport and packaging.

The nearer an organisation is to tertiary production the stronger is the relationship between marketing and production, so that in the pure service industries the marketing function *is* the production function.

3 Personnel

Even the smallest organisation, public or private, has a personnel function. People are an organisation's main resource. It is the personnel department, with the help of the other departments, which will implement any manpower policies by recruiting, selecting and training all employees. Employee development is a crucial function in organisations.

4 Finance

The use of money is common to all organisations. Financial accounting not only provides records of transactions such as the payment of wages or the purchase of equipment, but also it provides control techniques which show how the organisation is performing. Finance is the common yardstick whereby the use of resources is measured, consequently public and private institutions use the financial accounting in all departments to see how efficient each department is.

—— Formal organisation structures ——

The formal relationship between departments is defined by policies, rules and regulations and is illustrated by the familiar hierarchical organisation chart (Fig. 3.1, opposite).

This traditional form of organisation is the most common form and is found in all kinds of organisation from the army and civil service to ICI. The lines of communication within the organisation are upwards and downwards (normally downwards). In this type of organisation, where instructions are passed along lines in the hierarchy, the functions in the pyramid are called line functions and the system is referred to as *line management*. Some advisory or consultative functions such as research or legal advice often cut across departments and consequently are outside the line framework. These advisory or specialist support services are called staff functions.

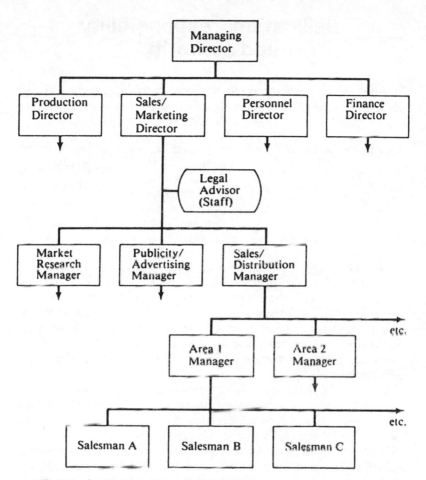

Fig. 3.1 A typical formal organisational structure (pyramid) in a marketing department

Delegation: responsibility _____ and authority

In order to carry out the policy decision, each department and each employee will be given tasks or objectives which will help the organisation to achieve its aims: this is *delegation* (Fig. 3.2, below).

Set **Aims** ➝ *Decide* **Policy** ➝ *Organise* **Tactical** ➝ *Appraise* **the**
Action Process
Set short-term
departmental
objectives and
delegate tasks

Fig. 3.2   The policy implementation process

Very often, departmental objectives are achieved by routine tasks such as filing, recording or assembling. There are few tasks which will be creative or which will require exceptional skill and judgment. Those jobs which do require skill and judgment are normally given greater responsibility and status in the organisation. The people who are employed to lead the organisation are given the greatest responsibility and then all operation will stem from the top: tasks will have been delegated down the pyramid.

Responsibility for tasks cannot be delegated: a superior is always responsible for the actions of his subordinates. For example, government ministers have resigned because they are accountable to Parliament for mistakes made by junior civil servants – mistakes of which the minister had no personal knowledge. Superiors can assign duties and activities which naturally carry responsibility, since the subordinate with his superior will be held accountable if things go wrong. Everyone in an organisation has some responsibility, but this cannot be delegated: the higher a person is in the hierarchy, the more responsibility he will have.

Authority or the right to use power, on the other hand, can be delegated. In a formal structure, this right is defined by the hierarchy, and no one should be given responsibilities which do not correspond to his position in the formal structure. For example, it would be unwise to send a buyer overseas with the responsibility for acquiring expensive equipment if he did not have the authority to sign orders.

The informal organisation

Social groups within organisations create informal pressure because their own beliefs, objectives and aspirations can sometimes conflict with the organisation's objectives. This type of activity is referred to as 'the informal organisation'. Informal behaviour is often different from, and can be opposed to, the needs and expectations of the formal organisation. For example, a board of directors might decide, on economic grounds, that a firm should be relocated from London to Liverpool, but evidence shows that informal pressure by the directors' wives to remain in London will probably have more influence on the decision than formal business arguments. In policy decisions, all organisations must recognise that the implementation of the policy is a subtle and complicated process, and decision-makers should consider the nature of informal organisational pressure on policy implementation.

Management principles in policy implementation

There are principles which have evolved during the twentieth century which provide basic rules on how policy should be implemented. Managers are often experts in a particular departmental function such as finance or marketing, but nevertheless the basic principles of policy implementation will apply to each and every manager. The following list was first produced by Henri Fayol (1841–1925), who was one of the pioneers of management thought and organisation theory.

1 Planning

Policy formulation is undertaken by people who are at the top of the organisation's hierarchy. For example, in private enterprise the board of directors makes policy decisions; in government departments, the ministers and senior civil servants decide on policy. The first stage in policy implementation is planning (Fig. 3.3). The managers must plan how the organisation's resources are to be used, and this involves setting targets for each department.

Set Aims ⟶ *Decide* Policy ⟶ *Organise* Tactical ⟶ *Appraise* the
            Strategic and   **Action**   **Process**
            long-term   Set short-term
            planning   objectives
                             Departmental
                             planning

Fig. 3.3 Stages in the planning process

Business Plans

The preparation and revision of a Business Plan is a common activity in many different organisations. A Business Plan enables managers to identify the most important features of future activity and in doing so encourages efficient work. The Plan can also be used to raise money: most banks, for instance, insist on seeing a Business Plan when a loan is being considered. The main features of a Business Plan are marketing and finance. At a minimum the Plan should identify the nature of the product or service, the main competitors in the market and a prediction of future sales. Using this prediction a financial statement of revenue and costs can be compiled, and the need for additional resources, such as accommodation or new employees, can be identified.

2 Coordinating

Departmental plans must interrelate with those of other departments. To avoid unnecessary tasks or a duplication of departmental activity, managers must encourage communication between departments. This ensures that corporate action takes place. Communication often takes place through inter-departmental committees, and coordination is one of the main reasons why managers in all types of organisation spend time in committee work.

3 Organising

In order to achieve departmental objectives, a manager will organise people by delegating tasks which have been allocated to the department. Naturally, these jobs will reflect the function of the department: marketing will employ salesmen, finance will employ accountants, production will employ technicians.

The main function of a manager is to get the best out of his subordinates; this implies that he must communicate with them, and communication takes time. Thus the number of subordinates any one manager can supervise is limited by the need to communicate and by the nature of the communication.

A further principle in organising people is the 'unity of command' principle. This means that subordinates should at best report to only one supervisor, and the command over one individual should not be shared between different managers.

4 Staffing

People are the most important resource in an organisation, therefore a manager must ensure through recruitment and selection procedures that the most appropriate people are engaged in the organisation. This means analysing the type of work to be done and deciding on the aptitude, experience and personality which the employee will require. The staffing function also includes schemes for improving and safeguarding the welfare of employees.

5 Directing

Directing does not simply mean issuing orders: once employees have been engaged, a manager must supervise and help them to maximise their potential. Directing people involves frequent communication with them to ensure that they understand the tasks for which they are responsible, and to reward them for work which they have done well. Motivation of employees through direction and guidance is one of the most important managerial functions.

6 Budgeting

Budget standards can be decided at policy level. For example, a production manager might have to meet a certain level of production, a college principal might have to provide a given number of courses within a cash limit, a sales manager might have to achieve a fixed level of sales. In government departments, minimum standards of performance are laid down by statute. For instance, outside the metropolitan areas each County Council must provide a police force and an adequate fire service. On a tactical level, a manager might want to reduce bad debts by 20%. A transport manager might attempt to deliver to customers within seven days instead of ten. In many instances, departmental targets are expressed in, or converted to, financial terms; these budgets are a guide to managerial efficiency.

7 Reporting

The control of policy implementation requires an accurate and speedy flow of information. One function of a manager is to provide facts on his department's performance. This information is processed and the manager is subsequently given feedback on his performance. The analysis of information takes place in all activities: stock levels, output, sales, expenses, etc., and it provides top managers with the facts of control current policy implementation and also helps them to formulate future policy (see Fig. 3.4).

Set →	*Decide* →	*Organise* →	*Appraise* →	*Review*
Aims	**Policy**	**Tactical**	**the Process**	**Policy**
		Action	Reporting	
		Planning		
		Coordinating		
		Organising		
		Staffing		
		Directing		
		Budgeting		

Fig. 3.4 The managerial process

Exercises

Comprehension

1   List the main functions which exist in business organisations.

2   Define 'informal organisation'.

3   Outline the main aspects of a Business Plan.

4   List the main principles of management.

5   Define 'delegation'.

Research

1 Explain what is meant by 'policy implementation'.

2 Do you consider it necessary to distinguish between 'responsibility' and 'authority'? Explain your answer.

3 Explain the difference between formal and informal structures in an organisation.

Project

Construct a diagram which shows the structure of any organisation with which you are familiar.

4

THE ACCOUNTABILITY —— AND SOCIAL —— RESPONSIBILITY OF ORGANISATIONS

In public and private corporations, the main duty of a manager is to satisfy those who own the company. The Board of Directors must satisfy the shareholders that their policies and performance are acceptable. Similarly, the boards of the nationalised industries must satisfy the minister and Parliament that their performance is adequate. If in each case the performance was not satisfactory, then the board or the chair would be asked to resign.

This form of commercial accountability runs through all types of organisations and is an obvious requirement of profit-based institutions. Less obvious is the need for organisations to be responsible to society. Social obligations of publicly-owned institutions are an integral part of their aims and objectives, and they are frequently imposed by law when the organisation is created. There are legal requirements for private organisations which impose social obligations on them – for example, the Health and Safety at Work Act, 1975. However, for private organisations social duty lies beyond legal requirements, and it is the exceptional company which pursues social responsibilities at the expense of commercial considerations.

———— Value systems ————

The balance between a free market system and government intervention is not purely a question of economics or organisational efficiency, it is also an ideological and political issue. In some cases, it is a matter of opinion whether a certain course of action is more effective, efficient or safe. For example, the use of nuclear power rather than other forms of energy is a matter of debate. A value judgment has to be made when factual evidence is not adequate and in such instances the decision about which course of action to follow is based on political philosophy.

——— Competition and planning ———

The free market system encourages competition between organisations. Planning, or a centrally-planned economy, describes a socialist system where State ownership of organisations, as distinct from private ownership, is common. Economic and business activity in the United Kingdom is a mixture of the two. Most of the businesses in Britain are in competition: they operate in a market system. But their activities take place in a local and central government framework which is managed by the State.

In the United Kingdom, privately-owned organisations are not entirely unrestricted. Government intervention takes place for several reasons:

1 Regulation. To ensure minimum standards are upheld by organisations in such areas as pollution and waste disposal, health and safety of employees and consumer relations.

2 Financial restrictions. Taxes such as VAT, Corporation Tax, National Insurance Contributions and local government rates reduce the profits of companies and are levied so that the government can fund welfare activities such as education, health and social security.

3 Public provision. Activities which are related to national security can only be carried out by the Government, so the management of the armed forces and the police is always State controlled.

———— Public ownership policy ————

During the 1980s around fifty State-owned corporations were privatised, i.e. sold by the Government to private shareholders. By 1990 25% of all adults in the UK owned shares compared with only 7% in 1980.

The main sales were:
- 1981 British Aerospace (51%)
- 1982 National Freight
- 1983 British Petroleum
- 1984 British Telecom
- 1985 British Aerospace (49%)
- 1986 British Gas
- 1987 British Airways
- 1988 British Steel
- 1989 Water Authorities

These big, well publicised sales were not the only form of privatisation. During the same period may local authority services, such as rubbish collection, leisure services, catering services and cleaning services were privatised.

The main justification for privatisation is that the businesses will become more efficient, and will respond better to market forces. However, opponents of privatisation argue that many of the organisations remain monopolies and do not have to respond to competition.

———— Private organisations ————

The first responsibility of a private organisation is to the shareholders. The reason why people invest in business is to obtain a return on their capital, and if firms are unable to make profits, then either the company will go into liquidation or the shareholders will find managers who can make a profit.

But private enterprise is an organ of society: it exists to serve society, and social costs do result from private business. The following are examples arising from the interaction between firms and society:

Social benefits
1 The creation of wealth (roads, houses, energy, durable goods, etc.).
2 The provision of employment and job security.
3 The creation of social facilities in health, education and welfare.

Social costs
1 Pollution resulting from industrial activity adds to health risks and to the cost of the NHS.
2 Restrictive practices. Some firms can take advantage of events to improve their profitability at the expense of the customers. For example, increases in the price of oil during 1979 or the change to decimalisation gave some unscrupulous companies the opportunity to charge excessive prices. In all economic transactions, excessive gains are made at someone else's expense.
3 Congestion. High concentrations of business in a locality can lead to transport problems, causing delays and accidents the cost of which, although hidden, will fall on business and society. An example is the congestion on the M25.

The interests of society do not necessary conflict with commercial aims. For example, increases in productivity could result from improvements in morale caused by welfare policies which make provisions over and above the legal requirements in employment protection and health and safety. The problem is to find a balance between normal commercial goals and social goals.

Local authorities and government departments

Government institutions have to operate within a financial framework. The budgets or cash limits which are imposed on government organisations give them responsibilities which are not dissimilar to those of large private organisations. The substantial difference is of course that local authorities and government departments do not make profits: they are given funds from government revenue which they allocate to different (and competing) projects according to political policy.

The social duties of a government institution are frequently laid down by statute. Most local authorities, for example, are required by law to provide services in housing, roads, education and social welfare. In the rare event of a failure to meet statutory requirement, those responsible will be compelled by law to rectify the situation.

With the development of local and central government services, a complex system of checks and balances to ensure the maintenance of standards and the elimination of corruption has evolved. The following is a list of the bodies and procedures which scrutinise government institutions.

1 The electorate. In a democracy, government organisations are accountable to the people. The electorate is the strongest pressure group in the country. During election periods the Government in power has to explain its performance and, if the people are not satisfied, then an alternative government will be given power. In this process, some government organisations can find themselves eliminated.

2 Parliament. The representatives of the people in Parliament systematically examine the performance of government departments. This is done both in the House and in committees. The methods of examination are: Parliamentary Questions, debates in the House, the Public Accounts Committee, the Expenditure Committee and Select Committees (non-financial).

3 Financial control. The Government, in association with the Civil Service, has developed its own committees and techniques for evaluating departmental performance. The three most important are: the Public Expenditure Survey Committee (PESC), Programme Analysis and Review (PAR), and the Central Policy Review Staff (CPRS). These methods of review, and the long-established district and internal audit procedures, maintain financial control on local authorities and government departments, and they make financial accountability an integral feature of policy formulation.

4 Ombudsmen. In recent years Commissioners have been created for Parliament, local government and the Health Service to ensure that maladministration is kept to a minimum. The Commissioners respond to complaints about a particular service and, by insisting on the examination of all relevant documents, have instituted a degree of accountability which private organisations would consider excessive.

—————————— **Exercises** ——————————

Comprehension

1 Define 'market system'.

2 Give three reasons why governments interfere with the market system in the UK.

3 List the ways in which business companies are accountable.

4 Give five examples of competition between firms in your locality.

5 List the industries which were privatised in the 1980s.

Research

1 Explain what is meant by 'social costs'.

2 Examine the benefits and the disadvantages of privatisation.

3 Do you think that private firms have social responsibilities? Explain your answer.

Project

Compile a list of headings which you think should be included in a policy statement on environmental issues to be made by any large organisation.

PART TWO

The Organisation and its Resources

5

———— FINANCE ————

People and organisations do not exist in isolation. They depend on other people and other organisations to produce goods or services for their own needs. In primitive economies, people exchange their products for crops and goods which they need. But this is a clumsy method of exchange. It assumes that an organisation or a person will be able to find someone who not only wants the goods that the organisation has produced, but also has the product or service which the organisation could use. This primitive method of exchange is complicated and it restricted the development of business.

The creation of money made business transactions much easier. Money can be exchanged into any type of good or service, and it is therefore a *medium* of exchange: it 'lubricates' business operations.

———— The functions of money ————

1 Money is a medium of exchange

People will exchange any good or service for money: this is its most important function. In order to be a medium of exchange, money must be acceptable: everyone must have confidence in the medium. Initially, this confidence was created by using metals like gold and silver which in themselves were valuable. The coins, notes and cheques which are used as money today are not in themselves worth what they represent. Nevertheless, they are accepted by everyone in business transactions.

2 Money measures value

The value of goods and services is expressed in money terms so that there is no problem in comparing different products. Money provides a standard measurement in business – an employee knows how much he is worth to an employer; and he also knows the range of products and services his 'worth' will obtain. Similarly, firms can use profit as a measure of success, and by using financial values they have a good idea of the range of expenditure and investment projects which they can undertake. A current problem however, which will be examined later in this chapter, is *inflation*. Constantly-changing prices make money as a measure of value less reliable, especially for comparisons over a period of time.

3 Money can be saved

Money can be stored away and generally it will not deteriorate. Until the 1960s in Britain it was reasonable to claim that money would not lose its value. However, as we have seen, increases in the rate of inflation have made money an unreliable store of value. As a result, many people now look for alternative ways of storing their wealth – by buying items which tend to maintain or even increase their value such as antiques, works of art, or land. It is unwise for a business to keep cash during inflationary periods.

4 Money can record debts

There are many transactions in business when payment is not made straight away. Money gives organisations the facility to record any deferred payments, and to receive the money either in instalments or in one payment at a later date. Inflation makes it unwise to give extended credit to customers, since the business will be losing cash as the value of the debt in real terms decreases. Conversely, most businesses will seek to defer their own payments to suppliers.

5 One-way payments can be made

Government organisations often provide a service when there is no direct exchange taking place. For example, such services as education, health, police and defence do not have to be paid for directly: they are financed out of taxation. Taxes are one-way payments which ensure that only those capable of making the payments actually do so.

Business cannot function without money. It enables all organisations to obtain resources. It enables commercial organisations to earn a reward for their product or service. It enables the government to raise revenue.

_____ The financial needs of _____ organisations

Revenue expenditure: short-term expenditure

The activities of an organisation are a continuous process. Money is flowing in and out of business all of the time. The constant demand which organisations have for resources means that they are constantly faced with expenses. In order to meet these expenses, organisations must obtain revenue from their activities – they must keep the cash flowing.

The flow of cash through commercial organisations is circular, as shown in Fig. 5.1. The money obtained from selling goods or services is used to finance further production. Although the flow of cash never ceases in a viable commercial organisation, at regular intervals the firm will produce, in a profit and loss account, details of the transactions which have taken place. The *Profit and Loss Account* is a summary of the resources a firm has acquired and how they have been allocated during the financial period (usually twelve months).

The Profit and Loss Account

Table 5.1 shows the items which are often included in a profit and loss account and illustrates the main resources which most firms would acquire. The expenses on these resources are then deducted from the income obtained from trading during the same period to give an idea of the profit (or loss) which has been made.

An important point is that a Profit and Loss Account does not show

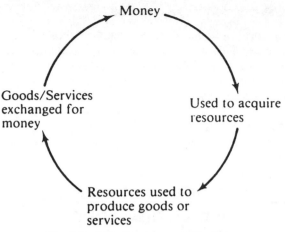

Fig. 5.1 Cash flow in an organisation

whether the flow of income into a business has been sufficient to pay for immediate expenses. Any major delay in receiving money will probably cause a firm to have cash flow problems and run into financial difficulties.

Table 5.1 The Profit and Loss Account and the organisation's resources

Expenditure (£)	*Type of resource (factors of production)*
Stocks of raw materials	Natural resources or producer goods
Wages and salaries	People
Directors' fees	People
Lighting and heating	Energy
Rent and rates	Land
Interest on loans	Capital finance
Hire of plant or leasing	Capital equipment

Capital expenditure: the acquisition of fixed assets

The short-term expenditure of companies loses its value as soon as it is expended. Naturally it helps the firm to earn income, but the payment of rent or electricity bills is a 'one-off' exercise. Where a company spends money but does not obtain a permanent asset, the expenditure is termed 'revenue expenditure'. When a company purchases plant or equipment which will be used over a long period of time, this expenditure is termed 'capital expenditure'.

The distinction between revenue and capital expenditure is not always simple. Clearly the payment of the heating bill is revenue expenditure, and the purchase of a computer is capital expenditure. But there are some items which cannot easily be categorised. For example, any transport costs when using British Rail would be a revenue expense. The purchase of a van to perform the same function, on the other hand, would be a capital expense. Similarly, the leasing or hiring of equipment is revenue expenditure, whereas purchase of the same equipment is capital expenditure.

In spite of the lack of clarity it is apparent that organisations will require large sums of money to purchase long-term assets. Investment in fixed assets is necessary for three main reasons:

1 Expansion and growth. New capital resources in an organisation provide the capacity for expansion. The purchase of more aircraft by an airline, or the construction of more colleges by the Government, allows the 'industry' to grow and output to increase.

2 Efficiency. The replacement of obsolete fixed assets by new machinery or new equipment can help to improve the productivity of an industry. For example, developments in computers have increased the efficiency of many administrative departments. New technology in heavy industries such as steel and ship-building has made the UK's competitors more efficient.

One of the problems with fixed assets as a resource is that their use cannot be changed. Once capital investment has taken place in specific plant, such as a steel rolling mill, the capital cost is so large that the plant has to be employed for many years even when it is obsolete.

3 Increased competitive power. Improved efficiency also improves competitive power. Organisations have to invest in order to be competitive. The above examples of ship-building and steel production are illustrations of the impact of technology on competition.

The need for capital investment creates five main problems for organisations:

(a) How to raise the money. It is unlikely that companies will earn enough revenue to finance their initial capital projects from their own resources.

(b) What balance to have between different sources of finance.

(c) Which alternative investment project to choose.

(d) How to build into the organisation provision for expensive purchases in the future.

(e) What rate of return to try to get on the investment (pricing policy).

—— Sources of commercial finance ——

Commercial organisations will rely on the revenue obtained from sales to pay for the day-to-day running of the firm. Surpluses will be 'ploughed back' into the organisation to finance expensive investment, so that profit can be a major source of finance. Quite frequently, however, firms will require money either in sums larger than their profits or more quickly than their profit is created. In these circumstances, organisations will use additional sources of finance.

Short-term sources of finance and resources

1 **Bank overdrafts** are one of the most common sources of business finance and used for current rather than long-term needs. The amount borrowed varies according to need. Since interest is paid only on the amount overdrawn on the account, the cost of borrowing varies as needs change. Overdrafts provide a flexible source of short-term finance which tends to be cheaper than bank loans.

2 **Bank loans.** A bank loan is a fixed sum which will be paid back during an agreed period. Firms normally take out a bank loan in order to finance a specific long-term project. Loans tend to be more expensive than overdrafts; there is very little flexibility in a loan and the interest charged is often at a higher rate than for overdrafts.

3 **Hire purchase.** Like consumers, firms can acquire goods through hire purchase. In hire purchase a finance company pays for the goods, which are then obtained through a normal supplier. Ownership remains with the finance company until the end of the payment period. The cost of borrowing the money is added to the purchase price, and the debt is then paid in instalments. This is an expensive source of finance, however, and only small businesses tend to use it, mainly when other forms of credit are not available.

4 Leasing is becoming a popular method of acquiring equipment. An operating lease separates the use of equipment from ownership. This contrasts with a mortgage or hire-purchase agreement, where the user either owns the equipment or property from the start of the contract or has the option of acquiring it during or at the end of the payment period. Under an operating lease, the leasing company will hire the equipment to another user. A finance lease, however, is similar to hire purchase in that the user has the option of purchase at the end of the leasing period.

Under a leasing agreement, the cost of the capital equipment is paid for out of revenue expenditure. The advantages of leasing compared to outright purchase are:

(a) No large sums of money are required to obtain capital equipment. This means that the user has a lot of flexibility in the use of fixed assets.

(b) The payments are fixed in advance and this enables the organisation to calculate the true cost of the asset over its expected period of use, and therefore to budget more effectively.

5 Trade credit. The initial capital which is acquired by paying in arrears for goods and services is important to small firms. When firms are in cash-flow difficulties, they can resort to acquiring short-term funds by delaying the payment of bills, by running down stocks, and by not putting income into some form of reserve. During inflation it is profitable to delay the payment of creditors, and of course the money acquired in this way does not bear interest. But it is a practice which has its dangers, in that creditors are suppliers and they could refuse to supply raw materials or producer goods, etc., unless payment is reasonably prompt. Equally, depletion of stocks as well as inadequate reserve funding are measures which could have serious consequences in the long run.

6 Debt factoring is an arrangement which increases the rate of flow of cash into an organisation. Under the arrangement a factoring house 'buys' a firm's (the client's) trade debts as they occur: when the client issues the invoice the factor pays up to 80% of the debt, after deducting charges. The balance of 20% is paid by the factor to the client when the customer pays the factor. By this arrangement, a firm does not have to wait several weeks to obtain revenue from its sales – it can get the greater part almost immediately.

7 Sale of existing assets. Some organisations purchase Government Stock or shares in public companies, and these securities are convertible into cash at quite short notice. Other assets are not necessarily as easy to convert into money, but fixed assets can be a source of finance. Such items as cars, computers and office equipment have reasonable second-hand values.

The ease with which a firm can convert its assets into cash is known as *liquidity*. That is why when a firm is wound up, it goes into liquidation: it sells its assets. The liquidity of an item varies according to its market ability. Fig. 5.2 summarises the degree of liquidity of the more common business assets.

The sale of an asset to raise finance will be influenced by the asset's liquidity. The more liquid an asset is, the more quickly it can be converted into cash.

Current Assets Circulating Assets Floating Assets Liquid Capital	Fixed Assets Fixed Capital
TOTALLY LIQUID ASSETS	*LEAST LIQUID ASSETS*

◄──

| Cash in Hand | Cash at Bank | Savings Account | Short Term Deposits | Debtors | Stocks | Investments | Motor Vehicles | Office Equipment | Machinery | Land and Buildings | Specialist Plant |

Fig. 5.2 Relative liquidity of business assets

Long-term borrowing

1 **Shares.** Incorporated public or private companies can issue shares in order to raise large amounts of money. The purchase of shares gives a person part-ownership in the company, with voting rights at shareholders' meetings. Because shareholders provide capital for a company, the company has a responsibility to try to earn sufficient profit to pay a dividend to shareholders. The size of any dividend varies according to the type of share:

(a) Ordinary shares – equities. Ordinary shareholders have voting rights (equity) at shareholders' meetings. But they are not entitled to a fixed rate of dividend. The size of the ordinary shareholders'

dividend varies according to the size of the profits and the directors' decision on the proportion to be retained by the company.

(b) *Preference shares.* As the name implies, preference shareholders are given preference over ordinary shareholders in the payment of dividends. Preference shares always carry a fixed rate of dividend, but the nature of its payment will vary according to the nature of the preference. For example, some – cumulative preference shares – can accumulate fixed dividends over time.

(c) *Deferred shares.* Deferred shareholders are generally few in number and only receive a dividend after ordinary shareholders have been given a stated minimum. This minimum, and deferred shareholders' voting rights, depend on the terms of the issue. Deferred shares are normally held by the founders of the company and carry valuable rights.

2 Debentures – loan stock. When a limited company borrows money, it commonly does so by issuing loan certificates called debentures. A debenture certificate holder is a creditor of the company, not a member, and thus does not have voting rights. Debentures are long-term loans to companies; they bear a fixed rate of interest and will be redeemed at the end of a stated period. The interest on debentures must be paid whether the company makes a profit or a loss, so that in effect debenture interest is a fixed expense which will be shown in the Profit and Loss Account. Failure to pay the interest means that debenture holders can exercise a legal charge on the assets of the company.

3 Mortgage. The issuing of shares and debentures are methods of raising money which are available only to incorporated associations. Sole traders and partnerships will require long-term finance to provide for large capital outlays such as the purchase of premises, and for this purpose they will sometimes take out a mortgage. A mortgage is a long-term loan against which the property is offered as security. Failure to pay the interest and capital charges means that the Building Society or mortgagor can exercise a legal charge on the property secured.

4 Government assistance. Successive governments have provided investment or cash incentives to certain sectors of British industry. The following list gives examples of the type of assistance which has been provided in recent years:

(*a*)　Small Business Loan Guarantee Scheme. The Government will supply loans up to £75000 to small businesses.

(*b*)　Regional Enterprise Grants. These are available to firms in Development Areas which have less than 25 employees.

(*c*)　Consultancy Initiatives. Advice is provided by the Department of Employment to businesses throughout the UK.

—— Sources of public finance ——

Commercial organisations in the public sector have very similar financial problems to private companies: they have to be profitable and they have to ensure that there is an adequate flow of money to acquire resources. The non-commercial organisations do not sell their services and therefore do not have the problem of cash flow. They are given money by the Government and have to work within strict cash limits.

The general philosophy in cash limits is that organisations have relative freedom to spend within the limit, but no freedom to spend beyond the limit. The central government and the local authorities are left with the problem of how to raise the money. The following measures are the main ones used:

Direct taxation

1　Personal taxation.　Earned income is taxed. Income earners are able to deduct certain allowances from their gross income, and any remaining income is then taxed. The proportion of tax paid increases as taxable income increases.

2　Corporation Tax.　This is a tax levied on company profits. Companies, like individuals, can deduct allowances from their gross profits. The allowances are in effect items of expenditure. The remaining net profit is then taxed at a standard rate.

3　Capital-Gains Tax.　When individuals sell an asset, it is assumed by the Inland Revenue that this is trade and consequently any profit or gain is taxed. The assets which are charged include all forms of property such as securities, works of art, and land. Exemptions are granted on certain assets such as a person's home.

4 Inheritance Tax.   This tax applies to transfers on personal wealth in three main areas: lifetime gifts, transfers on death and transfers relating to property. The tax is charged on a cumulative basis in respect of lifetime transfers as they occur. Transfers made on death are taxed as though the deceased had made the transfer just before death.

Indirect taxation

1 Value Added Tax (VAT).   This is imposed on products and services at every stage of production. The rate of tax remains constant and as the product increases in value (value added), the more revenue will be collected. Certain items such as food, fuel and power and books are zero-rated, and some services – such as education and health – are exempt; but zero-rating and exemptions cause problems in collection. For example, children's clothes are zero-rated – the problem is to define 'children's clothes'.

2 Customs and Excise Duties.   Apart from goods from EEC countries, most imported goods are subject to customs duty. Excise duty is levied on home-products such as alcohol, petrol and cigarettes. The demand for these products is fairly inelastic, so the government can be fairly sure of the amount of revenue it will create.

Other forms of taxation

1 National Insurance contributions.   This is a form of direct tax which is shared between the employers and the employees. The rates of contributions, which are made both by employers and employees, depend on the earnings of employees and whether the employment is contracted out of the scheme. Unlike other taxes, this tax is raised specifically for the social security and industrial injury benefits, the National Health Service, and the Redundancy Fund.

2 Motor vehicle duty.   Ownership of a motor vehicle incurs a tax which for cars is at a standard rate, regardless of the size of the car.

3 Local government income.   The arrangement of the financing of local government in the UK was radically reformed in 1990 with the introduction of the Community Charge. The reform included a Non Domestic Rate charge on local businesses. However, these arrangements have not generally been accepted and reform of the financing of local authorities and the wider issue of reform of the local government itself is not yet finalised.

Borrowing by local authorities and central government

When government expenditure exceeds the revenue obtained from taxation it then has to borrow from private individuals and organisations; this is known as the Public Sector Borrowing Requirement (PSBR).

The main sources of government borrowing are:

1 The issue of loan stock. The local authorities and the central government issue loan stock which is similar to debentures in private corporations. Government stock is issued on the Stock Exchange and the loan certificates can be purchased by any individuals or firms. Since the borrower is the Government, such stock is termed *gilt-edged*: the lender is guaranteed a fixed rate of interest as well as repayment of the loan. Local authorities also issue loan stock to the general public, as well as borrowing directly from the Government.

Table 5.2 Central government income, by source

	% of total
Taxes on income	
Paid by persons	27.1
Paid by corporations	12.6
Taxes on expenditure	
Customs and Excise duties (inc. VAT)	31.0
Other indirect taxes	3.4
National insurance and national health contributions	
Paid by employees	8.4
Paid by employers	10.1
Transfer payments	0.1
Rent, interest, dividends, royalties, and other current income	6.8
Taxes on capital (inc. capital transfer tax and capital gains tax)	2.4
Borrowing requirement	−2.8
Other financial receipts	0.9
Total	100.0

2 Funds from overseas. Overseas investors who want to hold their money in sterling can purchase government stock.

3 Treasury bills. These are used to borrow money on a short-term basis (usually 91 days). Because such loans are short-term, the rate of interest is usually lower than for long-term loans.

—— Internal sources of finance ——

Internal funds are extremely important to organisations. Not only do they provide money for day-to-day operations (working capital), but they also provide finance for future investment. It has been estimated that internal funds account for more than two-thirds of funds from all sources.

Profits

The amount of profit a business makes is not always easy to calculate. One of the main problems, especially during inflation, is the valuation of a firm's assets. For example, the price of property is constantly changing and consequently the value of premises is often difficult to assess. The problems of inflation are outlined in more detail later in this chapter.

Accountants have conventionally used two definitions of profit:

1 Increase in assets. Profit or loss is the increase or decrease in net assets which results from normal business activity. The sale of existing assets and long-term capital transactions are excluded from the calculation.

2 Revenue less expenses. Profit or loss is the difference between total revenue from sales less any resources or assets used in the process.

Tax has to be paid on any profit and the shareholders will decide how the remainder will be allocated. Profit can be distributed as dividends to shareholders and/or be put into a reserve fund. It is the reserve fund which is the source of internal finance.

Depreciation

A second method which commercial organisations use to provide for future purchases is depreciation. The purpose of depreciation is to reduce the cost of a fixed asset to a scrap or realisable value. The amount of money used to reduce the cost is deducted from the initial capital outlay in the Balance Sheet and is also treated as a legitimate expense in the Profit and Loss Account.

There are several methods of depreciation. Two more popular ones are:

1   **Straight-line method.**   The scrap value of the asset is deducted from its initial cost and the remainder is written off over the estimated life of the project on a constant or fixed-instalment basis. *

2   **Reducing balance method.**   This method recognises that the value of an asset is higher during the first years of ownership. The depreciation charge is a fixed percentage of the remaining balance, so that each year the actual charge gradually reduces. *

Problems of inflation: falling money values

Money is not constant in its value; during inflation the cash in an organisation becomes an unreliable measure of value. Inflation distorts the calculation of profit and the valuation of assets. The following is a summary of the problems caused by falling money values:

1   **Asset values.**   During inflation the 'book' or recorded value of an asset tends to be inaccurate. Constantly increasing prices make many asset values on Balance Sheets too low.

2   **Depreciation.**   When fixed asset values are low, the depreciation charges will also be too low. A major reason for setting money on one side is to provide for future purchases. Inflation can make such provision inadequate.

* For an example, see Appendix 4.

3   Stock.   There is a temptation for firms to include the increased value of stocks in their profits. But a firm has to be careful not to distribute such increases to shareholders because the extra value will be needed to replace stock.

4   Cash.   Cash resources lose their value during inflation but this loss is not shown in the accounts.

5   Borrowing.   It pays to be in debt during inflation because often the rate of interest does not adequately reflect inflation rates. Any 'gain' by borrowing is not shown in the accounts.

6   Growth.   The growth of a firm is difficult to assess because the changing value of money makes measurement difficult.

The problems caused by inflation have been recognised as serious; and in 1970 the accountancy bodies set up an Accounting Standards Committee which publishes Statements of Standard Accounting Practice (SSAP). The main objectives of their publication are to improve the levels of comparability between firms by narrowing the difference between accounting methods which firms use, and to establish basic rules of accounting procedures which deal with inflation.

Balancing different sources of finance

Private corporations – capital gearing

Since there are many sources of finance open to large organisations, they have to make a choice on the balance between them. The choice will be influenced by three considerations:

1   The cost of the source.
2   The proportion of fixed assets to current assets. A high proportion of fixed assets in an organisation would indicate that a high proportion of 'permanent' capital is required.
3   The need for working capital. Loans for immediate cash needs are usually obtained from short-term sources, especially commercial bank borrowing.

The capital structure of a company can be assessed by various ratios. One of the most important ratios for this purpose is the *gearing* of the company. The gearing is the ratio between a company's equity (ordinary shares and dividend capital) and its permanent loan capital (preference shares and debentures). A company must pay interest on its permanent loan capital before it can decide on the dividend to award to ordinary shareholders, and therefore the ratio between the two will affect dividends. Debenture and preference shareholders have a prior charge. (Examples of how the gearing is calculated will be found in Appendix 4 along with other financial ratios.)

What is the 'right' gearing ratio depends on the degree of risk the company faces and the nature of the industry. Those firms likely to make very different amounts of profit (or even loss) from year to year should avoid having too much permanent loan capital – a high gearing. The Capital Market consists of a wide variety of people and institutions, and they will differ in the degree of risk they are willing to take as well as the amount of return they will expect from their investment. Companies have to take into account these differences when deciding on which source of finance to use. The cost of the source plus the company's own expected yield will ultimately influence the balance between the different sources.

Smaller businesses are less fortunate than public limited liability companies. They do not have the advantage of being able to choose between a wide variety of sources; they mainly rely on their profits and borrowing from commercial banks to finance their activities.

The balance in public finance

The government has the problem of deciding on the balance between revenue from taxation and public borrowing, as well as between direct and indirect taxation.

Revenue and borrowing

The expenditure patterns of governments are not fixed, but a high proportion of government services must be provided by law. In addition to this constraint, established patterns of spending mean established patterns of resource utilisation. These patterns are difficult to change. For example, once a hospital has been constructed, it is difficult to change its use.

It is difficult, then, to change either the size or the pattern of government expenditure. Naturally, in the first instance, it is the established level of spending which will determine how much money is required by the Government. But it is not the only consideration which will influence the level of government revenue and the public borrowing requirement. Another important factor is the Government's assessment of the economic situation.

Budgeting for a deficit. In budgeting for a deficit, the Government intends to spend more than it collects in taxes. The reason for this is the need to stimulate the economy by giving consumers more to spend, through tax reductions, and by increasing government spending on social services and capital projects. The excess in expenditure will be financed through government borrowing. The issuing of loan stock in the Capital Market will have an effect on the general supply of money: as treasury bills increase, so will the money supply increase.

Budgeting for a surplus. The Government can reduce Public Expenditure and/or increase taxation when it wants to reduce total spending in the economy. This policy is normally adopted when there is inflationary pressure in the economy and the Government wants business activity to contract. A danger is that high levels of taxation might discourage effort and at the same time encourage high wage demands, both of which could lead to higher inflation.

A neutral or balanced budget occurs when the Government considers that neither stimulus nor restraint is necessary. However, since there are millions of independent decisions made every day, many of which will be affected by government spending, it is extremely unlikely that a budget can in fact be wholly neutral.

Direct and indirect taxation

There are two main forms of taxation: direct taxation and indirect taxation. Direct taxes are those which are levied on income or capital; for example, Income Tax, Corporation Tax, Inheritance Tax and National Insurance contributions. Indirect taxes are levied on expenditure and include VAT, Petrol Tax, Customs and Excise Duties and Alcohol Tax. Table 5.3 outlines the advantages and disadvantages of direct and indirect taxation.

The raising of public revenue is more complicated than the earning of sales revenue by commercial organisations. Governments do not impose taxes simply to obtain money: it the prime reason but not the only one. As we have seen, taxation is also used to influence the pattern of consumers' expenditure and to stimulate the economy.

Table 5.3 Direct versus indirect taxation

		Advantages		Disadvantages
Direct Taxation	1	Relatively cheap and easy to collect.	1	Discourages hard work and enterprise.
	2	Equitable in that it falls on those who can afford to pay.	2	Increases the time and resources spent on tax avoidance.
	3	Gives the Government fairly direct control over people's spending.	3	The tax on company profits tends to reduce investment.
Indirect Taxation	1	Does not discourage effort.	1	Indirect taxes are regressive: as a proportion of income they fall more heavily on the poor.
	2	Can be used for specific social policies such as reducing smoking or gambling.	2	Can be difficult and costly to collect.
	3	People have a degree of choice in whether they will pay the tax.	3	The amount of revenue to be raised by VAT cannot easily be predicted.

Deciding between investment alternatives

The two elements which an organisation will take into account in an investment decision are the *cost* of the project and the expected *benefits* which the project will bring. These two factors will be considered regardless of whether the investment is made by a public or private organisation. The cost of a project is fairly easy to estimate since the price of machinery or plant or equipment is known. Organisations can also make reliable estimates of running and maintenance costs. The benefit side of a project, however, is not so easy to predict: the degree of risk, the timing of the benefits, as well as the missed opportunity to invest the money elsewhere, make the assessment of the rewards from investment unreliable.

The degree of risk

A significant difference between commercial and non-commercial investment decisions is that commercial investment carries a degree of risk. Competition from other organisations makes predictions of the rewards from an investment project unreliable. The risk of failure, especially in marketing new products, is high: 80% of all new products fail to become established.

The timing of the benefits

Investment is forward-looking, in that it will only produce results in the future. A major feature of investment decisions is the time lag between the initial investment and the eventual return. Money, in effect, buys the time between the initial outlay and the eventual return. To complicate the issue is the fact that money received at different times has a different value. The sooner an organisation receives a return, the sooner it can employ the money to earn further rewards. A delay in obtaining earnings from an investment decreases the value of the earnings. Tables have been devised which discount future money earnings back to a present value, as shown in Table 5.4.

From the table it can be seen that the present value of £1 which is to be received in four years' time and discounted at 5% per annum is only

Table 5.4 A discount table showing the present value of £1 receivable or payable in future years

Year	Rate of Discount	
	2%	5%
1	0.9804	0.9524
2	0.9612	0.9070
3	0.9423	0.8638
4	0.9238	0.8227
5	0.9057	0.7835

£0.8227. Tables have been compiled for all rates of discount up to 48% and for periods up to fifty years.

Missed opportunities to invest – opportunity cost

A notion which runs through all investment decisions is the one of opportunity cost. The benefits from an investment project are produced over a number of years, and during that time the money used on the project might have been used more profitably elsewhere. The true cost of an expenditure is the lost opportunity of spending the money on alternative schemes. Normally, the benefits which would have arisen from an alternative scheme will never be known. But a common and constant indicator is the return that would have been obtained if the money had been lent to someone else – the rate of interest. If an organisation chooses to lend money rather than buy resources, it can make a reliable estimate of the reward it would obtain. When using discount tables, the rates of discount vary from 1% to 48%, and a problem is which rate of discount to select. A good guide is the rate of interest one would get if the money was lent.

Table 5.4 shows quite clearly that the longer returns are delayed, the lower the present value of the £1 becomes. This fall in value should not be confused with the falling value in money caused by inflation. Discount tables simply show how the value of the £1 falls at a particular rate of interest; even if the inflation rate were zero, money would still lose its value over time because delay costs either income which could have been earned had the £1 been 'in the hand', or interest paid on the borrowed £1.

Techniques which incorporate the above ideas of timing and opportunity cost have been devised to help businessmen to decide between different investment alternatives. The risk element is always present in commercial ventures, and although market research and other management techniques can help to reduce the element of risk, it can never be eliminated. On the other hand, discount tables can be used to overcome the problem of timing of the returns, because estimates of the income can be discounted to present values which allows fair comparisons to be made. If the rate of interest used in the discount tables is the same as that which could be earned by lending the initial capital, then the notion of 'opportunity cost' has effectively been included in the comparison.

Pay back

This is the crudest method of investment appraisal. The pay-back period is the time taken for an investment to generate sufficient revenue to recover the initial outlay. The investment programme which is selected is the one which repays the initial cost in the shortest possible time. Therefore the pay-back method emphasises the project which brings immediate reward.*

Average rate of return

The average rate of return is the ratio of profit (after depreciation) to capital outlay. Net profit is more commonly used than gross profit. The capital outlay can be the initial sum invested or the outflow of cash over the live of the project. Although the average rate of return is not as crude as the pay-back method, it ignores the timing of the cash flows and therefore is not ideal. Time is an important factor in all investment projects.*

Internal rate of return (IRR)

One of the most common investment appraisal techniques is the internal rate of return method, which uses the discount tables to compare alternative projects. The method takes into account the cost of the project as well as the timing of the inflow of cash. IRR uses the net present value of the £ to find a rate of interest which will discount the cash flows of a proposed investment to zero.*

—— Cost-benefit analysis (CBA) ——

Commercial organisations in the private and public sectors will use discounted cash flow (DCF) techniques. The yardsticks for measuring commercial investment cannot, however, be used to assess investment in schools, hospitals, defence, etc. Instead, *cost-benefit analysis* (CBA) is applied.

The idea of discounted cash flow is used in cost-benefit analysis, but

* For an example, see Appendix 5.

unlike the internal rate of return method, CBA takes into account all costs and all benefits which accrue to society, whether actual payments or receipts are involved or not. These costs and benefits (which will be given financial values) will be discounted to present values. This form of analysis is most often used in connection with projects which have social as well as economic implications, such as the construction of motorways, bridges, airports, dams, etc.

Social costs

The main difference between CBA and commercial methods of appraisal is that CBA takes into account social or 'hidden' costs as well as financial costs. For example, if it were proposed to build a new toll bridge across an estuary like the Severn, then the crude costs and benefits shown in Table 5.5 could be considered.

This example is only a simplified illustration. Evaluating the costs and benefits associated with a particular project can be very complex. In spite of this, CBA does allow public administrators to compare investment alternatives, and not only does it clarify financial considerations, but it also highlights social implications, such as conservation and pollution.

Table 5.5 Cost-benefit analysis

	Costs	*Benefits*
FINANCIAL (visible)	Construction of the bridge. Approach road construction. Repairs and maintenance. Provision of lighting. Wages of toll keepers. Administrative costs.	Income from tolls.
SOCIAL (hidden)	Noise pollution. Fumes pollution. Congestion at peak times. More accidents from increased traffic.	Saving of time and distance. Fewer public vehicles required. Saving of fuel. Less wear and tear on other roads. More economic activity.

— Obtaining a return on investment —

Non-commercial organisations allocate their services according to need. In commercial organisations, market forces – prices – determine how products or services are distributed. The price of a product also determines how much income an organisation will obtain from a capital project. It greatly influences the cash flow into an organisation, and consequently affects its acquisition of additional resources.

The pricing policy of commercial organisations can be a constantly changing process. The setting of prices requires technical understanding of market forces, such as elasticity of demand, as well as practical knowledge of changes in fashion, design and competitors' strategies. The degree of control a firm has over its prices depends on the competition it faces, that is, the number of other firms producing similar products.

The main factors which will influence a company's pricing policy are:

1 The cost of the product.
2 The planned return on capital investment.
3 The company's need for liquidity.
4 The supply of similar products.
5 The nature of demand and its elasticity.
6 How much of the existing market the company wants to obtain.

The pricing methods which exist are:

1 **Cost-plus pricing.** This is probably the most common form of pricing. Firms need to have a good knowledge of their expenses, because to set the price they have to calculate the average cost of the product and then add a profit margin.

2 **Marginal-cost pricing** is a system which is adopted by organisations in imperfect competition - for example the public utilities. It is a method which in theory *maximises* the profit a company can earn.

3 **Variable pricing, Price discrimination, Price differential.** Many organisations are able to charge different prices for the same product, commonly through quantity or cash discounts. Off-peak pricing practised by British Rail, the telephone service and many hotels provides another example. The reason for off-peak pricing is to try to switch demand to periods when capital resources such as railway stock, telephone exchanges and hotel bedrooms are lying idle.

4 Corporate pricing. Organisations which produce a variety of goods sometimes have a corporate pricing strategy. This system is adopted either when the company wants to establish a reputation for stable prices or to cross-subsidise weaker products. For example, the Rank Organisation subsidised its investment in hotels with profits from Rank Xerox.

5 Bidding for tenders. Government and local authority contracts are awarded to those organisations which *tender* the best bargain. The price, which will often be set for the one contract, and delivery times are the most important factors which are considered when bids are judged.

Exercises

Comprehension

1 List the functions of money.

2 Define 'revenue expenditure'.

3 List the main sources of commercial finance.

4 Describe the ways in which governments raise revenue.

5 Find examples of different pricing arrangements used by British Rail.

Research

1 Using examples, explain the difference between 'direct taxation' and 'indirect taxation'.

2 Explain what is meant by the phrase 'true cost is sacrificed alternatives'.

3 Explain why high levels of inflation are not desirable.

Project

Select any major domestic project in DIY or gardening and compile a detailed cost-benefit analysis of it.

6

PEPLE IN ORGANISATIONS

Organisations employ three main resources or factors of production: *natural resources*, such as land and raw materials; *man-made resources*, such as buildings, machinery and equipment; and *people*. Of these, people are arguably the most important asset to any organisation.

Specialisation

Most people in organisations are specialists. The degree of special skill which is required in a job obviously varies, but it is important to realise that almost everyone in employment is a specialist to some degree. This simply means that in a job we concentrate on specific or specialised tasks – only sole traders perform all the functions in their organisations.

One of the main reasons for the growth in the economy during the nineteenth and twentieth centuries has been the development of specialisation. Specialisation occurs when people, regions or even countries concentrate on what they can do best. Specialisation is common in all organisations and takes place when the total operation is broken down into a series of sub-tasks. The mass production of motor cars provides a good example: in car production, hundreds of different components are manufactured separately: the components are then assembled on a production line where each employee performs a repetitive specialist task.

The advantages of specialisation are:

1 People can concentrate on what they are best at. Given the ability, a person can choose to become a secretary or an engineer.
2 Repetition of the same task increases a person's skill and improves efficiency.
3 Constant employment in the same job can lead to suggestions for improved methods of operation.
4 Breaking operations into sub-routines encourages automation, so that mass production and economies of scale can take place. This advantage is double edged: automation increases productivity and wealth, but at the same time can lead to redundancy and unemployment.

There are also disadvantages which specialisation creates:

1 Many tasks are so repetitive that they are boring. Those jobs which do not require much imagination or creativity can cause boredom which leads to frustration, discontent and low morale. Such tasks tend, however, to be those which can most easily be automated.
2 Even when jobs require imagination, the total operation can be so large and so complex that employees do not understand how their work contributes to the total process. This, like boredom, can cause feelings of uselessness and frustration.
3 Specialisation creates interdependence which reduces self-reliance. People and organisations who are dependent on one another become vulnerable to strikes and similar activities by other people.
4 Specialisation can lead to poor control of people, particularly in large organisations. Communication lines become long and weak and organisation structures become complex. All this makes the job of managing people in an organisation more difficult.

—— The nature of labour markets ——

The range of occupations in business is extremely wide and it is unwise to make too many generalisations and comparisons between different occupations. One of the most basic and standard indicators of what people are worth is the amount of money an organisation is willing to pay them. Salaries and wages are the price of people in organisations, and reflect the supply of and demand for particular skills and knowledge. The difference between labour markets is the difference in people's knowledge and skills.

A person does not necessarily belong to only one labour market, but can apply for a variety of jobs. For example, almost every able-bodied person could do unskilled work, therefore the supply of people in this labour market is very large and consequently the price is relatively low. However, the more skill and knowledge a person has, the more specialised he tends to be and his 'rarity value' will give him a high price.

The factors which determine the labour market to which a person will normally belong are:

1 **Qualifications.** Academic and professional qualifications are one of the main indicators employers use to assess people. Where an occupation requires long periods of study, then people in those markets tend to be in short supply, and therefore they command a high price. For example, it takes several years of study for architects and doctors to become qualified, but when they are qualified and experienced they are highly paid.

2 **Experience.** Many employers are unhappy about employing 'raw recruits'. There are circumstances where a firm would like to train its own personnel from the beginning of their employment, particularly in fields which require initiative and new ideas. But advertisements for many occupations ranging from typists to sales directors state that experience is an essential requirement.

3 **Aptitude.** Some people are fortunate to possess skills which are rare. Sports 'stars', pop 'stars' and others in the entertainment industry are paid high salaries because their skills are much in demand but short in supply. Individual talent in this category cannot easily be acquired by training and education – it is often an inherent gift. Natural gifts are not confined to jobs in entertainment, but also apply to inventors, designers, artists and so on.

4 **Social skills – personality.** Almost all employees in the service industries have to be able to cooperate with the general public, and some occupations put particular emphasis on certain types of social skill. The

shop assistant and the salesman require the ability to persuade. People employed in the social services require the special skill of listening to the problems of others and of suggesting remedies or solutions. Employees in the hotel and catering industry have to be able to deal with difficult customers, and even in the manufacturing industry an employer will always consider how well a new recruit is likely to 'fit in' with the existing workforce. Where delegation and participation are common, *all* employees require the ability to communicate and the ability to listen.

Job description and job specification

An interesting feature of the labour markets is that many organisations do not specify the type of person they require: instead they will provide the details of a job or task in a job specification. The Department of Employment has given the following definitions of a job description and job specification:

Job description: A *broad* statement of the purpose, scope, duties and responsibilities of a particular job.

Job specification: A *detailed* statement of the physical and mental activities involved in the job and, when relevant, of social and physical environmental matters. The specification is usually expressed in terms of behaviour: what the worker does, what knowledge he uses in doing it, the judgement he makes and the factors he takes into account when making them.

The skills and knowledge which organisations need

The enormous variety of job specifications which exist in business illustrate the range of diversity and specialisation in occupations. It is not presumed that the five categories outlined below cover this wide range, but they do provide a guide to the role of people in organisations.

1   Unskilled.   Many jobs do not require any training or previous experience, for example manual labour or assembly work. These occupations are often highly repetitive and boring, as well as being poorly paid. Much unskilled work could be performed by machines, but the capital cost would be too high. Almost all businesses have such jobs and they tend to be at the bottom of the organisational hierarchy.

2 Mechanical or motor skills. There are some tasks in business which are performed by machines which require an operator. The more complicated the machine, then generally the more skilled the operator has to be. Jobs which require motor skills can range from the semi-skilled occupations, such as a machine operator in an office or factory, to highly skilled occupations, such as an airline pilot.

3 Intelligence and knowledge. Occupations which require a high level of motor skill sometimes also demand a high level of intelligence and aptitude. An airline pilot is a good example. There are jobs in business which do not need mechanical skills but make exacting demands on people's knowledge. The professions of law, finance and insurance, and the jobs in research and design, are examples of this.

4 Administrative or managerial skills. The ability to organise other people is a fairly rare skill. It not only requires knowledge and understanding of the functions within an organisation, but also the ability to motivate people: to persuade them to give their best towards the aims of the organisation. In addition to this knowledge and ability to motivate, managers must be able to organise non-human resources using techniques of forecasting, planning, coordinating and controlling. These are techniques which require judgment as well as knowledge.

5 Decision-making skills and initiative. Decision-making is an everyday occurrence for everyone. We decide what to eat, what to wear, when to go out, and so on. Similarly, decisions are part of an organisation's everyday activities. Routine tasks, by their very nature, exclude the employee from the decision-making process, but middle and top management will be using their judgment every day. It is important for senior managers in an organisation to develop skills in decision-making. People at the top of an organisation are employed to have initiative – to make decisions. For example, boards of directors are employed to make policy decisions in investment, manpower and marketing. The risks which all organisations face mean that organisations have to be run by people who have the ability to diagnose and assess the risk, and the capacity to decide on the correct strategy. Business is constantly changing and organisations require people with enterprise and initiative in order to survive.

The five categories outlined above can be placed in a hierarchical pyramid (Fig. 6.1) which indicates the relative size of the labour markets for each category. The pyramid also illustrates an organisation's hierarchy.

Fig. 6.1 Labour markets and the organisational pyramid

The recruitment of human resources

The recruitment of people into an organisation is normally carried out by the personnel department. The steps in the recruitment process are:

1 Analyse the task – job analysis

The objectives of an organisation are sub-divided into a series of separate specialist tasks or jobs. The personnel department will analyse the delegated tasks in order to find out what type of labour skills and knowledge are required. The purpose of job analysis is to produce a job description or job specification.

2 Provide details of the job – job specification

The job analysis should provide the personnel department with sufficient information to compile details of the skills and knowledge which the job requires. These details normally specify:

(a) *The craft skills required.* This describes what the employee actually does, and the nature of the machinery and equipment which the work involves.

(b) *The mental skills required.* This is a description of the knowledge needed to perform the task.

(c) *The decision skills required.* This specifies the degree of judgment and initiative which the employee will have to use.

3 Advertise the job – recruit employees

Some posts are restricted to internal applicants and in these cases the job will be advertised on an organisation's notice board and in internal circulars. The reasons for internal appointments are, firstly, that promotion within a company improves morale, and secondly, that they allow an organisation to reduce its workforce if that is necessary (natural wastage).

Most employees, however, are recruited from outside the organisation from the following sources:

(a) *Press advertisements.* Many newspapers and journals display columns of 'situations vacant', which is the most popular method of advertising a post. Occasionally, firms use box numbers rather than disclose the company's name. This happens when there are details, such as salary policy, which the organisation wishes to keep secret.

(b) *Government agencies, Job Centres.* Many occupations, but particularly unskilled and semi-skilled vacancies, are advertised in Job Centres which are administered by the Department of Employment.

(c) *Private agencies.* These are private firms which perform a similar function to government Job Centres, except that they will help organisations to recruit in markets where labour is in short supply – that is, where the skills that jobs require are rare.

(d) *Further and higher education.* Many employers approach universities and colleges directly. Higher educational institutions employ full-time careers guidance officers who liaise between employers and students and assist both in employment problems.

(e) *Direct applications.* Anyone can approach an organisation at any time and ask for a job. This is true for all levels of employment. Where labour skills are rare or where a person is particularly talented, it is common for organisations to approach individuals directly.

4 Interview and select the applicants

Interviewing is the most widely-used method of assessing people. Normally, an organisation will draw up a shortlist of those candidates whose skills and knowledge are closest to the job specification. There are legal rules in this process which an organisation should observe. The Sex Discrimination Act, 1975, as amended by the Sex Discrimination Act, 1986, and the Race Relations Act, 1976, make it illegal to discriminate in all aspects of employment.

The candidate who is selected is the one who, in the opinion of the interviewing panel, has the qualities and skills demanded by the job specification.

5 Appoint the candidate: the contract of employment

The appointment of a person is a contract between the employer and the employee. The employer makes the offer of the job and the employee accepts the offer in writing.

——— Conditions of employment ———

The employer is obliged to provide certain details of the conditions under which the job is to be performed. These obligations arise from two Acts of Parliament: the Contracts of Employment Act, 1972, and the Employment Protection Act, 1975.

According to the 1972 Act, an employment contract must contain:

(a) The name of the employer and employee.
(b) The date when employment commenced.
(c) Details of the pay or how the pay is to be calculated.

(d) When the payment of wages or salaries will be made (usually weekly or monthly).

(e) The terms and conditions of work (hours, holiday pay, sick pay, pension scheme).

(f) The length of notice required on each side.

(g) Trade union rights.

The Employment Protection Act, 1975, adds further requirements: the contract of employment must also contain:

(a) The title of the job.

(b) Details of whether previous employment counts towards the period of employment for notice purposes.

(c) Guidance on the rules relating to disciplinary and grievance procedures.

The Trade Union Act, 1984, was introduced in order to increase democracy within the trade unions by ensuring that elections for positions on a union's executive and decisions to conduct strike action are subject to a secret ballot of the members.

How organisations manage people: personnel policies

Induction: first impressions

Induction is the act of introducing a new employee to an organisation. Its purpose is to help new recruits to become part of the organisational structure by introducing them to their jobs and their working environment.

The methods which are commonly used are: *(a)* visits to the departments within the organisation; *(b)* lectures and talks by senior management; *(c)* films on the organisation's activities; and *(d)* introductions to colleagues and supervisors.

The content of an induction programme can include: *(a)* the organisation's rules and policies; *(b)* the organisation structure; *(c)* health and safety measures; *(d)* welfare facilities; and *(e)* the organisation's services and products.

Development of people: training and education

People are an employer's most important resource and so it is in the interests of an organisation to try to develop the skills and knowledge of its employees. The benefits which result from training and education are:

1 Increased productivity and output.
2 Improvements in the quality of output.
3 Greater flexibility of skills of the employees.
4 Greater job satisfaction.
5 Reduced turnover of labour.
6 Improved employee morale.
7 Improved promotion prospects for employees.
8 Improved safety awareness.

In 1991 a new framework for the promotion of training and enterprise was established. The principles on which it was based were that employers and individuals should take responsibility for training and its costs; and that there should be national standards of competence (NVQs) recognised by a National Council of Vocational Qualifications (NCVQ).

The NCVQ works in close cooperation with employers to ensure that vocational qualifications measure competence in a job, and that there is an appropriate qualification for the broad skills which are required at each level of employment.

Skill Training

Every industry needs people with basic craft skills. The following list, although it is very limited, gives some indication of how wide the range of skills which are needed in British industry is: chefs, waiters, motor mechanics, machine operators, bricklayers, plumbers, electricians, typists, receptionists and hairdressers. Almost all occupations require an employee to be competent in a basic skill. The most common way to learn a skill is either by training courses in a college or by gaining experience in an appropriate workplace.

Social skills: relating to other people

The growth of the service industries, and a better understanding of how people work together, has led to an increased interest in the improvement of social skills: the ability to relate to other people. Social skills are not exclusive to the service industries: all occupations require employees to have the ability to cooperate with people. Social skills include:

1   The ability to communicate.   Misunderstanding can occur between employer and employee and often leads to conflict. The knowledge of how to present a point of view, either in written or spoken form, is vital to employer–employee relationships. An employee's willingness to participate in an organisation will often be influenced by his ability to communicate.

2   The ability to listen.   As we have seen, many occupations comprise delegated tasks: they are small specialised parts of a total effort. In order to carry out delegated tasks and duties, an employee must understand them. The ability to listen to what has been said improves the employee's understanding.

3   Awareness of other people.   People's attitudes and perceptions vary according to their personality and experience. Managers in particular have to be aware of the needs of their subordinates in order to motivate them. All employees have to work with one another, and understanding of each others' needs and attitudes leads to greater cooperation and increased job satisfaction.

The methods used to develop these abilities in employees are very similar to those used in management and supervisory training, which are outlined below.

Supervisory and management skills

The skill which managers require above all is the ability to manage people: to motivate them to improve their performance. In addition, top managers must be able to make decisions, and this requires a knowledge of the constraints on decisions as well as the techniques which help decision-making.

The methods of training and education which are used to develop managers are:

1   Formal lectures.   The purpose of formal lectures is to pass on knowledge. Normally, the content of management lectures will deal with organisation and motivation theories, constraints on decisions, and management techniques.

2 Case studies, simulation exercises, role-playing. One of the problems of management training is to make the learning environment as realistic as possible. Case studies, simulation exercises and role-playing give students practical awareness of the problems of managing people and of making decisions. They enable students to participate in realistic problems.

3 Discussion groups. There are no absolute solutions to problems which occur in business. Discussion groups enable managers to exchange ideas and experiences so that they can learn that there are many aspects and different points of view on solutions to business problems.

4 Business games simulate a commercial environment. Teams of management students analyse the relationship between such variables as price, quality and output, as well as employer–employee relationships, and decide on a team strategy. The advantages of this exercise are, firstly, that students can apply theories and principles, and, secondly, that they can learn to cooperate in working groups.

Manpower planning

Manpower planning is where an organisation systematically anticipates the type of staff it will need. Such a scheme should be based on policy and forward planning. The questions which require considerations are:

(a) What new developments are planned and what staffing is required?

(b) What training and staff development programmes are required to ensure that the employees have the appropriate skills and knowledge?

(c) Are there likely to be fluctuations in the organisation's demand for labour, e.g. seasonal variations in selling or production?

(d) What are the systems for staff appraisal and related policies such as promotion and transfer of staff?

(e) What is the age profile of the existing workforce and what effect will this have on the proportion of retirements?

——— The welfare of employees ———

The difference between development and welfare schemes is not always clear. As we have seen, employee development concentrates on improving knowledge and skills; and these will undoubtedly improve the employee's welfare. However, most welfare programmes are specifically concerned with the physical and social well-being of people rather than their abilities.

Some welfare facilities are required by law. The Health and Safety at Work Act, 1974, required organisations to provide:

1 Hygiene facilities, such as lavatories, cloakrooms and drinking water.

2 Safety programmes, which must include the maintenance of safe plant and equipment as well as training and supervision in accident prevention.

3 Safety devices and clothing. Some occupations are dangerous because of the high level of fumes, dust, sparks or noise. Protective clothing and equipment must be supplied by the employer.

4 A safe working environment in relation to space, lighting, heating and ventilation.

Some organisations will provide welfare facilities above the legal minimum, for example:

Social and sports clubs. People enjoy social contact outside work and it helps the organisation if employees form relationships through their social and sports clubs. Such relationships strengthen the bonds between organisations and employees.

Fringe benefits. Successive governments have imposed restrictions on pay and this has led to an increased growth in alternative financial rewards such as pension schemes, sick pay, subsidised meals, company cars, and private health care.

——— The informal organisation ———

The welfare facilities which are provided by the organisation are, to some extent, the formal organisation's recognition of the informal organisation. The formal organisation is symbolised by policies, rules and regulations, and above all by the hierarchical pyramid of authority. During the past sixty years, it has been recognised that people in organisations have their own aims, ambitions, expectations, needs and behaviour patterns which will be different from, and sometimes in conflict with, the aims and policies of the formal organisation. The real power and influence in an organisation is not necessarily represented by the formal organisational chart.

——— The Human Relations School ———

Modern motivation theory, and our understanding of the behaviour of working groups, stems from the research into the informal organisation by social psychologists. The most influential work has been published by four writers:

Elton Mayo

The importance of the informal organisation was first discovered by Elton Mayo at the Hawthorne factory of the Western Electric Company, near Chicago, between 1927 and 1932. Mayo and his colleagues discovered that pressure within the informal group could increase output even when the working environment was made worse. Conversely, the informal group's attitudes could serve to restrict output even when financial incentives were offered to individuals.

Up to 1930, it has been assumed that individuals were fairly isolated within organisations. After the Hawthorne experiments, managers began to appreciate that people work in informal social groups; and that the pressure within informal groups frequently exceeds the strength of formal rules and regulations.

Douglas McGregor

The theory developed by McGregor questioned basic assumptions about the motivation of employees. These basic assumptions McGregor called Theory X. In Theory X it is assumed that most people dislike work, avoid responsibility and respond to authoritarian leadership. In contrast, McGregor maintained in his Theory Y that most people find work natural and pleasing, do not need external controls when motivated, enjoy responsibility and enjoy participating in solving problems.

The contrast is between work-centred management (Theory X) and people-centred management (Theory Y). Douglas McGregor advocated the latter.

A. H. Maslow

Maslow's theory is that the needs of employees are very complex and that they occur at different levels. He argued that in order to motivate people, managers should understand the different needs and different levels of need of employees. The levels are in an ascending or hierarchical scale: the second level cannot be satisfied unless the first one is, and so on. Maslow classified the needs into five levels:

First level: Basic needs
hunger
thirst
sleep

Second level: Security needs
warmth
housing
security

Third level: Affection needs
companionship
recognition
friendship

Fourth level: Status needs
praise/esteem
possessions
power

Fifth level: Self-actualisation
personal development
creativity
use of full potential

The pressure of these needs will vary within individuals and between individuals. An interesting observation is that the first, second and, to some extent, the fourth levels can be satisfied by financial reward. But such needs as recognition and personal development require managers to look for additional methods to motivate people.

Frederick Herzberg

Herzberg contrasted the factors which he found gave job satisfaction with those which created dissatisfaction. He argued that the provision of satisfying factors would motivate people. The 'motivators' include recognition of work done, responsibility for tasks, sense of achievement and promotion prospects.

On the other hand, Herzberg said that there were factors which, although absolutely necessary in a job, would not motivate people. Inadequate provision of the maintenance factors – wages and salaries, fringe benefits, rules and regulations, and relationships within the organisation – would tend to cause dissatisfaction.

The satisfying factors or 'motivators' are not the opposite of dissatisfying or 'maintenance' factors. It is significant that those elements which had to be adequate to maintain a person in a job would not, according to Herzberg, motivate a person.

The findings of the industrial social psychologists (Human Relations School) show that motivation is an intricate thing. Financial reward is an important but complex method of motivating people. But money is not the only motivator: equally important are recognition and responsibility. As a result of the work of the Human Relations School, new methods of motivation are being adopted by organisations. These include job rotation, job enlargement and job enrichment.

— Employee/employer relationships —

Although people are an organisation's most important resource, they are also a very costly resource. It is inevitable that some conflict will occur between employer and employee, since an employee will want to maximise his wages, and an employer will want to minimise his wage costs.

In order to secure benefits from employers, many groups of employees have organised themselves and formed trade unions. The objectives of organised labour are:

1 To increase wages and salaries.
2 To improve the conditions of employment (hours of work, overtime, shift-work, etc.).

3   To improve the working environment (space, lighting, heating, ventilation and safety).
4   To protect the employees from unfair or even illegal practices, such as unfair dismissal.
5   To represent individual employees in cases of dispute.
6   To ensure that all employees receive adequate training.

Between 1979 and 1988 trade union membership fell by a quarter from 13.4 million to 10.2 million. During their development, and up to the present time, trade unions have been subject to legal rules. The landmarks in trade union history are:

The Tolpuddle Martyrs (1834)
Trade Union Act (1871)
Taff Vale Judgment (1901)
Trade Disputes Act (1927)
Industrial Relations Act (1971)
Trade Union and Labour Relations Act (1974)
Trade Union Act (1984)

The Employment Act, 1982 made important detailed changes to the existing legislation. The main changes were:

(a)   Exclusion of the legal immunity of trade unions in certain circumstances e.g. secondary picketing.
(b)   Extended protection for individuals from compulsion to join a closed shop.
(c)   Tighter balloting requirements.
(d)   Amendments to the rules affecting compensation and relief for union related dismissal.
(e)   New provisions affecting legal proceedings against trade unions.
(f)   Directors' reports to contain a statement on how employee participation will be developed.

Trade Union Act, 1984

The Trade Union Act, 1984, provided for:

(a)   Members of the governing bodies of trade unions to be directly elected by individual secret ballot of the union's membership.
(b)   Trade unions' immunity from legal action for organising industrial

action to be made conditional on the holding of secret and properly conducted strike ballots.

(c) Members of trade unions with political funds to be enabled to vote at regular intervals on whether their union should continue to spend money on political parties.

Trades Union Congress (TUC)

Most trade unions are affiliated to the Trades Union Congress, which was formed in 1868. The main objective of the TUC is to act as a pressure group to influence government and business decisions. It also promotes research and publicity on behalf of organised labour.

Employers' associations

Employers have formed associations which help members in their industrial relations problems and provide assistance in trade matters. The large national associations are called Employers' Federations. Employers' associations provide a wide range of services for their members and will:

1 Negotiate and deal with organised labour.
2 Help with technical problems.
3 Liaise with other organisations, especially the Government, local authorities and professional bodies.
4 Seek to improve customer relations.
5 Encourage cooperation in research.

Confederation of British Industry (CBI)

Many trade associations are members of the Confederation of British Industry. The CBI was formed in 1965 under a Royal Charter, and its aims are to formulate and influence industrial and economic policy. The CBI also encourages the development of methods to improve efficiency in British industry. It is the managers' counterpart of the TUC and as such is one of the best-known pressure groups in business affairs.

Collective bargaining

The parties in collective bargaining are the trade unions and the individual employer or employers' association or federation; and the bargaining is generally about wages and salaries, conditions of work and productivity arrangements. The distinction between joint consultation and collective bargaining is that in collective bargaining, *negotiation* rather than *consultation* takes place, and any agreement becomes a formal agreement rather than an 'understanding'. Normally, collective bargaining is held at national level, but it can take place within an organisation. Legislation such as the Health and Safety at Work Act, 1974, and the Employment Protection Act, 1975, however, has tended to put more emphasis on local rather than national agreements, and in so doing has narrowed the difference between collective bargaining and joint consultation. Disputes in collective bargaining will normally go to arbitration.

Disputes

The causes of a breakdown in employer–employee relationships can be very complex. The most common cause is pay and conditions of work. However, poor management practice such as inadequate communication, lack of consultation and no recognition of work well done will often create low morale and lead to disputes.

In a dispute, the action which employees can take against their employers are:

Absenteeism. Frequently, employees who are dissatisfied with their job will not turn up for work. Absenteeism accounts for more working days lost than strikes. Of course, many workers absent themselves because of genuine illness or domestic difficulties. These reasons apart, it is a form of 'informal' protest many individuals use against their employers.

Go-slow, work-to-rule, refusal to cooperate. The specialisation which dominates human activity in organisations requires well-defined rules and regulations. The rules are a flexible framework for tasks – they are open to interpretation. If employees work to rule, they will rigidly interpret all rules and obey them to the letter. In addition, employees can limit their cooperation by refusing to work overtime or to attend joint consultative committees. In a work-to-rule the organisation can still function, but not without problems.

Strike action. Withdrawal of labour from an organisation is a drastic form of action. Not only is the organisation unable to function properly, but also the employees who are on strike will not be paid by the firm.

Where the trade union agrees with the strike, then it is deemed 'official'. Unofficial strikes occur when the employees have not obtained central union approval for their action.

Conciliation and arbitration

Parliament has established several statutory bodies which help to settle industrial relations problems. Two of the most important are:

1   Industrial Tribunals deal with a variety of problems, including discrimination, equal pay, unfair dismissal and redundancy. They are similar to courts of law in that they attempt to decide what is the most reasonable case in a dispute. Appeals can be made by dissatisfied parties to a higher court, but only on a point of law. The chairman of a tribunal is an independent, legally qualified person and the other members are representatives of employers and trade unions.

2   The Advisory Conciliation and Arbitration Service (ACAS)
ACAS was established by the Employment Protection Act, 1975, and is an independent body with the following powers and duties:

(a)   To improve employer–employee relationships.
(b)   To help solve disputes when requested.
(c)   To investigate voluntarily any industrial relations problem and publish the findings.
(d)   To investigate terms and conditions of employment and the recognition of trade unions.
(e)   To prepare codes of practice for the conduct of employer–employee relationships.

—— **Termination of employment** ——

Resignation, giving notice

Employment is a contract between the organisation and the employee which can be ended at any time by either party. Employees do not have to give reasons for leaving an organisation, but an employer has to be careful not to infringe the Employment Protection Act, 1975. The period of notice which either party must give is normally written into the contract of employment and varies according to the length of service. An employee may bring a case for wrongful dismissal when insufficient notice is given by an employer.

Dismissal without notice

An employee is dismissed when an employer terminates the contract of employment. Employers can legally dismiss a person without notice for serious misconduct, and examples of conduct which might warrant instant dismissal are:

1 Stealing from the employer.
2 Fighting on the employer's premises.
3 Repeated absence from work.
4 Refusal to obey a reasonable instruction.
5 Serious neglect of duties or continued inability to perform delegated tasks.

Dismissal with notice

Employees whose conduct does not warrant instant dismissal can ask the employer to give reasons for the dismissal, and to show that no discrimination has taken place and that the dismissal is fair. There are three Acts of Parliament which prevent employers from discriminating against employees: the Equal Pay Act, 1970, the Sex Discrimination Act, 1975, and the Race Relations Act, 1976. In addition, the Trade Union and Labour Relations Act, 1974, protects employees against *unfair* dismissal. Employers can legitimately dismiss an employee for only three reasons:

1 Persistent inadequate performance or conduct, after due warning.
2 The post has become redundant.
3 Statutory requirements: employment cannot continue without contravening the law. For example, if the Government were to enforce strict legislation on the publication of pornographic material, then those employees who specialise in producing such material could legitimately be dismissed.

Any other reason would be classified unfair for those employees who have more than 26 weeks' service and are employed for more than 21 hours a week. Employees who have been unfairly dismissed can complain to an industrial tribunal.

Redundancy

Under the Redundancy Payments Act, 1965, an employee is considered to be redundant when his job is no longer required by the organisation. Redundancy often occurs when an organisation closes down, but can also occur when reorganisation takes place.

An employee who has two years' service and has worked for at least 21 hours a week is entitled to minimum rates of redundancy pay (which are tax free). For each year of employment: *(a)* between ages 18 and 21, half a week's pay, *(b)* between ages 22 and 40, one week's pay; and *(c)* between ages 41 and 65 (60 for women), one-and-a-half weeks' pay. Industrial tribunals hear disputed cases of redundancy.

Retirement

Women can retire from work at 60 and men at 65; they are then entitled to a retirement pension. Some organisations prepare people for retirement by providing pre-retirement courses, reductions in the working week and longer holidays. Welfare and social facilities are sometimes available for those who have retired.

——— Employment legislation ———

There has been a good deal of legislation dealing with the employment of people in organisations. The following are some of the most important Acts passed since 1970:

Equal Pay Act, 1970, amended by the Employment Act, 1982

Under this legislation, employers must give men and women equally favourable terms and conditions of employment if they are engaged on:

Like work, which is work that is of broadly similar type and involves the same skills.

Work of equal value. This provision was instituted in 1984 and allows an independent assessor, appointed by an industrial tribunal, to determine whether a man's and a woman's work, though different, is of equal value. The factors which the assessor can take into account are experience, training, skill and adaptability.

Work rates as equivalent. This occurs when a job evaluation study gives equal points to two entirely different jobs.

Sex Discrimination Act, 1975 and 1986

This Act complements the Equal Pay legislation, and makes it unlawful for an employer to discriminate against female employees in personnel functions such as recruitment, selection, promotion, training and dismissal. The Act established the Equal Opportunities Commission and gave it full powers to investigate cases where sex discrimination in employment has been reported.

Race Relations Act, 1976

This legislation is similar to the Sex Discrimination Act, and makes it an offence for an employer to discriminate against an employee on the grounds of race, colour or nationality. The Act set up the Commission for Racial Equality, which investigates cases of racial discrimination.

Wages Council Act, 1979

A wages council comprises representatives from trade unions, employers and public bodies and the function of the councils is to regulate the pay and conditions of workers in certain occupations. The 1979 Act gave the Minister of Employment powers to establish a wages council in various occupations.

—————— Exercises ——————

Comprehension

1   List the advantages and disadvantages of specialisation.

2   What is the difference between a 'job description' and a 'job specification'?

3   Give the methods which employers can use to recruit people.

4   Define 'self-actualisation'.

5   In what ways can a person's employment be terminated?

Research

1 Explain McGregor's Theory X and Theory Y. Your explanation should include examples.

2 Examine the ways in which an employer might discriminate against women.

3 Explain why training and education are considered to be important for a business.

Project

Collect information from newspapers relating to disputes between employers and trade unions and compile:
(i)   A list of reasons for the disputes.
(ii) Details of how the disputes were resolved.

7

INFORMATION IN ORGANISATIONS

The purpose of information processing

The nature and flow of information determines how 'sensitive' an organisation is to customers, employees, changes in the market, levels of sales, and so on. The purpose in processing information is to plan, record, control and report the activities of the organisation.

Planning. Managers need information to be able to plan how an organisation's resources are to be used. This can be a complex process since each department's plans must interrelate with the other departments.

Recording. Under the Companies Acts, firms are obliged to keep financial information. In addition, a business will maintain many other kinds of records dealing with such functions as sales, personnel, purchasing and production.

Controlling. There are many activities in business where immediate or 'real time' information is necessary so that the activity can be controlled directly. These activities include stock control, budgetary control and quality control.

Reporting. Many different kinds of reports exist in business: they range from weekly sales reports to financial reports at an Annual General Meeting. Every function within an organisation is constantly monitored and reported on. This requires firms to have accurate information produced in a fast and acceptable form.

The integrated nature of business information

The various functions within a business have to be coordinated, and the information process within an organisation is therefore an integrated one. Table 7.1 gives examples of the types of information which is processed in business, and illustrates its integrative nature.

The advantages of electronic data processing

Organisations look to advances in technology to reduce office costs, and information processing is one of the main areas where technological development, especially in electronics, is having a great influence.

The reason for this influence is that electronic information processing has many advantages over traditional manual and mechanical systems of information processing. These are:

Speed. Information on almost any aspect of an organisation's activities can be recorded, sorted, analysed, stored and retrieved almost instantly.

Accuracy. Mistakes by people are the main cause of errors in information. There is far less human involvement in electronic information processing; consequently, errors are reduced. For example, standard letters to customers are typed only once and then stored for future use.

Reliability. Microelectronic equipment is more reliable than people and mechanical equipment. People at work often make mistakes because they are tired or distracted. Mechanical equipment has many moving

Table 7.1 Types of information processed in business

Purpose in Processing	Type of Information (Examples)
Planning	
Financial planning	Departmental costs
	Budget targets
	Income received
Production planning	Market statistics
	Orders received
	Orders dispatched
	Work in progress
Recording	
Payroll	Wages and salaries
Invoicing	Orders dispatched
	Accounts not paid
Turnover	Sales data
	Orders received
Purchases	Orders issued
Controlling	
Stock control	Purchases received
	Stocks used
	Work in progress
Budgetary control	Budget targets
	Departmental costs
Quality control	Work in progress
Reporting	
Financial reports	Sales data
	Departmental costs
	Budget targets
Personnel reports	Wages and salaries
	Training costs
	Recruitment data

parts, any one of which can fail, causing the machine to break down. Failure in electronic equipment is far less frequent.

Flexibility. Electronic information processing means that the analysis of information is both accurate and sophisticated. Microprocessors can be programmed to perform many operations which previously would have been too complicated or taken too long.

Improved quality. The finished copy of written communication is greatly improved by word processing. In addition, the content can be improved. For example, financial and statistical information is easily updated in reports. Information becomes less historical, and therefore more useful.

——— Financial information ———

Financial information in an organisation enables managers to perform three functions:

1 To record. The money values of resources and of transactions in any organisation can be recorded using accounting techniques. The records enable companies to produce periodic statements of the value of assets, liabilities and capital.

2 To analyse. The presentation of financial information is required by law for many organisations, and so accounting conventions have developed as to how financial information should be presented. The standardised or conventional methods of accounting enable organisations to analyse financial information; and to make comparisons of performance between one year and another (intra-firm comparisons), and between similar organisations (inter-firm comparisons).

3 To control. Organisations can maintain a degree of control over departments by examining and regulating their expenditure. Accountancy provides reliable technique for the internal management of organisations.

——— Recording transactions ———

There are three reasons why organisations should record their transactions:

1 The Companies Acts impose statutory requirements on companies

to publish their accounts. Public limited companies, the nationalised industries, and non-exempt private companies must keep and publish a proper record of transactions with respect to *(a)* receipts and expenses, *(b)* sales and purchases, and *(c)* assets and liabilities. The accounts must give a 'true and fair view' of a company's affairs.

2   Private commercial organisations have to pay tax on any surpluses which are earned through trading. Consequently, they must keep proper books of accounts which represent in a fair way all transactions. These books will be examined by the Inland Revenue.

3   It is in the interests of a public company to publish its financial information in a form which is readily understood. Public limited companies require long-term finance from the general public, and the shareholders' and potential investors' assessment of a company is normally obtained through its published financial record.

The recording and presentation of financial information is carried out according to accounting conventions. The two most important standard documents are the Profit and Loss Account, and the Balance Sheet.

——— The Profit and Loss Account ———

The Profit and Loss Account records what has happened during a particular period (normally the financial year), and the conventional presentation is shown in Fig. 7.1. (See also Appendix 4.)

The Profit and Loss Account is a summary of a firm's activities during a financial period: it does not show that income and expenditure are constantly taking place. Every working day, sales will be made and resources will be acquired.

Profit performs two important functions. As the Profit and Loss Account shows, if a firm makes sufficient profit after tax, then some money can be 'ploughed back' into the organisation through a reserve fund. Profit enables a company to grow. Equally important is the second function of profit: it provides short-term funds (working capital) to meet day-to-day expenses. So profit provides both long-term and short-term finance.

In spite of the development of standards in the presentation of the

Trading Account		£
add	Income from sales	+ sales
deduct	Costs directly related to production	− direct
	e.g. cost of raw materials	costs
	wages of operatives	
	fuel to drive machines	
gives	the Gross Profit on trading	= gross profit
add	Gross Profit on trading	+ gross profit
add	any Income other than from sales	+ additional
		income
deduct	any Expenses not directly incurred in	− indirect
	trading/manufacturing	costs
	e.g. depreciation of fixed assets	
	debenture interest	
	directors' fees	
	salaries	
	rent and rates	
gives	the Net Profit (loss) before taxation	= net profit

Appropriation Account

Taxation

add	Net Profit	+ net profit
deduct	Taxation	− taxation
gives	the Net Profit after Taxation	= net profit
		after tax

Other Appropriations

add	Net Profit after Tax	+ net profit
		after tax
add	Balance carried forward from previous year	+ previous
		balance
deduct	Gross Dividends paid or proposed to be paid	− dividends
deduct	Redemption of debentures or other loans	− redemptions
deduct	Transfers to reserve (plough-back)	− reserves
gives	the Balance on the Profit and Loss Account	
	which will be shown in the Balance Sheet	= balance

Fig. 7.1 Profit and Loss Account of *XYZ* Ltd for the year ending—19...

Profit and Loss Account, there are problems in assessing and measuring profit.

1 **Profit is a relative measure.**   Profit has more meaning when it is seen in relation to the amount of capital employed in its creation. For

example, if Company *ABC* has assets of £2000m and makes £2m net profit, and Company *XYZ* has assets of £200m and makes £2m net profit, it would be unreasonable to conclude that both companies were equally successful. Net profit is a relative figure. It needs some qualification if it is to be used as a test of efficiency.

2 Timing. Profits can fluctuate from year to year, and therefore annual Profit and Loss Accounts describe the fortunes of a company only for a limited period. For example, compare the profit performance of the two companies in Table 7.2. Investors and directors would generally prefer the consistent profits of Company *XYZ* rather than the erratic performance of Company *ABC*. The Profit and Loss Account for one year does not show these fluctuations.

3 Inflation. Money as a measure of value is not reliable during periods of inflation. Consequently, organisations have problems in valuing stocks or in deciding on the amount to set aside for the depreciation of fixed assets (see Chapter 5). Since there is an element of choice regarding the presentation of certain money values in the Profit and Loss Account, the accounts do not always give a 'true and fair view' of the performance of a firm.

4 Allocation of costs in large organisations. In large organisations, the cost of some items is not easy to apportion to particular trading activities. For example, where a large corporation spends money on corporate advertising, or on centralised research and development, the cost of these activities is not easy to allocate. Poor allocation of costs could hide unprofitable ventures and distort profit figures.

Table 7.2 Profit and losses after tax (£m)

Year	1	2	3	4	5	Total
Company *ABC*	+19	+3	+11	−5	+14	42
Company *XYZ*	+10	+9	+ 7	+8	+ 8	42

——————— The Balance Sheet ———————

The Balance Sheet is a statement of the financial position of a company at a certain date. It provides details on the assets, liabilities and owners' equity; and is required by law to be produced once during a financial year. Some companies produce 'interim' statements to show the position at a quarter or half year.

The purposes of a Balance Sheet are:

(a) To show, at a specified time, the total capital employed in the business (share capital, loans and amounts due to creditors).

(b) To show how the organisation has converted money into 'real' or 'productive' assets.

(c) To provide a record which allows auditors and owners to keep a check on the assets of a company.

(d) To provide a record which can be analysed to show how the organisation is performing. The Balance Sheet shows the gearing of the company, the balance between fixed assets and current assets, and the balance between current assets and current liabilities.

The fixed and current assets of a company are the resources which the company employs in addition to people in order to produce goods and services. Assets are acquired by incurring liabilities and by using shareholders' equity. Therefore the fixed and current assets should equal the equity (which includes any reserves and retained profit) and liabilities of a company. If a company's books are correctly kept, then both sides of the Balance Sheet should balance:

$$\text{Assets} = \text{Liabilities} + \text{Owner's Equity}$$

The apparent precision of a Balance Sheet is misleading. The techniques of accounting, if they are carried out correctly, will ensure that a Balance Sheet will always balance. But the information which is disclosed can be deceptive. The problems of inflation and changing money values (see Chapter 5) affect the accuracy of Balance Sheets. Fixed Assets, such as premises, do not necessarily represent their actual values. Similarly the value of stocks and the allowance for bad debts can only be estimated. It would be unwise to assume that the guesses of accountants are always accurate. A Balance Sheet represents the accountant's fairest view of the position of a company and, like a Profit and Loss Account, it is not an absolute record. (See also Appendix 4.)

Schedule 4 of the Companies Act, 1985 requires firms to disclose financial information in a specified format, and Fig. 7.2 shows the minimum headings which are required to be included in a Balance Sheet presented in vertical format 1.

	£ ·	£
Called-up Share Capital Not Paid		0000
Fixed Assets		
Intangible assets	000	
Tangible assets	000	
Investments	000	0000
Current Assets		
Stocks	000	
Debtors	000	
Investments	000	
Cash	000	0000
Prepayments and Accrued Income		0000
Creditors: Amounts falling due		
within one year		(000)
Net Current Assets (Liabilities)		0000
Total Assets *less* Current Liabilities		0000
Creditors: Amounts falling due		
after more than one year		(0000)
Provisions for Liabilities and Charges		(0000)
Accruals and Deferred Income		(0000)
Net Worth of the Company		___
The above is financed by:		
Capital and Reserves		
Called-up share capital	000	
Share premium account	000	
Revaluation reserve	000	
Other reserves	000	
		0000
Profit and Loss Account		0000

Note: Items shown in brackets () are minus figures.

Fig. 7.2   Balance Sheet of *XYZ* Ltd as at—19... – vertical format 1

The presentation of the Balance Sheet in a vertical format is a relatively recent practice. The traditional form of presentation is a horizontal format; and a simplified example of the layout is given in Fig. 7.3. The information which is included in both the vertical and the horizontal formats is similar: it customary in both formats to show assets and liabilities in order of liquidity – the least liquid item is shown first and the most liquid last. The two advantages of the vertical format are that,

	£		£
Share Capital	0000	Fixed Assets shown at cost *less*	0000
Reserves	0000	depreciation to give written-down value	
Liabilities and Provisions	0000		
Current Liabilities	0000	Current Assets	0000
	£		£

Fig. 7.3 Balance Sheet of *XYZ* Ltd as at—19... – horizontal format

firstly, it is generally easier to understand. For example, the horizontal layout shows shareholders' capital as a liability and this can cause confusion. Secondly, it emphasises important features such as the working capital and net worth of a company.

Exercises

Comprehension

1 List the purposes of processing information in a business.

2 Give examples of information which is used in a business.

3 What are the advantages in processing information electronically?

4 Why should organisations record their transactions?

5 What is a 'Profit and Loss Account'?

Research

1 Explain why the profit which a company makes in one particular year may not necessarily be a good guide to the success of the business.

2 Do you think that there are any disadvantages in processing business information electronically? Explain your answer.

3 Explain the purpose of a Balance Sheet.

Project

Compile a table of examples of electronic business information which you have received in your home over a period of four months.

8

EFFICIENCY IN ORGANISATIONS

Money, as we saw in Chapter 5, is a measure of value. An organisation's efficiency, or the value it gets from its use of resources, is represented by how much money the organisation spends on different items in relation to the output it gains from its expenditure. For example, if there are two breweries producing identical amounts and types of beer, the brewery with the lower costs of production would be considered to be more efficient. Efficiency, then, is the relationship between costs (use of resources) and output.

Types of costs

Costs are the expenses which are incurred in producing and distributing either goods or services, and there are two types of costs in all organisations.

Fixed costs are those which an organisation would have to pay even when production is not taking place – for example, rent for the premises (land and buildings); taxes paid to the local authority (land and buildings); interest paid on loans (capital equipment); and depreciation (capital equipment).

These examples illustrate the fairly obvious fact that money which is spent on fixed assets such as plant and equipment is a permanent or fixed cost. Fixed costs are those expenses which are primarily used to provide long-term capital resources, and additional expenses, such as staff salaries, which will be incurred regardless of the level of production.

Variable costs are those which vary with output, and any costs which are not fixed are considered to be variable – for example, expenditure on raw materials, fuel, lighting and heating, and the wages of those directly engaged in production.

Difficulties in the classification of costs

In practical terms, it is not always easy to differentiate between fixed and variable costs. For example, some administrative costs – such as telephone bills or postage expenses – will have a tendency to vary with output, although the relationship between them and output is not as strong as it is between raw material costs and output. However, some administrative costs are fairly fixed: the salaries of managers and staff have to be paid regardless of output. But salaries are not as fixed as capital costs, because managers can be made redundant when production remains low for a long time.

A second difficulty occurs in relation to capital costs. The provision for depreciation is classified as a fixed cost, but the actual deterioration of a machine is related to how frequently it is used. Production does create a cost of capital equipment through wear and tear. Equally, time makes equipment obsolete and leads to a deterioration in plant and buildings. In effect, therefore, all costs are variable in the long term. Fig. 8.1 illustrates the degree of permanence of various costs in the short term.

Unit costs

The total costs of production are made up by variable costs and fixed costs. An organisation, however, is not necessarily interested in total costs but in how much each *unit* of production costs. This is particularly true if a firm is confident that it can sell every unit at a certain price. It is the unit costs rather than the total costs which give a better representation of the efficiency of organisations.

Fig. 8.1 The short-term variability of costs

The relationship between output and costs

Time has an important effect on costs, in that all costs will eventually vary. Equally, output itself has an effect on the unit costs of an organisation: unit costs can never remain constant. Assuming that everything else remains constant as production increases, then unit costs will fall. A simple example illustrates this point in Table 8.1. Assume that Company Toy produces jigsaw puzzles for which the fixed costs are £400, and the variable costs £1.00 per puzzle. As production increases, so total costs will increase (Fig. 8.2(*a*)), but unit costs will fall (Fig. 8.2(*b*)).

The reason or the fall in unit costs is that, as output increases, the fixed cost element becomes a smaller and smaller proportion of total costs. In the initial stages of production, however, the impact of fixed costs on total costs, and therefore on unit costs, is very great.

Table 8.1

Units produced	Fixed costs £		Variable costs £		Total costs £	Unit costs £
0	400	+	0	=	400	∞
1	400	+	1	=	401	401.00
10	400	+	10	=	410	41.00
50	400	+	50	=	450	9.00
100	400	+	100	=	500	5.00
250	400	+	250	=	650	2.60
500	400	+	500	=	900	1.80
1000	400	+	1000	=	1400	1.40

Unit costs get nearer and nearer to variable costs, but of course they can never become equal to variable costs.

Fig. 8.2 Behaviour of costs

Economies of scale

All organisations, particularly those with high fixed costs, will benefit from producing on a large scale, because increased output reduces the percentage of fixed costs to total costs. The reductions in unit costs which result from increases in output are known as the 'economies of scale'. The following are examples:

Set-up costs. The motor car industry has to spend large sums of money to establish or 'set up' a production and assembly line. Similarly, the printing industry 'sets up' presses to produce newspapers or books. The long production runs which this type of industry can then undertake reduces the fixed costs to a smaller and smaller proportion of total costs; and unit costs become lower at each stage of output.

Marketing costs. Advertising expenditure is not directly related to production. The more units a firm produces, the smaller advertising expenditure becomes as a proportion of total costs.

Administrative costs. A complex computer installation or a research and development team are relatively expensive administrative costs which are fixed. Large firms can afford such costs only when they' form a small percentage of total costs.

Efficiency, productivity and scale

We have seen that increased output automatically makes fixed costs a small proportion of total costs and therefore reduces unit costs. So large-scale production does create some savings or economies, but these economies are not increases in efficiency or productivity. The real test of efficiency is to reduce *in absolute terms* either the variable costs or the fixed costs.

An increase in productivity can occur in two ways:

1 When output increases and costs remain constant. Costs represent factors of production or resources, so a test of efficiency is to get more out of existing resources.

2 When output remains constant and costs fall. If an organisation can use fewer resources – raw materials, energy, people – and yet maintain production levels, then productivity has increased.

The expansion of output not only reduces the percentage of fixed costs to total costs, but also provides organisations with opportunities for increasing productivity. For example, other economies of scale are:

Capital cost saving. The capital cost of some fixed assets does not increase in direct proportion to size. For example, the design size of oil tankers can be doubled from 100 000 tonnes to 200 000 tonnes, but the materials which are required do not double. Jumbo jets do not cost twice as much as other passenger jets to build and yet they can carry twice the number of passengers.

Improved purchasing power. Large firms can benefit from reduced purchasing costs because they can obtain their supplies in bulk. Similarly they can afford to buy equipment which is up to date and more efficient. For example, computer-aided design systems which combine design, production, stock control and finance are more efficient than traditional manual methods.

Savings in finance. Large organisations can attract investors and are able to 'shop around' for the cheaper sources of finance. Not only do their funds tend to cost less, but finance is easier to obtain and therefore borrowing requires less effort and less time.

People. Large organisations can afford to employ specialists who are skilled in such management techniques as work study or organisation and methods, which will help to improve the efficiency of the organisation. They can also afford to train their own management staff in motivation and similar skills which will improve the performance of employees.

It would be wrong to assume that only large organisations can improve productivity. Increases in output and size provide organisations with the above opportunities for reducing fixed and variable costs; but there are techniques for improving efficiency which *any* organisation can use, regardless of its size.

_____ Techniques for improving _____ efficiency

1 Improved methods of work and operation: work study

An organisation can systematically analyse its existing procedures by:

(a) Identifying the goals of particular tasks.
(b) Recording in a systematic manner (using a flow chart) how a task is performed.

(c) Examining the record made in *(b)* with the intention of eliminating duplicated and wasted effort.

(d) Designing and introducing a revised and improved method.

(e) Making periodic checks to ensure that the new procedures operate as planned.

Work study can improve the performance of many employees, particularly those who are engaged in repetitive tasks such as assembly work. It can also be used to improve the layout of a factory, hospital ward, office, etc., so that space is used more effectively.

2 Organisation & Method (O&M)

O&M originated in the Civil Service during the 1940s, and is particularly useful in administrative departments. O&M is in effect the application of work study ideas to the office. It uses the same type of systematic analysis, with the objective of simplifying and improving office methods. The benefits which can result from O&M are:

(a) Improved flow and speed of information (e.g. accounting records).

(b) Better records and easier access to information (e.g. staff records).

(c) Closer control of operations (e.g. quicker response to customer complaints).

(d) Avoidance of bottle-necks caused by delays (e.g. the processing of customers' orders).

(e) Improved security procedures (e.g. handling cash and confidential documents).

3 Standardisation

A common approach is useful in all areas of business activity – tools, equipment, procedures, forms, etc. Conversion from one system to another either costs time and money or is impossible. Standardisation eliminates conversion problems and reduces obsolescence of equipment.

The following are examples of standardisation from which the whole of business can benefit:

(a) Standard basic components, such as the threads on nuts and bolts.

(b) Standard measurements, such as metric.

(c) Standard terminology and procedures, such as airport procedures.

(d) Standard equipment, such as containers for lorries and ships.

Organisations can benefit too from internal standardisation. For example:

(a) Standard packaging, which makes the storage and transport of finished goods cheaper and easier.

(b) Standard methods of production and the interchangeability of parts (e.g. when the tools used in the production of one car are used again in the production of another model).

(c) Standard communication procedures (e.g. standard forms and reports make recording and filing much simpler).

A danger in standardisation is that it can make organisations inflexible because of 'red tape', and it can make the reaction to change slow.

4 Statistical techniques/Operational Research (OR)

Because change and risk are so prevalent in business, the application of probability theory can help organisations to predict when events might go wrong; and it can help them to select the best course of action – to decide on the best alternative. OR describes a series of techniques which can assist managers in planning and decision-making. All of the techniques have a mathematical basis, and their practical application is complex. The main OR techniques are:

(a) *Critical Path Analysis (CPA)* can shorten the time of projects, especially construction projects such as bridges, roads, buildings and ships. The technique can be refined to indicate the best time to allocate resources.

(b) *Simulation/queuing theory.* In simulation techniques, a mathematical model is constructed to represent the many variables which exist in a real system. Different combinations of variables are tested to find the most efficient allocation of resources or to find the solution to a problem. For example, it helps to solve queuing problems such as aircraft waiting to land, goods waiting to be processed, customers waiting for buses, or customers waiting for telephone calls.

(c) *Game theory: competitive strategies.* This technique is used by the armed forces to test different battle strategies. Its commercial application is in marketing, where the reaction of competitors to different marketing strategies is predicted.

(d) *Quality control.* The quality of products can be controlled by using statistical techniques which help human or machine errors to be detected quickly.

(e) *Stock control.* Stocks (of raw materials, stationery, spare parts, etc.) are kept by all types of organisation and techniques have been developed which help organisations to keep sufficient stock without running out, and at the same time to minimise the cost of holding stock.

5 Productivity/incentive schemes

Productivity agreements enable employees to become more effective and so reduce wages costs. The terms which can be included in a productivity agreement are:

(a) Payment by results, bonuses, fringe benefits.
(b) Reduction in overtime. Wage costs are more expensive when overtime is worked.
(c) Flexible working hours.
(d) Elimination of rigid demarcation between different jobs.
(e) Elimination of time-wasting.

Financial reward does motivate people, but it is limited in its capacity to act as an incentive. In the long run, employees have to be given other rewards as well as recognition and responsibility if they are to maximise their contribution to an organisation.

6 Technology and automation

Improved efficiency is often achieved by developments in machinery and equipment. A most revolutionary impact has been made, and is being made, on business by developments in microelectronics. Silicon-chip technology will affect all organisations, for example stock control in retailing, data processing in the small business, word processing in administration, and so on. (See also Part 5.)

7 Strategic quality management

In recent years the techniques for improving efficiency have been absorbed into the working practices of many organisations under the umbrella of strategic quality management programmes. These programmes are seen as a process within an organisation which, once started, never ends.

An organisation which practises strategic quality management should carry out the following operations:

(a) *Vision and purpose.*   Define the main purpose of the organisation.

(b) *Strategy.*   Determine priorities, set objectives and establish a plan to fulfil these objectives.

(c) *Management.*   Describe the roles of senior staff and describe the responsibilities and functions of all employees. Set performance criteria for staff.

(d) *Involvement.*   Establish effective methods of communication and set up appropriate training and development programmes.

(e) *Resources.*   Apply the appropriate techniques for improving efficiency and ensure that the systems for control and checking accountability are in place.

(f) *Quality improvement.*   Determine the characteristics of quality which will be assessed and set attainable standards which can be measured.

— Costs and geographical location —

The efficiency of an organisation is not decided simply by its size and its management practices. The geographical location of an organisation will affect its costs. For example, office accommodation is more expensive in central London than in Aberystwyth. On the other hand there are advantages in being located in London, such as the speed of communication or the large market of office employees, which can offset the high rents and cause offices to be London-based. These advantages are called *external economies.*

When deciding on its location, an organisation will try to get maximum savings and incur minimum costs from the immediate environment. But not all organisations have a choice of where they will be situated – coal mining can only take place where there is coal, docks can only be located in sheltered waters – so the location decision of an organisation cannot always be in terms of costs. The factors which influence the location of organisations are:

1   Historical reasons: industrial inertia.   Many industries became established in particular areas because of the nearness of certain supplies, especially energy. For example, the manufacture of wool was established in Yorkshire because of the availability of water power in the Pennine valleys. Steel production was located in Sheffield because of the availability of coal as well as iron ore and limestone. Even though the initial advantage has declined, many industries have remained in their first locations because of 'industrial inertia'. Other advantages, such as a skilled workforce, have replaced the initial attraction.

2   The distribution of 'nature's gifts'.   Extractive industries have very little choice of location: mining, quarrying and oil drilling must be based at the source of the product. Similarly, the location and type of farm is influenced by topography and climate. The fishing industry is located near to harbours and fishing grounds.

3   The current availability of resources.   Manufacturing industry requires raw materials, energy and labour in order to produce, and will often be located close to an essential resource. The Ford Motor Company was established in Dagenham, Essex, because of the supply of labour. Modern steel production is located close to ports where iron ore can be imported.

4   Closeness to a market.   The service industries have very little choice in location decisions – they must be situated where the demand for their service exists. Thus insurance and banking are located in commercial centres; hairdressing salons, restaurants, retail outlets, and central and local government services are located in populated areas. Those firms which produce finished products which are fragile or valuable will also want to be located near to a market, to minimise the cost of damage or loss during transit.

5   Cost of transport.   Those organisations which manufacture a product must choose either to be located near to the supply of raw materials or near to their market. The decision will be influenced by the costs of transport. If the finished product is bulkier and heavier than the raw materials, then the production will be situated near to the market. Generally speaking, raw materials are cheaper to transport than finished foods, so that industries which produce furniture, clothes and durable goods tend to be located close to the supplies of labour which are also consumer markets.

As we can see from Fig. 8.3, the two sectors of business which have very little choice in location are the primary and tertiary industries. The

Nature's gifts	Raw materials	Transport costs	Working population	Customers and clients

←——————————————————————————————————→

Primary industries have little choice	Secondary industries can choose	Service industries have little choice

Fig. 8.3 Factors determining location of primary, secondary and tertiary sectors

manufacturing sector has much greater choice, and it is the cost of transport which will influence most firms' decisions on location. They will balance the cost of transporting the raw materials against the cost of transporting the finished product.

———————— **External economies** ————————

Once an industry becomes established in a particular location, there are advantages which accrue. It is these advantages which cause 'inertia' or lack of mobility in the system. The benefits are:

1 Local authority and central government services. The National Health Service, Education and Housing become established wherever people are. Some of these services, such as courses at the local technical college, can become specifically geared to the needs of local organisations.

2 Commercial facilities. Banking, insurance, and security organisations will adapt their services to meet the needs of a local industry. They become familiar with the particular problems of local organisations and provide a specialised service. In addition, local chambers of trade and employers' associations develop, and then provide, specialised assistance in research and cooperation.

3 Marketing and distribution facilities. An established industry will encourage the provision of specialised haulage and warehousing facilities, as well as the creation of local mailing agencies.

4 Ancillary support industries. Interdependence, which is a dominant feature of modern business, means that ancillary organisations will develop around established producers. For example, car production in the Midlands has encouraged the siting of hundreds of car component manufacturers in that area.

Organisations and production systems

The nature of an organisation's product or service will greatly influence its location; similarly it will also determine the type of 'system' through which the organisation will achieve its aims. Because of the nature of their product/service, most organisations do not have any choice in the type of system they will adopt. For example, mining has to be carried on in an 'extractive' system. Although one system will dominate the business of an organisation, it will generally use more than one system. All industrial organisations, for example, have a production function which forms part of the manufacturing system, a financial function in the administrative system, and a marketing function in the service system.

The systems which are described below are general illustrations of the types of arrangement which can dominate the activities of an organisation, and which will influence the organisation's efficiency. It would be wrong to believe that every organisation fits neatly into one particular category.

1 The extractive system.   Mining, quarrying, fishing and farming are engaged in the extraction of products and produce from nature. Developments in technology have made the extractive industries more capital-intensive, but traditionally they require a high proportion of their total costs to be spent on labour in order to produce.

2 The manufacturing system: flow production.   In manufacturing it is common for the operations to be broken down into a series of repetitive tasks where components are assembled to form a finished product, such as a car. The mass production of durable goods such as radios, vacuum cleaners, refrigerators, etc., requires high capital investment in fixed assets to set up the production process. The people employed in assembly or flow production tend to be unskilled or semi-skilled.

3   The construction system.   There are products which cannot be created on a 'massive' scale. Some, like power stations, roads or bridges, can only be produced once. Other products, such as houses, are normally produced in batches. The organisations in a construction system tend to be more flexible than those in manufacturing because their investment in fixed assets tends to be a smaller proportion of total assets. On the other hand, they will employ highly skilled people who can adapt to different work situations.

4   The communications system.   The transport industries and the post and telecommunications services provide a communications system; they produce the facilities for people and organisations to make contact. The industries in this system require both high capital investment in advanced technology, and a large number of employees, many of whom are highly skilled.

5   The service system.   Most organisations have a relationship with the service system; for example, the marketing function is part of distribution. The service system includes commercial industries such as retailing, hotels and catering, and hairdressing, as well as the public services such as health, education and social welfare. A significant feature of the service system is that the organisations which use it are dispersed throughout the country in direct relation to the population. The system is labour intensive.

6   The administrative system.   Organisations are dominated by the administrative system when their main aim is to control and produce information. Naturally, administrative systems exist in all organisations, but the activities of some institutions, such as the Civil Service, the commercial banks, the building societies and insurance companies, are primarily administrative – they manage information. The developments in computers and electronic information processing are making these organisations more capital-intensive, but they remain large employers of people.

The different methods of efficiency which the various systems create can be summarised in chart form (Table 8.2).

Table 8.2 Organisations and production systems

Type of system	Examples	Nature of the fixed assets	Nature of the labour
Extractive	Mining Quarrying Fishing Farming Oil Gas	Has become more capital intensive using highly specialised capital equipment	Employs a small % of working population. Dangerous work
Manufacturing	Durable goods Vehicles Food processing Printing Chemicals	High 'set up' costs	Large number of employees. Low-skilled assembly work
Construction	Roads Bridges Aircraft Ships Houses	Equipment has to be adaptable as well as highly specialised	High technical and motor skills required. Labour has to be mobile in some cases
Communications	Rail Road Sea Air Post Telecommunications	Highly expensive fixed assets required. Assets soon obsolete	Labour intensive industries. Employ all types of labour
Service	Retailing Hotel & catering Health Education Social welfare	Premises tend to be the main capital asset	Labour intensive industry. Social skills important
Administration	Civil services Banking Insurance Local govt.	The main capital assets are premises and data-processing equipment	Becoming less labour intensive. Employs mainly 'professional' people

Position regarding the economics of scale	Location decision	Efficiency Methods used	Comments
Growth limited by 'Nature's Gifts'	No choice in location	Productivity and incentive schemes	Coal and some oil production are nationalised. Farming controlled by EEC policy
Long production runs and high output. Economics of scale	Choice between raw materials and labour supply	Standardisation Quality control Stock control	Traditionally known as 'flow production'. Includes many well-known corporations: ICI, BL, Unilever
Short production runs and high-cost products	Apart from 'batch' production very little choice in location	Standardisation Critical path analysis Simulation models	Design plays a very important part in the system. Very competitive system
Organisations tend to be monopolistic and large-scale	Provides a communications service for almost all the population	Research and development Queuing theory	Most organisations in this sector are monopolies and were privatised in the 1980s
There are many small units in the commercial sector	Can be situated any-where near to population (market)	Stock control Queuing theory	Competition in the commercial sector is high. The public organisations are the most expensive govt. services
Problems of coordination and communication. Decentralisation common	Main organisa-tions are based in London. Exist in all areas of population	Organisation & Methods	Administration is a function found in all organisations

_ The law of diminishing returns and _ the diseconomies of scale

The efficiency of a business is influenced by the way it is managed; and by organisational features such as system, location and scale of operations. Set against these influences, there are two important principles regarding inefficiency which apply to all organisations, particularly those which expand. The two principles are: the law of diminishing returns, and the diseconomies of scale.

The law of diminishing returns

The law of diminishing returns states that as more and more resources are allocated to a fixed asset, then eventually output will diminish (Fig. 8.4).

Fixed resources have a finite capacity. For example, there is a limit to the number of animals which can graze in a field, or to the number of tables which can be placed in a restaurant. There are some assets,

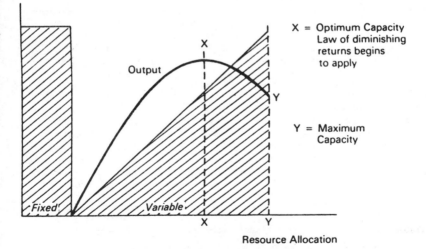

Fig. 8.4 Optimum and maximum capacities – the law of diminishing returns

however, where it is difficult to assess their capacity. What, for example, is the maximum capacity of the road system? Although it is efficient to use resources as much as possible, it is a mistake to believe that a resource is always most effective when it is worked at maximum capacity. Employment to maximum capacity of most resources will result in delays, bottlenecks, breakdowns, congestion and all the other factors which cause inefficiency, for example the M25.

In all systems there is an *optimum* mix of resources which will maximise output, and this mix can often be assessed by OR techniques. Since it is rare for the optimum capacity to be the same as maximum capacity, the managers, when they want to allocate resources most effectively, should use management techniques to assess the optimum use of their resources and so avoid the onset of the law of diminishing returns.

The diseconomies of scale

One of the problems of large organisations is that, although increased size brings the benefits of large-scale operations, they will probably run into the diseconomies of scale. For example:

1 Communication problems. Large organisations can have problems with internal and external communication. The lines of communication become extended and 'red tape' develops. For example, customers find it difficult to complain when organisations are large, and employees feel that the firm is impersonal.

2 Poor coordination and control. Central control can become difficult. The skills and knowledge which are needed to control and coordinate large organisations are rare. A lack of control might allow managers to develop their own aims and objectives so that they build up their department at the expense of other departments in order to get increased status or more power.

3 Slow reaction to change. The need for standardised procedures in large organisations can make them so inflexible that they reject good ideas and plans which do not fit into the standard pattern. Highly centralised organisations can be slow to adapt to change.

4 Obsolescent equipment. The purchase of expensive fixed assets is easier in large organisations but it can be costly and create inflexibility. Some of the former nationalised industries provide good examples of capital equipment which is obsolescent – rail stock, telephone exchanges, power stations, steel plants. Although such equipment is less efficient than contemporary equipment, once it is installed it is too costly to change for a long time.

__ Analysis of financial information: __ measures of efficiency

Several techniques have evolved which enable businessmen to compare the performance of an organisation from year to year, and to compare similar organisations. The following are three important methods of financial analysis.

1 Working capital

Without finance, a business cannot obtain resources and therefore it cannot operate. The fixed assets in an organisation need to be used as frequently as possible – it is very costly and inefficient to have plant and machinery lying idle. There are many necessities which are required before fixed assets can operate, the most important being people, raw materials and energy. Money and other highly liquid assets (those assets which can quickly be turned into cash) are the lifeblood of business activity because they help an organisation to acquire these three important resources on a continuous and current basis. Liquid assets are the capital which help to lubricate the fixed assets in an organisation.

It is not surprising that one of the most important areas of financial analysis is that which is concerned with this 'working capital'. Working capital is the current assets minus current claims which could be made on those assets (Fig. 8.5).

It is important to remember that the flow of money through an organisation is a continuous process.

If the working capital is insufficient, then it is likely that the organisation will run into difficulties. Fig. 8.6 illustrates the flow of circulating capital through an organisation, but it also indicates some of the difficulties which could occur. For example:

Current assets
Cash in hand
Cash at bank
Payments in advance
Debtors
Stock of raw materials
Stock of finished goods

less

Current liabilities
Trade creditors (for goods supplied)
Expense creditors (for services)
Taxation payable
Dividends recommended
Debenture interest due
Bank overdrafts

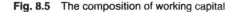

Fig. 8.5 The composition of working capital

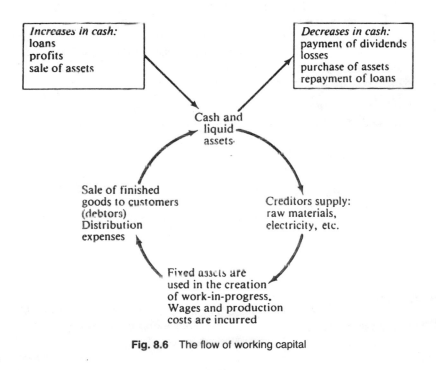

Fig. 8.6 The flow of working capital

(a) Insufficient cash to pay creditors means that the organisation is unable to purchase raw materials, fuel, etc., and is unable to pay wages.

(b) Holding too much cash is an expensive and inefficient practice, especially during periods of high inflation. Money has to be employed if it is to generate profit.

(c) If stocks of raw materials are low, then production could be held up and the delivery of finished goods delayed.

(d) Holding too much stock can cause deterioration and obsolescence.

By analysing its working capital on a regular basis, an organisation can attempt to avoid these problems.

2 Ratio analysis

The relationship between items on the Profit and Loss Account and the Balance Sheet can be clarified by using financial ratios. Their main use is that they provide additional information over and above single items in the recorded accounts.

A ratio, like any statistic, is useful only when it is compared with the same ratio from a previous year or from a similar organisation. There are more than one hundred ratios which *could* be calculated, but the most useful ones are described below (see also Appendix 4).

Tests of liquidity
These ratios help the organisation to analyse the flow of cash through an organisation.

(a) *Current ratio*
current assets: current liabilities.
The current ratio is a way of quickly assessing the nature of the working capital. If the ratio is less than 2:1 then the firm could be running into liquidity problems and might find it difficult to pay its way.

(b) *Acid test ratio*
current assets *less* stock: current liabilities.
The current ratio includes stock, but stocks are not easily converted into cash. The acid test ratio excludes stock, and illustrates the relationship between highly liquid current assets and all current liabilities. Analysts would normally look for an acid test ratio of 1:1 – the ability to meet immediately all current liabilities.

(c)   *The average period of the collection of trade debts*
Debtors: annual sales.
This ratio shows how quickly an organisation could convert the money owed by the debtors into cash in hand. For example, a ratio of 1:4 would indicate that the average period is three months, 1:2 is six months, and so on. The longer the period, the less liquid the debts are.

Tests of profitability

(d)   *Rate of return on capital*
net profit: capital employed (fixed assets *plus* working capital).
A company would hope to obtain a consistent return on capital which, if the organisation is successful, is higher than that achieved by similar organisations.

(e)   *Profit to sales*
net profit: sales *or* gross profit: sales.
This ratio illustrates the relationship between profitability and turnover. It is sometimes used in conjunction with break-even analysis.

Ratios in themselves have only a limited value if they are used purely for comparisons within the business. Firms can increase the value of such ratios by subscribing to the Centre for Inter-firm Comparisons. This body provides a confidential service and helps companies to compare their own ratios, costs, sales, output, etc., with other similar (but unidentified) organisations. If the comparisons are unfavourable, then it is a sign that the management of the organisation could be inefficient.

3   Break-even analysis

A firm breaks even when its total costs equal total sales revenue. Once the total sales revenue exceeds total costs, then the firm is making a profit. This relationship between revenue and costs can be illustrated diagrammatically with a break-even chart (Fig. 8.7). The volume of production/sales is plotted on the horizontal axis, and the revenue and costs on the vertical axis. The chart illustrates the amount of profit or loss at various volumes of sales/production.

There are three assumptions in the construction of break-even charts which could be unrealistic. The diagrams show the effect if the assumptions are *not* realised.

— **123** —

Fig. 8.7 The break-even chart

(a) All of the goods which are produced will be sold (Fig. 8.8).
(b) Costs, selling price and product mix remain constant (Fig. 8.9).
(c) The capacity, technology and the fixed assets of the organisation remain unchanged (Fig. 8.10).

The effects of changes in the many variables of price, costs and technology can be incorporated in break-even analysis, however. A chart which does take account of these will be complicated, but more realistic and therefore more useful. The main advantages of break-even analysis are that it enables businessmen to:

(a) Assess the impact of changes in turnover on profitability.
(b) Predict the effect of changes in price and forecast the percentage change in turnover which would occur when the selling price changed.
(c) Analyse the relationship between fixed and variable costs.
(d) Predict the effect on profitability of changes in efficiency or changes in costs.

Fig. 8.8 The break-even chart – sales below production

X shows actual sales

Y shows actual production based on predicted sales

Demand has fallen short of expectation and the company is selling below the margin of safety and is therefore making a loss. The company will be left with unsold finished stock

Margin of Safety

Break-even point

Production Sales

Fig. 8.9 The break-even chart – selling price falls

Y shows the production capacity of the firm.

If the selling price falls, then sales revenue decreases: the area of profit and the margin of safety decrease

Margin of safety 1

Break-even point 2

Break-even point 1

Production/Sales

Fig. 8.10 The break-even chart – capacity increases by acquisition of extra fixed assets

(e) Assess the effect of changes in the capacity of the plant brought about by investment in new fixed assets. (See Appendix 3.)

Financial control

Since money represents the allocation of resources in any organisation, the best method of controlling the efficiency of a business is by watching and directing expenditure. Financial control is exercised internally by accountants and managers, and externally by auditors.

Internal control-budgeting

A budget is a plan which is based on estimates of future revenue and spending. It establishes the allocation of costs and expenses in relation to a given objective over a defined period of time. A budget can include the employment of capital, as well as plans related to daily income and expenditure. The procedure for budgeting (Fig. 8.11) is to:

1 Define departmental goals and allocate expenditure to specific programmes.
2 Set, in consultation with the departments, standards of operation of programmes in relation to costs.
3 Obtain the information on actual spending in a systematic manner.
4 Compare the actual performance (spending) with the set standard. These comparisons will take place at different times according to the nature of an organisation's operations. A government department or a manufacturing organisation will probably set targets annually and analyse them every six, or even three months. A retail outlet might set its standards every six months, to coincide with seasonal variations in demand, and analyse them every month.
5 Take action when market variations occur between the actual and the planned spending: then either the plan is revised or the operation and the efficiency of the department are examined in detail. This is the stage in the budgeting process when organisations can attempt to become more efficient, by questioning the validity of departmental objectives and by considering alternative methods of operation.

The recording and analysis of the Profit and Loss Account and the Balance Sheet is an operation which is restricted to commercial organisations. Budgeting, however, is practised by all types of public bodies as well as by private organisations. For example, 'Output Budgeting' or 'PPBS' (planning-programming-budgeting-systems) is carried out by government departments in consultation with the Treasury. In PPBS,

Define→*Set* ⟶ *Obtain* ⟶ *Compare* ⟶ *Revise*
goals standards information actual plans and
in cost on actual performance examine
terms costs with plan alternative
strategies

Define →etc. ◄
new goals

Fig. 8.11 The budgetary control process

department objectives are defined and funds allocated to broad areas. Then on regular, and on an *ad hoc* basis, systematic review of particular sectors of expenditure takes places.

The advantages of budgetary control are that it:

1 Clarifies the aims and policies of organisations in relation to specific departments, and helps the organisation to translate its policies into departmental programmes.
2 Clarifies departmental objectives and helps managers to define lines of authority and responsibility.
3 Helps the development of corporate strategies and stimulates departmental cooperation.
4 Improves central control. Actual performance can be compared with planned or budgeted performance.
5 Helps to improve efficiency. It shows which resources are used in relation to specific activities, and how well they are being used.

Auditing

External auditors provide a means of control which is required by law. The Companies Act, 1985, codifies in some detail the appointment and resignation of the external auditor, and strengthens the auditor's position in relation to the disclosure of information by company officials and access to company records. The auditor performs these functions by systematically examining on a sample basis all relevant documents.

The functions of an external auditor are to:

1 Examine documents such as invoices, receipts and contracts in order to verify their accuracy.
2 Examine administrative procedures to prevent and discourage fraud and embezzlement.
3 Certify that proper records have been kept and that the recorded accounts agree with the details of transactions in the organisation's books.
4 Certify and report that the accounts give a 'true and fair view' of the company's affairs.

The external auditors who check the accounts of companies will report to the shareholders at the Annual General Meeting. A similar reporting function is carried out by District Auditors in local and central government. District Auditors not only perform similar duties to private auditors; they check the accuracy of the financial records of government bodies and local authorities; but they also assess whether public expenditure has been within the law (*ultra vires*). Local authorities and government organisations cannot spend money outside their statutory authority. For example, at one stage councillors in Clay Cross refused to obey the law and increase council house rents; in effect they subsidised rent payers by £6985. The District Auditor surcharged the members of the council for the £6985.

Many organisations in the public and private sectors have their own system of internal auditing. Although by law the internal auditors cannot replace external auditors, they perform similar functions. Internal auditors also help to improve the efficiency of organisations by:

1 Helping to maintain the policies and procedures within an organisation.
2 Promoting accuracy in record keeping, and helping to reduce errors.
3 Guarding against misappropriations such as theft, fraud and embezzlement.

Exercises

Comprehension

1 Give examples of 'economies of scale'.

2 Define 'productivity'.

3 List the main methods a firm can use to improve its efficiency.

4 What is meant by 'external economies'?

5 Define 'working capital'.

Research

1 Explain why, in the long term, fixed costs can become variable.

2   Do you agree that a business cannot afford not to practise Strategic Quality Management?

3   Assess the relationship between costs and the geographical location of a business.

Project

Construct your own table which shows the relationship between output and costs.

9

THE CONSTRAINTS ON ORGANISATIONS

Legal constraints

Legal rules govern the relationship between people and organisations, between people and people, and between organisations and organisations. For example, rules apply to the establishment of an organisation, to an organisation's relationship with employees, and to an organisation's relationship with customers/clients. Although the influence of law is present in all business activity, the rules are mainly applied when conflict or uncertainty occur.

Sources of law

Statutes – Acts of Parliament

Legal rules are created by Parliament, primarily at the instigation of the Government. Acts of Parliament or Statues have to be approved by the House of Commons, the House of Lords and the Queen. The Government translates its policies into Bills (Public Bills), and because most governments have a majority in the House of Commons, the Executive dominates the introduction of legislation into Parliament. However, individual Members of Parliament are allowed time to introduce their own Public Bills (Private Members' Bills) into the process, and outside bodies such as local authorities can have private legislation (Private Bills) introduced.

Delegated legislation

The process of creating law can be complicated and difficult, especially when technical and detailed rules are required. Parliament does not have the time, nor even the expertise, to design some complex rules – for example, building regulations or regulations regarding aircraft. In such instances, Parliament provides the principles and framework of legal rules but delegates the power to draft the more technical rules and regulations to local authorities and government departments. The local authorities produce by-laws, and the government departments issue statutory instruments.

This subordinate or delegated legislation has become a major feature of the legal constraints which are imposed on business.

The decisions of judges: judicial precedent

Although the parliamentary process is rigorous, and every attempt is made to ensure that the language in statutes is unambiguous, all legislation requires interpretation. The interpretation of Acts is made by judges. The decisions of judges in higher courts on interpretation must be followed by the lower courts, and decisions made by courts of equal rank are taken into account by one another. The procedure is that judges explain the legal principles on which they have based their interpretation (known as *ratio decidendi*), and the decision becomes a judicial precedent. This process, although it is slow, creates certainty and fairness in the application of legal rules.

Custom

General customs laid the foundation for many legal rules when law was becoming established. But custom is not now as important as Statutes as a source of law. However, regular practice will become law if it is recognised by a valid court. Such recognition occurs when the custom is not reasonable, has existed for as long as anyone can remember, and the court can clearly identify who benefits.

——— The classification of law ———

Legal rules can be classified into two distinct groups: Public Law and Private or Civil Law. The distinction is important in that Public Law provides the rules for behaviour in the community at large; and Private Law provides the legal framework for relationships between individuals and organisations.

Public Law

1 Constitutional law.   The United Kingdom does not have a written constitution, and many of the rules which govern the activities of constitutional bodies are based on custom and convention rather than legal rules. For example, the collective responsibility of the Cabinet is an unwritten convention. However, the power of government ministers and of local authorities is primarily governed by Statute Law.

2 Criminal law.   The behaviour of some people is anti-social; in business, for example, fraud, misrepresentation and misappropriation of funds occur. The purpose of criminal law is to suppress behaviour which either disturbs the peace or disrupts the well-being of others. In effect, the criminal law allows the State to protect the property of persons and organisations, and to protect persons from others, by punishing the offenders.

Private (Civil) Law

Private Law provides legal rules on a much wider basis than Public Law – rules which relate to marriage, the family, inheritance and trusts. In effect, the Civil Law clarifies the rights and duties of people and organisations towards each other. The two main aspects of Civil Law which directly affect business are:

1 Law of Contract   Agreements or contracts are the most common form of relationship in business. There are contracts of employment, contracts of sale, contracts of work, and so on. The Law of Contract provides the rules and conditions on agreements between people and/or organisations.

2 Law of Torts.   The Law of Torts (wrongs) clarifies the position of organisations and individuals when they have suffered injury or an infringement of their rights. Thus when a person or an organisation has been negligent, has trespassed, caused a nuisance or defamed a person's character, the Law of Torts provides the rules under which damages can be recovered for any injury which has been sustained. In order to recover damages, the injured party must prove that the defendant has done something he should not have done, or has failed to do something he should have done; and has intentionally or negligently caused injury, and that the 'injured' party has suffered loss.

Liability

When a dispute occurs, the courts decide which person or organisation represented in the case is liable for any wrongful act. Wrongful acts can be both criminal and civil, and they can regulated at the same time by criminal and civil actions. This is known as *double liability*. For example, if a trader gives a false description of an article which he is selling, he is liable to criminal prosecution under the Trades Description Act, 1968; and at the same time, if any person has suffered loss as a result of the misrepresentation, that person could sue the trader for damages in the civil courts under the Misrepresentation Act 1967.

Vicarious liability

Liability can be *strict* in that the specific party which commits the tort can be held liable, even when that party is unaware of his/her negligence or nuisance. In addition, organisations have to be careful in the way in which they operate, because they can be held vicariously liable for the actions of their employees. For example, employers can be vicariously liable for any torts (negligence, nuisance, etc.) committed by an employee when the employer is in charge of the employee's operations. Similarly, members of a partnership can be held to be vicariously liable for the torts of other members which are committed during the course of business.

——— The law on contracts ———

A contract is a legal agreement. Bargains and agreements are the essential ingredients of commercial activity, and any form of trade implies that agreements or 'contracts' have been made. Consequently the law relating to contracts has been evolving over several hundred years, and in some aspects is still being refined. Basically, the legal rule in contract is that if an agreement is not carried out, or not performed correctly, then the 'injured' party has the legal right to claim some form of redress.

The essential features of an agreement – all of which have to be satisfied to make a contract legally valid – are:

1 Offer and acceptance. To make an agreement legally valid one party must make an offer to perform some function or to pay a particular price, and the other party to the agreement must unconditionally accept that offer. It is important that all the terms in the offer are accepted. For example, if an employer offers to engage someone at £10000 per annum, and the person writes to accept the offer but says in his letter that he requires a salary of £11000 per annum, then there is no contract of employment.

An interesting feature of the sale of goods is that it is the *purchaser* who makes the offer to buy at a particular price. The price on an article is *not* an offer, but is an invitation to offer. The retailer can accept or reject the purchaser's offer – obviously he invariably accepts.

2 Consideration. Another important element of a contract is consideration, which is something performed, given or suffered, in return for the benefits received. Both parties to a contract must show consideration. The most common example of consideration is money exchanged for goods or services; as well as goods exchanged for goods, or goods exchanged for services, and so on.

3 Intention. Parties to a contract must intend to create a legally binding relationship. Arrangements where offer, acceptance and consideration have been made, for example social arrangements, will not be legally binding unless the parties intended that it should be so. It is assumed in business agreements that there is an intention to enter a legally binding relationship, unless it is formally stated that the agreement is 'binding in honour only'.

4 Capacity to contract. The law is designed to protect persons who might not be fit to enter a legally binding agreement. People who are under 18 years (minors), those who are mentally disabled, and drunken persons, do not have the capacity to enter a contract. With a few exceptions, contracts made by such persons are void or voidable.

It is a legal rule that the unauthorised use of a statutory power (*ultra vires*) is void and ineffective. Since governmental powers, and the powers of commercial corporations, are created by statute then this rule is important for almost all organisations. It means that statutory corporations such as local authorities cannot enter into contracts which are not authorised by statute. For example, a public corporation cannot sell a diversified range of products. Similarly private corporations, which are registered under the Companies Act, cannot make contracts which are not authorised by the Memorandum of Association. For example, a firm would be acting *ultra vires* if the Memorandum had only 'retailing' listed as the firm's activity, and then it made contracts to drill for oil; such contracts would not be valid.

5 Validity. Sometimes a contract will meet the four essential requirements which are given above, but will become invalid because of some other factors such as:

(a) Mistake. People are not infallible: error is common in all human activity. Error in a contract may make the agreement invalid. The most common error is mistaken identity, either of the parties or of the substance of the contract. However, this rule does not allow people to be careless or casual in business agreements: the mistake must be of a genuine and significant nature, otherwise the rule is *'caveat emptor'* – 'let the buyer beware, or be alert'.

(b) Misrepresentation. Some unscrupulous people make false statements to try to induce an agreement. Legislation such as the Trades Descriptions Act, 1968, makes misrepresentation a criminal offence. Any contract entered into because of misrepresentation can be voidable, and the injured party can claim damages in a civil action.

(c) Uberrimae fidei. It is important in some contracts that all facts which are material to the agreement should be declared, otherwise the contract is voidable. This is particularly true of insurance contracts. For example, life insurance contracts can require details of all previous illness and a family history of illness. Similarly, motor insurance contracts can require details of any previous accidents. Failure to provide the information at the time when the contract is drawn up can make the contract void.

(d) Unlawful intent. Some contracts are not enforceable because they are not lawful. Illegal contracts are invalid, and so too are any lawful contracts which require the performance of an illegal act. For example, contracts to misappropriate funds or to commit a public

nuisance might satisfy the four essentials of a valid contract, but, because they are unlawful, are not valid.

Inequality of bargaining power in contracts

The law will not enforce a contract against a party if the agreement was unduly influenced by the other party. This does not mean that if a person strikes a bad bargain through ignorance, miscalculation or economic weakness that the courts will interfere. Obviously, threats and other forms of duress would be regarded as 'unequal bargaining power' and the weaker party is protected. But what constitutes 'undue influence' is not always clear, and so Parliament has intervened in many different kinds of contracts, and passed legislation to protect the weaker party. Examples of such 'protection' occur in the legislation which controls rents, and that which controls hire-purchase agreements. An example of legislative intervention is in the field of exclusion clauses in contracts. The Unfair Contract Terms Act, 1977, clarified the position of exclusion clauses and established that:

1   An exclusion clause can only apply in a contract if it is fair and reasonable.
2   Exclusion for liability for injury or death is void.
3   Guarantees can never exclude or restrict liability for loss or damage caused by goods which are defective, or for services which are negligently performed.

Employment legislation

Contracts of employment

Between 1972 and 1986 several Acts of Parliament were passed which dealt with the rights and obligations of employees and employers in relation to contracts of employment. The main rules are:

1   **Offer of a job.**   The offer of a job is made by the employer, and the consideration shown by him, for the work performed by the employee, is

the payment of wages/salary. In return, the employee accepts that he will put himself at the disposal of the employer during agreed periods. At the time of the contract, the employee must guarantee that he is fit and competent to do the work which is required, and, in some cases, declare any conflict of interest. For example, public employees are not allowed to advance their private interests when working in the public service.

The law requires the following details in the contract of employment: the names of the employer and employee, the date when employment began; pay, or the method of calculating pay; when payment is to be made (weekly, monthly, etc); and the title of the job.

2 Conditions of employment. The conditions of service are often combined with the offer of work. The employer, once the employee starts work, has the right to supervise the employee's duties, and the right to decide how the work should be performed. In relation to the conditions of service, the contract of employment should give details of the hours of work, holiday pay, sick pay, fringe benefits, the grievance procedure and disciplinary rules.

3 Termination of the contract. The employment legislation requires an employer to give an employee details of how the contract of employment can be terminated. These details should include the period of notice which the employer is entitled to give and receive, and an indication of how much previous employment with another employer counts towards the period of notice.

Discrimination in employment

The three Acts which relate to discrimination in employment are the Equal Pay Act, 1970, the Sex Discrimination Act, 1975 and 1986, and the Race Relations Act, 1976. Discrimination occurs under these Acts when an employee, or an applicant, is treated less favourably than others because of his or her sex, colour or race. The rules apply to all aspects of employment and have far-reaching effects. For example:

1 Job advertisements must not specify the sex of the applicants sought. Many advertisements now use 'person' in place of 'man' or 'woman' – for example, 'herdsperson'.

2 Selection, promotion and training. When an organisation draws up a shortlist of internal employees or external candidates, it is illegal to exclude people because of their sex, colour or race.

3 Terms of employment. The law does not allow people to be given more favourable terms of employment than those of the opposite sex who are doing the same job. It is unlawful for any employer to set different retirement ages for men and women who work in similar posts.

4 Dismissal. It would be illegal for a company to make only women redundant simply because it was felt that the men had more pressing family commitments.

5 Equal pay. Both sexes should obtain equal pay for work of a similar and comparable nature.

Liability for discrimination is not restricted to the person who makes the decision to discriminate: employers are vicariously liable if their subordinates perform discriminatory acts. Individuals who feel that they have a grievance because of discrimination can complain to an *industrial tribunal*. If the tribunal finds in favour of the complainant, it may award an order declaring the rights of both parties, or award damages to be paid by the employer.

The Acts of 1975 and 1976 established Commissions to investigate discrimination in employment. The Sex Discrimination Act, 1975, set up the Equal Opportunities Commission, and the Race Relations Act established the Commission for Racial Equality. Both bodies can institute legal proceedings against persistent offenders; and they have an obligation to promote equal opportunity and eliminate discrimination.

Health and safety in employment

The legislation on health and safety applies to all working people, and to any of the general public who might be affected. The three statutes which relate to health and safety are the Factories Act, 1961, the Offices, Shops and Railway Premises Act, 1963, and the Health and Safety at Work Act, 1974.

The Acts of 1961 and 1963 laid down specific conditions which must exist in work places. These legal requirements still apply – for example, the temperature in offices should not be less than 16 degrees centigrade, there must be adequate ventilation and lighting in all places of work, premises should be kept clean, and so on. Legal rules also apply to the guarding of machinery, the maintenance of hoists and lifts, the maintenance of stairs, and the provision of fire escapes, drinking water, conveniences, protective clothing and first aid equipment.

The 1974 Act, in laying down the principles relating to health and safety, clarified the duties of the employer and employees, and provided the framework in which a Health and Safety Commission could operate.

The employer's duties under the Act are to maintain safe plant, equipment and systems; provide training and safety measures, and supervision in safety matters; produce a Safety Policy Statement, and communicate the Policy to all employees.

The employee's duties are to take reasonable care at all times and to cooperate with the employer on all safety matters.

Enforcement

The 1974 Act established the Health and Safety Commission which consists of representatives of employers, trade unions, local authorities and professional bodies. The Commission drafts detailed rules and regulations on health and safety (delegated legislation), and enforces them through an inspectorate. If the Commission's inspectors discover practices which are outside the legal rules, they can *(a)* stop the operation by serving a prohibition notice, *(b)* make the operation safer by serving an improvement notice, *(c)* or destroy any dangerous materials or substances, and *(d)* prosecute the offenders. The offenders could either by the management or individual employees. In addition to criminal prosecution, the offenders could face a civil action for negligence by any party who has suffered damage or injury.

The Control of Substances Hazardous to Health (COSHH)

The COSHH regulations were published in 1988 and have implications for almost all businesses covered by the Health & Safety at Work Act, 1974. The purpose of the regulations is to control the exposure of employees to any hazardous substances/chemicals which they might deal with at work.

Data protection

The Data Protection Act, 1984, regulates organisations in their use of information which is recorded and processed electronically.

The legislation imposes specific duties on data users and gives individuals certain rights. All individuals have the right to be informed whether an organisation holds personal data on them. If this is the case, then, subject to certain limited exceptions, they can request a copy of the information.

Individuals will be able to claim compensation from data users for any damage or distress they suffer as a result of:

(a) Loss of personal information.
(b) Destruction of the information without the authority of the data user.
(c) Unauthorised disclosure of the data.

The law on property

People are an organisation's most important resource, but businesses also require other basic resources. For example, all businesses need land and buildings. Most organisations do not own the land on which they operate: they lease the property for a specified period (*leasehold*). During the period of the lease, the organisation will have use of the property, and will pay the landlord rent in consideration for its use. An organisation can become the owner (landlord) of property by purchasing the *freehold*. For small businesses especially this can be an expensive acquisition, and many have to borrow the money by *mortgaging* the property. This means that the property is offered as security on the loan, and if the debt is not paid off, the bank, building society or whoever loaned the finance has a claim on the property.

Restrictive covenants

There may be agreements or covenants restricting the use of land, such that the organisation may not build on the land, or all buildings should be of a certain height, or an existing building should not be used as a shop, and so on. In the case of freehold property, restrictive covenants are enforceable in the original contract, and the restrictions are passed on to subsequent owners of the freehold. In leasehold contracts, the land-owner may make agreements with the lessee, and the terms create obligations which affect only the parties to that contract. Not all restrictions will be enforced. When making a decision on restrictive covenants, the courts will ensure that the covenant is negative – i.e. that it does restrict use, and that the restriction is, in some way, beneficial in protecting the land.

Duties of the occupier of premises

Under the Occupiers' Liability Act, 1957, the occupier of property owes a 'common duty of care' to all visitors, to ensure that visitors will be reasonably safe when using the premises for a permitted purpose. Warnings can free the owner from liability – for example, a notice saying: 'Beware! Overhead Cranes at Work'. However, the warning has to be adequate for visitors to take precautions. Visitors themselves have a duty to take care.

A *trespasser*, however, has to take property as he finds it: the law does not expect the occupier to safeguard a trespasser's interests. Trespass is direct interference with another's possession of land (which includes houses, shops, gardens and paths), and occurs when a person *(a)* enters land without permission, *(b)* remains on the land after the permission has expired, or *(c)* places any objects on land without permission. The remedies which the occupier has against trespass are *(a)* an action for damages, *(b)* an application for injunction to restrain the trespasser, and/or *(c)* throwing the trespasser out, without using excessive force.

Non-physical property

Goodwill. The reputation of a business, and its trade connections, are *intangible assets*, which are commonly referred to as 'goodwill'. When a business is sold, and 'goodwill' is included in the price, the purchaser has a right to the established trade connections. The value of 'goodwill' is determined by the comparative success of the business.

Trademarks. A trademark is a sign used in connection with goods and services, which helps customers and clients to identify a particular producer. Trademarks are registered for a set period, during which they can be sold, especially when the business is put up for sale.

Patents relate to inventions. Inventors apply for a patent to the Patents Office where experts examine the invention to ascertain its validity. When the validity is resolved, the Crown grants the inventor monopoly rights (a patent) for a set period. The purpose in granting monopoly rights is to encourage the full disclosure of new products and processes, with protection against 'pirating', while at the same time allowing the inventor a period in which to earn financial reward for his creativity. Patent rights can be sold, or another party can be granted a licence which allows it to use the invention.

Copyright is similar to a patent, except that it does not have to be applied for. A composer or writer has a monopoly right for fifty years in music, and for life plus fifty years in literature. As with patents, copyright can be sold or assigned.

_____ Bankruptcy and liquidation: _____ insolvency

Insolvency is the inability to pay debts when they are due, and it applies both to private individuals and private companies. The principles which deal with the regulation of insolvency are derived from several sources; the main legislation is:

Deeds of Arrangement Act, 1914
Bankruptcy Act, 1914
Deeds of Arrangement Rules, 1925
Bankruptcy (Amendments) Act, 1926
Companies Acts 1947, 1976
Insolvency Act, 1976
Employment Protection (Consolidation) Act, 1978

The inability to pay debts can be approached in several different ways, depending on the nature and size of the debts and the attitude of the creditors. The insolvency of individuals is treated in a slightly different fashion from that of companies; but the general aim is to protect the creditors.

Insolvency of individuals

1 Moratorium and informal arrangement. A moratorium is an authority to delay the payment of debts. Such informal arrangements are negotiated with the creditors and help the debtor avoid bankruptcy.

2 Deeds of arrangement. When a debtor enters into a deed of arrangement, he transfers his property to a trustee. Sometimes this form of arrangement allows the debtor to carry on with his business and to retain some assets.

3 Bankruptcy. The proceedings for bankruptcy are initiated by a petition to a court. The petition is usually made by the creditors or it can be made by the debtor. The effect is that the bankrupt is subject to legal restrictions. A bankrupt cannot:

(a)   Obtain credit of £50 or more without disclosing he is an undischarged bankrupt.

(b)   He cannot be a director of a company or manage its business.

Insolvency of companies

1   Moratorium and informal arrangements.   In a moratorium, the directors of the insolvent company arrange an informal meeting with the creditors. The purpose of the meeting is to inform the creditors of the financial position of the company and to negotiate an authority for a delay in the payment of the debts.

2   Scheme of arrangement.   This is an agreement between the insolvent company and the creditors which is drawn up under the Companies Act, 1948. An agreement, filed with the Registrar of Companies, which has the approval of three-quarters of the creditors attending the meeting is binding on all the creditors.

3   Members' voluntary liquidation.   This occurs when a company volunteers to pay all its debts in full within not more than 12 months. The assets of the company are sold off or liquidated. In such circumstances, it is technically incorrect to describe the company as insolvent, but voluntary liquidation often occurs when the company anticipates insolvency and the company is wound up.

4   Creditors' voluntary liquidation.   This occurs when the company volunteers to go into liquidation at the request of the creditors. It signifies that the company is insolvent. The directors of the insolvent company are required to present the creditors with a statement of the company's trading position. Once a liquidator has been appointed, he will take steps to realise the company's assets and to decide on the claims of the creditors.

5   Compulsory liquidation.   Compulsory winding-up is solely in the hands of the court and not in the control of the company, as it is in a creditors' voluntary liquidation. Many of the principles developed in relation to the bankruptcy of individuals apply to the compulsory liquidation of a company. If the assets of the company are insufficient to pay the creditors, then certain groups of creditors are given preference. They are:

(a) Governmental debts of rates, taxes, VAT, etc.
(b) Unpaid wages and salaries.

———— Economic constraints ————

The most obvious constraints which organisations face are legal restrictions. Generally these are easy to identify, and the sanctions or punishments which exist if the law is broken are readily understood by most people. The constraints imposed by general economic activity are not so easy to identify, and yet the consequences of not taking action to ensure that their detrimental effects are kept to a minimum can be very great. A firm can make substantial losses or, at worst, be driven out of business. The major economic constraints which businesses face are as follows:

Competition

Firms which operate in free market conditions might find that their competitors' products have improved in quality or design, or that other firms are pursuing a more rigorous marketing strategy. In both instances, the firm could find that it is losing customers. One of the most common forms of competition is in pricing policy; businesses sometimes cut their prices in an attempt to drive their competitors out of the market.

Technology

Changes in technology can make a firm's existing products redundant. For example, in the field of electronics, digital watches rivalled mechanical watches. Similarly, developments in polymer science have led to the replacement of many wood and metal products.

Changes in technology are not restricted to new variations on established products. Sometimes research and development creates goods which did not exist previously; such items as video recorders and home computers compete with traditional goods in the consumer goods market.

International developments

In recent years, Japan and many of the newly industrialised countries (NICs) in the Far East have successfully competed with the older industrial nations in such varied industries as shipbuilding, motor car manufacturing and microelectronics. As a result their economies have grown, while the UK and other European countries have had sluggish economic growth.

General level of economic activity

The sluggish growth in the British economy and the ideology of successive Conservative governments in the 1980s has meant that government investment has been relatively low, so that parts of the economic infrastructure have deteriorated. Unemployment, urban decay and low investment in industries such as construction have contributed to a reduction in business confidence, especially in the West and North. This lack of confidence has had an adverse effect on existing businesses.

Government regulations

Government regulations have the same constraining effects on businesses as legal restrictions. The planning requirements of many local authorities make it difficult for some firms to expand. Similarly, the imposition of tighter controls on weights and measures or transport can cause problems for some organisations.

Variations in the level of taxation will also have an effect on business activity. A general increase in taxes will increase the costs of firms, and in some instances the introduction of new taxation can affect a company's prices and reduce its turnover. For instance, the imposition of VAT on home extensions in the mid-1980s reduced the level of demand for building contractors.

—— Social and moral constraints ——

The consequences of social and moral constraints on organisations are generally the most difficult to assess. Nevertheless, demographic changes, changes in attitudes and values and changes in people's knowledge will create changes in the demand for goods and services as well as changes in the nature of employment. Social and moral constraints can be as restrictive as legal and economic ones.

Population changes

The wealth of the country is created by people who are employed. Their earnings contribute to the maintenance and welfare of the remainder. In the UK, the proportion of those who are engaged in wealth-creating activities is becoming smaller and so an increasingly smaller proportion of the population has to maintain those who are dependent such as the old, the sick and infirm and children. In 1990, out of a total population of 57 million less than half (28 million) were in employment.

Changes in the demographic structure can affect some firms directly. For instance, organisations which deal with children such as private maternity hospitals, infant schools and baby food producers quickly feel the effects of changes in the number of live births.

Employees' rights

One of the major changes which has occurred in employer/employee relationships has been the demand for improved rights of employed women and of minority groups. In some instances, the demand has led to legal constraints such as the Sex Discrimination Act, 1975, and the Race Relations Act, 1976. In addition, the awareness of the rights of employees generally has led to changes in the personnel policies of organisations.

Work and leisure

Attitudes to work and leisure have changed considerably since World War II. People tend to work a shorter week, to have longer holidays and to retire from work earlier. This has meant that organisations have had to develop manpower policies to cater for these changes; and some firms, in order to attract good labour, have had to improve the social and leisure amenities for their employees. Similarly, organisations in the public sector such as district councils have found that there has been an increasing demand for public leisure facilities which can only be provided at the expense of alternative claims for other public services.

Environmental issues

The public interest in the environment is increasing and those organisations which are seen to cause damage are subjected to increasing
pressure to change their policies. Damage to the environment can occur
in many different ways: congestion in towns and cities, noise from aircraft
and heavy traffic, smoke and chemical pollution, derelict land and buildings. Government restrictions exist to curb the worst malpractices, but
in addition many organisations find that they are subject to public
pressure if they are insensitive to local public opinion.

The legislation which affects most companies deals with water, air and
waste disposal.

Water. Water pollution was formerly regulated by the Rivers (Prevention of Pollution) Acts, 1951 and 1961. These have been extended
and rationalised by the Control of Pollution Act, 1974. Discharge into the
sea is closely controlled by the Food and Environment Protection Act,
1985.

Air. The Clean Air Acts, 1956 and 1968 regulate the emission of
smoke, dust and grit from chimneys.

Waste Disposal. The Control of Pollution and the Deposits of
Poisonous Waste Act, 1972 control the dumping of harmful waste.

Other environmental issues are becoming part of the policies of many
organisations. These policies deal with:

- Energy conservation
- Recycling of waste, especially paper
- Purchase of 'green' products
- Control of litter
- Use of unleaded petrol.

Health

People's increase concern for the environment stems from an increased
awareness of individual health and welfare. Consequently, there are
social and moral constraints placed on organisations in relation to public
health. Much of the pressure, like most effective forms of social pressure, has been transformed into legislative action. In recent years, for
instance, food manufacturers have had to disclose in detail the in-

gredients and additives in their products; and tobacco manufacturers have to disclose the hazards of smoking in their advertising.

Exercises

Comprehension

1 Give the four main sources of law.

2 Define 'vicarious liability'.

3 What are the essential features of a contract?

4 List the ways in which a company can go into liquidation.

5 Give examples of 'non-physical property' which can be owned by a business.

Research

1 Why do you think that legislation on health and safety in organisations is necessary?

2 Explain the difference between the 'economic' and the 'social and moral' constraints an organisation might encounter.

3 Do you think that a firm should pay directly for any pollution it causes? Explain your answer,

Project

Using past copies of the consumer magazine *Which?*, make a list of examples of disputes in contracts between consumers and business organisations.

— PART THREE —

The Organisation: Its Markets, Customers and Clients

10

THE DEMAND —— FOR GOODS —— AND SERVICES

In Business Studies, wants and needs are referred to as 'markets'. In general the term 'market' is used in connection with commercial activity; however, in a broader sense, there is a market for hospital beds, or for places in university, or for any other public service. Thus all organisations, both public and private, have some form of market in which they 'distribute' their product or service. Organisations exist because customers and clients have wants and needs.

Home demand for goods and services

As a general rule, when people purchase goods they are *customers*; when they receive a service they are *clients*. This distinction between customers and clients is not rigid. Many industries such as hotels and catering, transport, entertainment and retailing provide a service, but serve customers.

An important theoretical difference between a customer and a client is that a client receives specialist advice or help which is administered on a personal level. For example, people's *social needs* are mainly provided for, on a personal basis, by government services such as education, health and welfare. In addition to public social services there are private organisations, such as those engaged in banking, accountancy, insurance, and legal advice, which provide professional and commercial services for clients.

People's *material wants* are satisfied by the production of goods. The best illustration of the type of goods which people primarily need or want is given by the items which are included in the Index of Retail Prices. Table 10.1 shows the approximate proportion of total consumer expenditure which is spent on the main items.

Table 10.1 Proportions of total consumer expenditure

	%
Transport	18.4
Housing	14.5
Food	12.7
Recreation	9.3
Household goods	6.7
Alcoholic drink	6.6
Clothing	6.1
Fuel & Power	3.7
Tobacco	2.7
Other goods/services	19.3

Market types

Capital goods markets

It is important to realise that organisations themselves act as customers and clients. There are many firms which do not serve the public directly, but are involved in producing goods and services for other organisations. For example, the Government is a customer for computers; private corporations are clients of external auditors. Almost all producers have to buy finished, or partially finished, goods in order to complete a stage of production: a car manufacturer requires steel plate in order to make car bodies; a farmer requires a tractor to produce grain. Goods which are produced for other producers are referred to as *producer goods*.

Overseas markets

Britain is one of the world's leading trading nations, and has traditionally bought and sold goods all over the world. However, membership of the Common Market has changed the pattern of Britain's trade, and more and more trade is taking place within the EC. The nature of the United Kingdom's top export markets, and the destination of the exports, is illustrated by Tables 10.2 and 10.3.

Table 10.2   The nature of the UK's exports

	%
Machinery	42.0
Manufactured materials	15.6
Miscellaneous manufactured	13.1
Chemicals	13.0
Minerals/fuels	7.6
Food	4.1
Beverages/Tobacco	2.6
Crude materials	2.0

Table 10.3   The destination of the UK's exports

Destination of exports	% of total exports
European Economic Community	50
The rest of Western Europe	9
Developing countries	6
North America	16
OPEC countries	7
Other developed countries	11
Centrally-planned economies	1
Total	100%

—— The demand for resources ——

In addition to producer goods, every organisation requires resources in order to produce. Resources, or *factors of production*, fall into three categories:

1 The labour markets

Everyone who can work belongs to at least one labour market. Labour markets range from the demand for labours to the demand for highly skilled people such as doctors and architects. There is an immense variety of occupations, and Table 10.4 gives a general idea of the nature of labour markets which employ almost three-quarters of the male working population.

The main factors which determine to which market or markets a person belongs are education and training, previous experience and personality (see Chapter 6).

Table 10.4 Employees in employment: by industry

	%
Agriculture, forestry and fishing	1.4
Energy and water supply	2.1
Minerals and ore extraction	3.3
Engineering and motor vehicle manufacturing	10.1
Other manufactured goods	9.4
Construction	4.8
Catering and distribution	21.0
Transport and communication	6.0
Banking, finance and insurance	11.6
Other services	30.3

2 Raw materials markets: The commodity markets

Some of the most important goods in the raw materials markets are natural products, although developments in synthetic products are causing structural changes in the natural product markets. All material products contain natural ingredients, and the demand for these ingredients tends to remain steady throughout the year. The production of natural products is, however, often on a seasonal basis; consequently many commodities are sold through formal markets or *Exchanges*. For example, the London Commodity Exchange deals in a range of commodities including coffee, sugar, spices and gums. Other Exchanges concentrate entirely on one type of product, such as the Rubber Exchange and the Metal Exchange.

3 The finance markets

Many organisations require funds to finance production (see Chapter 5), and there are two main finance markets. The *Money Market* deals in short-term loans, and this market involves the Bank of England and the commercial and merchant banks, as well as the Discount Houses. Most loans which exceed 91 days are obtained from the *Capital Market*: organisations acquire medium- and long-term loans through such institutions as the Stock Exchange and Finance Corporations.

——— Determinants of demand ———

The various forms of market which were described above exist because people want that range of goods and services: the demand for goods and services is the basis of all business operations. However, people's wants and needs are never constant. The first part of this section examines the factors which determine demand; and analyses how and why people's wants and needs change.

— Factors which influence demand —

The producer's influence

Demand, in this context, means that customers and clients have the intention of acquiring the goods or services, as well as the money to pay for what they want. An analysis of the market as a mechanism does not include the wants and desires which people cannot afford. Having stated this assumption, it follows that the lower the *price* of a product then, generally, more people will be able to afford it, and consequently the demand will increase. Conversely, when the price increases, fewer people will buy the product, and the market will contract.*

Elasticity of demand. The relationship between price and demand is not straightforward: the extent to which demand responds to changes in

* See Appendix 2

price varies. For example, goods which are 'essential', such as tobacco, will be bought almost regardless of their price. When the price changes and change in demand is small, demand is said to be *inelastic*. On the other hand, if a product, such as fresh fruit, is produced by many competitors, then an increase in the price by one producer will probably lead to a reduction in the demand for that producer's goods, because people will simply buy the alternative producers' products. When demand does respond easily to changes in price, then it is said to be *elastic*. *

Price, then, is one of the main factors which encourages or discourages people from buying a good or a service; and producers can influence the demand for their products by altering the price.

The customer's/client's influence

Price is not the only factor which influences demand. Members of the public are always changing their minds, and altering their ideas. Even when the price remains constant, the demand for a product can change. Such changes are called *shifts* in demand, because the whole relationship between demand and price changes.

The producers of goods and services are aware that popularity is one of the most important external influences on demand; consequently they attempt, through sales promotion, to influence the opinions of customers. Naturally, changes in *tastes and fashions* are not entirely in the hands of sales promoters. There are other influences:

1 Changes in the age distribution of the population often create changes in demand. This is illustrated by the increasing need for homes for the elderly and for geriatric services as a larger proportion of the population becomes older.

2 The introduction of new products. People's tastes often change when products or services are replaced by new alternatives. For example, the development of television caused a sharp decline in cinema attendances; and the invention of the digital watch has severely affected the mechanical watch industry. Similarly, passenger ocean-going liners became less popular as jet air travel expanded.

3 Public pressure. Direct pressure by groups can influence people's tastes. There are groups which attempt to persuade the public to

* See Appendix 2

buy, or to avoid buying, certain products. An independent pressure group which has a semi-scientific basis for its recommendations is the Consumers' Association. The Association publishes *Which?*, a magazine which analyses products under 'laboratory' conditions, and influences the market by giving guidance on which products perform best.

Changes in people's income

An important factor which causes shifts in demand is changes in the real disposable income of customers and clients. Although income can come from many sources – profits, interest, dividends, rent, social security benefits – most income is in the form of salaries or wages.

The factors which influence what people have to spend are:

1 **Changes in real income.** Increases in real purchasing power arise from wage and salary increases, and from a change to an occupation where the pay is higher. Increases in real income enable people to become customers and clients for products and services which they previously could not afford. Even when the price of a product increases, people will often buy more of it when their real income increases. For example, the demand for foreign travel increased as earnings increased, even when 'package tours' increased in price. This does not of course apply generally to durable goods – a family would not normally buy a second washing machine, say, except to replace the present one.

2 **Changes in the price of other goods and services.** The demand for a good or service is sometimes affected by the price of other goods and services. Some items of personal expenditure are essential (inelastic demand) – for example, most people have to spend money on rent, rates and food. If the cost of these essential items increases, then there is less money remaining to buy other products and the demand for non-essential items, such as entertainment and luxury goods, falls (elastic demand).

3 **Changes in taxation.** The State's income is obtained through direct and indirect taxation. All taxation leads to a reduction in people's income, and therefore, when taxation levels are increased, there is an automatic reduction in the demand for the goods and services purchased by private citizens. However, the Government does spend the revenue which it has obtained on public services such as education, health and police, which keeps the money in the system.

Changes in tastes and income cause constant shifts in demand, and therefore are a perennial problem for producers. In order to survive, organisations can never remain static: they must always be responding to changes in society.

—————— Supply ——————

Since every organisation exists to serve customers or clients, it is essential that whatever the organisation creates – either products or services – should be consumed or used by people. Organisations function for the benefit of people: if they are unable to meet society's wants and needs, then they go out of business. This fact means that almost all organisations, both public and private, have to be very conscious of the needs and wants of people; and their production must be shaped to meet these needs.

Business activity (production) is usually divided into three sectors: primary, secondary and tertiary. The trend has been for the tertiary (service) sector to expand, and to become the most important sector for the employment of labour.

—— Competition and monopoly ——

The market as a mechanism

Business is the interaction between those who require goods and services, and those who produce goods and services. This interaction, which allows people's wants and needs to be satisfied, is made possible by the market acting as a mechanism. The degree of influence which market forces exert depends on the nature and extent of competition between producers.

Perfect competition. For a perfect market to exist two assumptions, both fairly unrealistic, have to be satisfied: *(a)* there are many producers, and they are all manufacturing identical products; and *(b)* every customer knows the price of each manufacturer's products. It is rare for manufacturers to produce identical products, and therefore perfect competition rarely exists in business. The best examples are the commodity markets such as the London Metal Exchange and the London Tea Auctions, and the finance markets such as the Stock Exchange and the Foreign Exchange market.

When these assumptions are met, as they are in the examples given, then the consumer is 'sovereign': everyone knows the price of the different products; and with this knowledge customers/clients will always purchase the cheapest item. Those firms which charge a higher price than their competitors, either because they are greedy or inefficient, will automatically go out of business. Competition thus leads to business efficiency. The price which is charged in a perfect market is determined by the interaction between consumers and the most efficient suppliers. The market mechanism sets the price, and determines how much is supplied.

Monopoly. The other extreme form of market control is when an organisation dominates, or monopolises, the market. A monopolist is able either to set the price of his product, or to decide how much to produce. The best examples of monopolistic producers in the UK are public utilities such as British Rail and the Electricity Board. Although private organisations are legally restrained from monopolising a market, there are some private businesses which are almost monopolistic (oligopoly) – for example, detergent manufacturers (Unilever and Proctor & Gamble), cereal producers (Kellogg's and Weetabix), and pharmaceuticals (Hoffmann and La Roche).

In practice, all organisations face a degree of competition. Even monopolistic organisations – for example, British Rail competes with road and air services, and British Coal competes with other fuel producers. The most important point to remember is that the degree of competition within an industry varies, and therefore the nature of the market mechanism varies. When there are many producers in the same market the consumer's influence is great; when the market is dominated by a few firms then the consumer's influence diminishes.

Marketing mix

The marketing mix of an organisation is, in effect, its marketing strategy. It is the company's combination of marketing functions such as promotional and advertising measures, methods of distribution, and pricing policy.

Costs of marketing

We have noted that selling goods and services in a competitive environment is a risky business, and that the main aim of the marketing function is to assist in the reduction or even elimination of the risks. A significant feature of the costs of marketing, unlike costs incurred in other parts of the organisation, is their unpredictability. The following examples illustrate the variable nature of some marketing costs.

1 Research costs

There is no guarantee that expenditure on research will eventually produce a marketable product. One market which depends very highly on research is the pharmaceutical market, and even though manufacturers of drugs adhere very strictly to extensive programmes of research to ensure that their products are safe, they cannot guarantee the eventual development of a safe and marketable drug.

2 Product development costs

Even when research creates a product which has good market potential, the development costs can deter some producers from making the product. The technique of office copying using xerography was invented in the 1940s, but many leading office-equipment manufacturers refused to develop the idea, and it was several years before a relatively unknown company called the Xerox Corporation took the risk and developed Xerox office copiers.

3 Market research costs

Market research is used to assess the potential demand for a product or service, but there is no certainty that the predictions will be accurate. So even when a product has been successfully researched and developed, the producer might find it difficult to sustain sales. Clive Sinclair's company launched the Sinclair C5 vehicle in 1985, but the market of the vehicle turned out to be much less than was predicted and the product was soon withdrawn.

4 Advertising costs

The effectiveness of an advertising campaign can be difficult to evaluate. Henry Ford said that fifty per cent of all advertising is wasted expenditure: the problem is to know which fifty per cent.

5 Selling costs

The volume of goods sold by a salesperson is not always predictable. Consequently, many firms, particularly those selling in a highly competitive market, do not pay salaries and wages to members of the sales force; instead, they pay a commission on the volume of goods sold. This means, of course, that the earnings of such salespeople can be difficult to predict.

Exercises

Comprehension

1 List the main items of consumer expenditure in the UK.
2 Give examples of the types of goods which the UK exports.
3 What is a 'perfect market'?
4 Classify the costs of marketing.
5 Define 'capital goods'.

Research

1   Examine the factors which influence demand for a product or service.

2   Assess the main factors which determine to which labour market(s) a person belongs to.

3   Explain how a person's real disposable income can change.

Project

Analyse the advertisements for jobs in your local newspaper and compile a table which shows the nature of labour markets in your area.

11

MARKETING: HOW ORGANISATIONS ___ INFLUENCE AND SATISFY DEMAND

——————————— Introduction ———————————

Selling goods and services in a competitive market is a risky business: a firm's price can be undercut, the market can be flooded with imported products, many goods are perishable and have to be sold quickly, new competitive products can appear on the market without warning, and so on. The main aim of marketing is to reduce the risks in selling goods and services, and there are several ways in which an organisation can try to eliminate some of the risks:

1 Undertake market research to identify the wants and needs of potential customers.
2 Design advertising and publicity literature to communicate with clients and customers.
3 Employ forecasting techniques to predict changes in the composition of the market and to help the firm plan for change.
4 Monitor the activities of competitors in order to learn of changes in their prices or designs or other changes in their marketing strategy.
5 Assist in the research and development of new products.

Marketing and production

Product life-cycle

The changing nature of demand makes cooperation and coordination between marketing and production essential in manufacturing organisations. Most products have a life-cycle similar to the one shown in Fig. 11.1. It is necessary for both the marketing and the production departments to be aware of the product's position in its 'life-cycle', so that corporate decisions on marketing and production can be made.

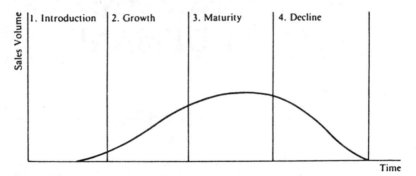

Fig. 11.1 The product life-cycle

Types of decisions which might be included in a corporate plan are:

Position of the product	*Type of corporate decisions*
1 Pre-production and introductory stage	(i) Capital investment
	(ii) Recruitment of new employees
	(iii) Retraining of existing employees
	(iv) Nature of product differentiation
2 The growth stage	(v) Changes in price
	(vi) Expansion of production
3 Maturity and saturation stage	(vii) New market strategies
	(viii) Change the product's design (marginally)
	(ix) Alter the product's quality
4 Decline	(x) Extend market to overseas
	(xi) Reduce the product's price
	(xii) Cease production

The product life-cycle provides a good reason why the marketing and production departments should cooperate. The following topics illustrate the areas where cooperation between the two functions is common.

Production planning

The production of goods requires careful planning: raw materials have to be ordered, machinery has to be bought and maintained, and people with the appropriate skills have to be employed. The capacity of a production unit is determined by the resources which the manager has at his disposal. To ensure full utilisation of resources production managers prefer sales orders to be near to, not above, the capacity of the plant. Therefore liaison takes place between marketing and production departments to ensure that orders do not exceed the plant's capacity. If orders are delayed, then delivery dates are not met and customers become dissatisfied.

Research and development: product design

Decisions on the design and the range of products (*product mix*) also entail cooperation between marketing and production. Production methods are more efficient when products are standardised. On the other hand, new products must have sufficient variety to attract customers. It is, therefore, important for R&D teams to cooperate, not only with the production department on the methods of production of new products, but also with the marketing department on the type of customer the product is likely to attract.

Price and costs: price determination

An organisation which has a monopoly in the production and selling of a product or service can, in theory, set the price of its product with little reference to outside influences. However, a firm which operates in a competitive market is not free to set the price of its own products or services: there are several factors, internal and external to the organisation, which determine the price of products and services. The two most important factors are supply and demand.

1   **Supply: production capacity.**   The level of supply in a particular market can be affected by various factors. For instance, improvements in efficiency or developments in technology can lead to increased produc-

tion. Conversely, rising costs of labour or raw materials can restrict a firm's output.

2 Demand: the customer's desire to buy.   One of the main influences on the demand for a product or service is fashion, i.e. the tastes and preferences of the customers. Another important influence is the general level of people's incomes. The amount of money people have to spend on goods and services is not only determined by the level of earnings but is also influenced by the price level of a range of products. For example, price increases in essential items such as electricity or mortgages will mean that most people have less to spend on other less essential items.

Packaging

An area where cooperation between production and marketing can improve efficiency is in the packaging of the finished product. The distribution of goods is regarded as a marketing function, but the actual despatch to customers is often made by a section of the production department. The nature of a product's packaging affects both despatch and sales. For example, problems in identification could occur in finished stock control if the products are packed in similar packages; on the other hand, identical product packaging can create *brand loyalty* in customers – for example, Heinz foods.

After-sales service

Durable products such as televisions, washing machines, cars and refrigerators have a 'life' of five to ten years, during which time they will require maintenance – after-sales service. Customer satisfaction is improved if the service keeps the product operational. This means that the production department has to manufacture spare parts – sometimes long after production of the model has ceased – and also has to train maintenance engineers. After-sales service is both a production and a marketing function: failure to provide spare parts or service facilities for 'discontinued' lines (for example 'out of production' cars) could deter existing customers from buying newer models from the same manufacturer.

——————————— Publicity ———————————

One of the most important methods which organisations use to try to change the nature of demand is publicity. The public image of the organisation, and its products or services, is at the root of the marketing function. It is unlikely that many organisations are able to create demand, but every organisation attempts to diagnose what people would like, through market research, and make them aware of its products and services. It may then use subtle methods to *persuade* customers and clients that its own particular product or service will best meet their needs.

There are three main methods of publicising products or services:

1 Advertising

This plays a very important part in business: over 1% of Britain's GNP is spent on it, and the purpose of such expenditure is to:

(a) Increase present sales by emphasising the desirable qualities of a product/service.
(b) Offset competition.
(c) Increase general market awareness of the range of products/ services.
(d) Create goodwill, and build a corporate company image.
(e) Introduce new products, models or services to customers and clients.

Much advertising is handled by specialised *agencies*, which perform the following functions for the producing organisation:

(a) Ascertain people's buying motives, and the type of advertising which has the most appeal.
(b) Select the most appropriate medium: newspapers, television, films, posters, etc.
(c) Create and design the advertisements.
(d) Appraise the results of an advertising campaign through market research.

Not all advertising is designed to persuade potential buyers to buy: some commercial advertising, and almost all government advertising, is designed to *inform* people about products or services. Private enterprise uses informative advertising to tell customers about new products and new variations on existing products. The Government uses advertising to explain regulations, to clarify citizen's rights and to give health warnings, and so on. However, most commercial organisations are in competition, and most advertising is used to persuade people that a firm's product is unique, and that the product's qualities are essential for the customer.

2 Sales promotion: 'below the line' advertising

Additional promotion methods – 'below the line' advertising – are often used to support an advertising campaign.

Examples of *(a)* displays at the point of sale; *(b)* free gifts, discount schemes and trading stamps; and *(c)* demonstrations and exhibitions.

3 Packaging and product differentiation

Producers often use packaging and labels *(trademarks)* to help customers to differentiate between their products and the products of close competitors. This technique is known as *branding*, and brand names are a common feature of everyday life (for example: Volvo cars, Parker pens, Wimpey houses). This technique can be so successful that customers often refer to a product by a brand name, such as 'Hoover', even when the product (in this case a vacuum cleaner) has been manufactured by a competitor. Producers hope to stress the brand image – 'Don't say brown say Hovis', 'Beanz meanz Heinz' were well-known examples – to such an extent that customers, when buying, ask for the brand rather than the product.

Branding has become such an important feature of sales promotion that some firms, in order to increase total sales, have created 'artificial' competition between brands, all of which are produced by the one firm. For example, there are only two major British manufacturers of soap powers and detergents – Unilever and Proctor & Gamble – but between them they produce eight different main brands. Another indication of the importance of branding is the fact that large retailers such as Tesco, Sainsbury and Boots use their own brand names on popular products like washing-up liquid, cereals and soft drinks.

Distribution – getting _____ products to the people

An integral part of an organisation's marketing strategy is the method it uses to get the products to the customers. Service industries do not generally face this problem, because the production of most services is at the market source. Producers can choose the following *channels of distribution*:

1 Traditional

Producer——▶ **Wholesaler**——▶ **Retailer**——▶ **Customer**
                Expert in   Offers a wide
                dealing in   range of choice
                bulk storage   and gives advice
                and distribution

Example: Tobacco and newspapers.

2 Eliminate the wholesaler

Producer————————————▶**Retailer**——▶ **Customer**
Example: Marks & Spencer, who perform their own 'middleman' functions.

3 Eliminate the retailer

Producer——▶ **Wholesaler**————————————▶**Customer**
Example: Discount stores, Hypermarkets and Mail Order companies which combine the functions of the wholesaler and retailer.

4 Direct service

Producer————————————————————▶**Client**
Example: Most services – banking, insurance, education and social services – fall into this category.

A producer will tend to use the full chain of distribution when the following conditions occur:

(a) High storage costs. Some technical products, such as components

for cars and electrical goods, are rarely demanded; and they are, therefore, expensive to hold in stock. Similarly, some expensive products such as cars and furniture are not always immediately available, but have to be ordered by the customer. Such products are held by the producer or wholesaler, and delivery to the retailer is made in response to customer requirements.

(b) *Perishability.*   The storage of some goods is often difficult because of their short life span. Perishable produce, such as fish, fruit and vegetables, are normally distributed through wholesale markets to retailers.

(c) *Seasonal production.*   Where production is seasonal, but demand is constant, stock holding costs can be very high. For example, imported food purchased on the commodity markets, such as grain, coffee, tea and sugar, is stored in large amounts. It is then distributed gradually through the full distribution chain.

Exercises

Comprehension

1   Define 'product life-cycle'.

2   Give examples of firms for which Research and Development (R&D) would be important.

3   Why do firms advertise?

4   What is 'below the line' advertising?

5   Describe the functions performed by advertising agencies.

Research

1   'The main aim of marketing is to reduce the risks in selling goods and services.' Do you agree with this statement? Explain your answer.

2   Do you think that the quality of the product or service is the most important aspect of a firm's marketing policy?

3 Examine the conditions when a producer will tend to use the full chain of distribution.

Project

Compile a list of examples of brand names and find out which companies own these products.

12

MARKETING INFORMATION

The markets which organisations serve are constantly changing. The demand for products and services is, as we saw in Chapter 10, influenced by many factors which are outside the control of business. In order to survive, organisations have to react to market changes. The elements of risk and uncertainty which exist in business are primarily caused by the shifting nature of demand. This chapter examines how organisations react to shifting demand, and how they contend with market forces.

All organisations, whether they are private or public, have to be aware of the needs of their customers and clients. Many of them will develop the marketing functions described below.

Research into the nature of wants and needs

The census of population, and government surveys

The statistics which are obtained in the Government's population census, which is carried out in detail every ten years, provide accurate information on the economic and social conditions of the population. Combined with the returns of the Registrar General on births, deaths and marriages, the census forms a factual basis for formulating the Government's social and economic policies. Government departments also carry out surveys on a regular basis to ascertain trends – for example, the National Food Survey, the New Earnings Survey, the Family Expenditure Survey, and Economic Trends.

Fig. 12.1 The marketing-oriented organisation

Field research

Commercial organisations use survey techniques to analyse the market. The process of acquiring information about people's wants and needs is highly technical. First, the market researcher examines a *sample* of the *relevant* population, and then, from the findings on the sample, assesses the tastes, attitudes, and habits of the total market population. *Questionnaires* are the main method used to obtain information, and those who are included in the sample can be asked to give a range of details about themselves and their buying habits.

Well-known examples of this technique are public opinion polls, which forecast the result of general elections. The prediction of the result is actually based on a very small proportion of the electorate. Similarly, many private organisations use field research to try to determine people's *reaction* to their product or service. This type of research is also used by public organisations – for example, the assessment of how many people watched a particular television programme is based on audience research methods using samples.

Desk research

Private organisations are interested not only in how customers' tastes are changing, but also in wider developments in the markets. An important method of acquiring information about market trends is to collect data from published sources – journals, magazines and newspapers, as well as specialised publications such as trade journals, company reports and other business publications. The Government's Statistical service publishes details of all aspects of business activity – prices, output, employment – and is one of the main sources of 'desk' or secondary information.

Elections

These too are a form of market research. The main method of deciding how the population feels about central and local government services is by having an election, and the future provision of public services (public policy) is influenced by the electorate's reaction to previous policy decisions. Elections are, in effect, extensive and accurate opinion polls.

____ Forecasting – the application ____ of market research

Forecasting is a semi-scientific prediction of the future. Forecasting changes in demand for a product or service is difficult: there is no way of ensuring that the predictions will be accurate, and this provides the risk element in business. The reliability of a forecast depends on three factors:

(a) The *accuracy* of the research information which is used in the calculation of the forecast. For example, when a sample is very small then the information which is obtained from it is less reliable.

(b) The *relevance* of the information which is included. For example, the buying habits of customers in Hong Kong are not a good indication of what might happen in Australia.

(c) The *number of unknown variables* which form part of the prediction. For example, there are many unknown variables when an entirely new product is being launched, and it is easier to predict people's reaction to existing types of products than to completely new developments.

As a general rule, forecasts in the short term, when more variables are known, are more accurate than long-term predictions. For example, the meteorological office can predict, with 90% accuracy, tomorrow's weather; but the accuracy of the forecasts of next month's weather is considerably less.

There are many types of forecast, of which three are important for businesses:

1 Sales forecasts

These predict shifts in demand. *Long-term forecasts* normally take place when the organisation intends to develop a new product, or to invest in plant or capital equipment. *Short-term forecasts* generally cover a financial year, and contribute to the setting of budget standards. Short-term sales forecasts also enable a commercial organisation to set its prices, and to help avoid cash-flow problems.

There are three methods of forecasting sales:

(a) Analysis of market research information, and assessment of the many variables which affect sales, such as the general economic outlook, trends in the existing market, the activities of competitors and recent sales performance.
(b) Statistical analysis of previous sales records.
(c) Speculation by sales executives based on past sales experience, and information from salesmen in the field.

2 Economic forecasts

The Government attempts to predict future economic activity by analysing trends in such economic variables as investment and expenditure. Economic predictions are often unreliable because the variables consist of millions of independent decisions which customers and clients make daily.

3 Technological forecasts

Forecasts which attempt to predict long-term technological change are used by the Government. For example, the Delphi method of forecasting requires experts to predict possible future problems in technology and related fields. Such forecasts are primarily based on opinions rather than quantitative information, and so tend to be unreliable; their application to commercial activity is limited.

Planning – the application of forecasts

The plans of organisations are based on their predictions of how customers and clients are going to act: plans are prepared courses of action for future events.

Planning at national level

The extent of State planning is determined by the degree of socialist philosophy which is present in the policy decisions. Britain has a *mixed economy*, which means that some State planning does take place; but most economic activity is left to the decisions of private organisations and private individuals (the market acting as a mechanism to allocate resources).

Government plans provide guidelines for business to follow: there are no legal sanctions which require the private sector to cooperate in the Government's plans. The procedure is to:

(a) *Define objectives.*   For example, a high rate of economic growth, an improvement on the balance of Payments, or a reduction in the rate of inflation.

(b) *Consult interested groups.*   In economic planning, for example, the Government consults employers, the trade unions and the City. In addition, there are 21 EDCs (Economic Development Councils) for individual industries where the consultation process deals with the more specific planning and development problems of the respective industry.

(c) *Determine policy.*   After examining economic forecasts, and after consultation, the Government formulates economic and social policy. For example, it will decide the level of public expenditure on such items as education, housing, health and social welfare.

Planning at organisational level

Organisations develop their plans within the framework of government policies. Two of the most important forms of planning at organisational level are:

1 Corporate planning. The first step in a corporate plan is a systematic study of the organisation's aims and objectives, especially in relation to the needs of customers and clients. Organisations then develop a corporate or unified strategy, which is designed to attain the goals outlined in the corporate plan. Thus, corporate plans highlight both objectives and strategies. In recent years, local authorities have used corporate planning techniques, and through them they have attempted to integrate the plans of different departments, such as education, housing, planning and transport, into one structure. The advantage of corporate planning is that quite separate departments in an organisation will be united in the pursuit of common goals and strategies.

2 Strategic planning
Many organisations feel that corporate planning is too inflexible and that it prevents a business from responding quickly to change. Strategic planning is considered to be more dynamic and more appropriate for modern business activity, especially if it incorporates an emphasis on improvements in quality in the organisation.

The process of strategic planning includes the following:

(a) Review the aims and objectives of the organisation.
(b) Assess performance against these objectives.
(c) Prepare consistent instructions to staff in line with the declared aims and objectives.
(d) Refine documents and methods of communication.
(e) Agree the plan and delegate tasks and duties to all employees.
(f) Ensure individual actions are accountable.
(g) Incorporate the plan into the management information system.
(h) Set up a reporting system.

3 Business plan
A business plan can be prepared for departments within large organisations or, if a business is small, can deal with the whole business. It helps a firm to establish operating objectives and to measure results on a realistic basis. Quite often a business plan is essential when a firm or department presents a case for financial support.

The essentials of a business plan are:

- Nature of the business.
- People employed in the business.
- Marketing and sales strategy.
- Profit and loss forecasts.
- Cash flow forecasts.
- Capital expenditure plans.
- Purchasing policy.
- Financial requirements.
- Management information systems.
- Action plan – key decision – target dates.

Exercises

Comprehension

1 What is the difference between 'field research' and 'desk research'?

2 List the factors which determine the reliability of forecasts.

3 What are the purposes of a Business Plan?

4 Give three methods which can be used to forecast sales.

5 Why do governments conduct a census of the population?

Research

1 Explain what a 'market-oriented' organisation is.

2 Compare 'corporate planning' with 'strategic planning'.

3 Why do you think that 'state planning' is not popular?

Project

Construct a questionnaire to ascertain consumers' attitudes to a product or service of your choice.

13

THE LEGAL
— CONSTRAINTS ON —
MARKETING

—————— Competition policy ——————

Monopoly

Producers do not like the uncertainties and risks of competition: many would prefer to monopolise the market. The reaction of most firms to the market mechanism is to try to minimise its harsh effects, and to obtain the *advantages* of being a monopoly. These are:

1 Prices can be fixed by the producer, and the risks and uncertainties of price competition can be reduced or even eliminated.
2 The benefits of price control make it possible for monopolistic producers to make larger profits.
3 The monopolist is in a position to set output at a certain level, which makes production planning and control easier.
4 Monopoly of a large market means that large-scale production can take place within one organisation. This brings economies of scale: finance is easier to obtain, more skilled and specialist personnel can be employed, distribution costs can be rationalised, and specialist equipment can be bought.

In order to reduce competition, producers can either combine with their competitors (integration (see Table 13.1)), or they can agree to co-operate (restrictive practice).

Integration

There are two types of amalgamation: *(a) Merger:* the firms concerned agree to amalgamate, and *(b) Takeover:* one firm, without necessarily having the consent of the other firm, acquires sufficient shares to have a controlling interest.

Table 13.1 Integration and diversification

	Benefits	Examples
Horizontal integration	Expansion in the organisation's existing activities which increases its share of the market	Habitat-Mothercare, BHS
Vertical integration	Provides greater security for the organisation by extending its activities into another stage of its existing production	Marks & Spencer and clothing manufacturers. Breweries and pubs: Guinness/Argyll/Distillers
Diversification	The organisation extends its range of products and its activities (Conglomerate). It therefore spreads the risks	Rank Organisation: hotels, bread, office copiers, entertainment

Restrictive practice

An alternative to formal combinations between organisations is when firms come to some understanding or agreement with one another to restrict competition. Such restrictive practices can be illegal. Under the Restrictive Trade Practices Acts of 1956 and 1968, all restrictive agreements must be registered with the Registrar of Restrictive Trading Agreements. The Restrictive Practices Court can give approval to agreements when they include the following 'gateways':

1 The restriction protects the public against injury.
2 Removal of the restriction would deny customers and clients sub-stantial benefits. For example, the Cement Makers' Federation

argued in the Court that prices were lower as a result of restrictive agreements, because the agreements reduced the degree of risk and kept many more firms in business.

3   Removal of the restriction would affect exports. Some firms have had long-standing agreements to cooperate in overseas markets. Such agreements may, however, be subject also to overseas legislation (for example, an Anti-Trust action brought in the United States was conceded by British book publishers, although the agreements in question were acceptable under British law).

4   Removal of the restriction would increase unemployment, since inefficient firms might go out of business.

5   The restriction does not directly or indirectly discourage competition.

Nevertheless, the main intention of many restrictive agreements has been to distort the market as a mechanism, and to attempt to gain some of the advantages of monopolistic control.

Office of Fair Trading

The Fair Trading Act, 1973 established the Office of Fair Trading. The Office has the power to investigate trading activities and to refer cases to the Monopolies and Mergers Commission. The Act also redefined 'Monopoly'. It is where one business has 25% or more of a particular market.

The Office of Fair Trading's powers were extended by the Competition Act, 1980 to include local authorities.

—————— Consumer legislation ——————

The Statutes which relate to consumer protection are many and varied, and establish legal rules covering prices, hygiene, false descriptions, dangerous goods, faulty services and restrictions on competition. Consumer legislation provides good examples of the distinction between public and private law. For example, it is a *criminal offence to*:

1   Sell food or drugs which are unfit for consumption, such as food which has been kept beyond its life date (Food and Drugs Act, 1955).

2   Sell goods which do not meet safety standards, such as electrical equipment or toys (Consumer Protection Act, 1961).
3   Give a false or misleading description of goods or services which are for sale (Trade Descriptions Act, 1968).
4   Demand payment for unsolicited goods (Unsolicited Goods and Services Act, 1971).
5   Restrict trade. For example, manufacturers cannot compel retailers to charge a certain price (Resale Prices Act, 1976).

In certain instances the law leaves it to the discretion of the individual to take *civil* action. A person can claim against, or sue, an organisation/individual when loss occurs as a result of:

1   Goods being sold which are not of 'merchantable quality' (Sale of Goods Act, 1893).
2   The person being induced to enter a contract by a false or misleading statement (Misrepresentation Act, 1967).
3   The person being deprived of his rights by unfair bargaining, such as unfair exclusion clauses (Supply of Goods (Implied Terms) Act, 1973).

Some of the most important Statutes are:

The Sale of Goods Act, 1893, which states that when goods are bought it is automatically implied that they correspond to their descriptions – for example, a garment described as 100% pure wool must not contain any other types of fibre. The Act also states that goods should be fit for the purpose for which they have been sold. A lawnmower, for example, should not break down the first time it is used. If goods do not meet these requirements, the seller can be sued for breach of contract in a civil action.

The Supply of Goods (Implied Terms) Act, 1973, which amended the Sale of Goods Act, 1893. Some traders had been able to deprive customers of their rights, under the Sale of Goods Act, by writing exclusion clauses into contracts – for example, clauses excluding liability for loss or damage to articles when they were being repaired. Under the 1973 Act such clauses have to be 'fair and reasonable', otherwise the customer can sue for negligence or breach of contract.

The Trade Descriptions Act, 1968, which makes it a criminal offence to give a false or misleading description. Descriptions include references to such features as the size, composition and strength of articles. It is, therefore, an offence to describe a coat as 'real leather' if it is made of synthetic materials. Less clear-cut cases have turned on the definition of terms such as 'waterproof'.

The Act also applies to comparisons between prices. It is an offence to advertise a price as a reduction unless the initial price has been charged for 28 consecutive days during the previous six months.

The Fair Trading Act, 1973, which set up the Office of Fair Trading, which acts as a 'watchdog' on traders who consistently break the law. Any agreements between organisations to restrict competition must be registered with the Office. The Office's Director General has wide-ranging powers to bring civil actions, in the *Restrictive Practices Court,* against those who do not obey the legal rules. He can, as a last resort, recommend to the Secretary of State for Prices that certain practices should be prohibited.

The Consumer Credit Act, 1974, which requires those businesses engaged in lending money to obtain a licence from the Office of Fair Trading. It also requires those organisations dealing in credit to disclose to their customers the true costs of borrowing the money, and the sources of information on credit-worthiness of individuals which the organisation used.

The Consumer Protection Act, 1987, gives the Secretary of State for Trade the power to issue safety regulations in order to prevent or reduce the risk of death or injury from the use of goods and products. The local authorities are empowered to employ trading standards officers who inspect and test all regulated goods.

Product liability

Product liability refers to a proposition that organisations should be strictly liable for injuries caused by any defective products which they have manufactured. The person who suffers from any injuries would not have to prove that the manufacturer was negligent: proof of cause of injury would be sufficient to entitle the plaintiff to damages.

This stricter interpretation of the liability of manufacturers was adopted by the European Council of Ministers in 1985 in an EEC directive on Product Liability. The intention of the directive is to impose strict liability on manufacturers for damages caused by defective goods.

——————— Exercises ———————

Comprehension

1 Give examples of mergers which have taken place between business organisations.

2 Define 'integration'.

3 Give examples of restrictive trade practices.

4 What are the functions of the Office of Fair Trading?

5 Define 'product liability'.

Research

1 'All business organisations would like to be in a monopolistic position in the market'. Do you agree? Explain your answer.

2 Explain why takeovers occur in business.

3 Why do you think that it is necessary to have legislation which protects the consumer?

Project

Compile a list of examples of descriptions of products which could be misleading.

—PART FOUR—

The Organisation in its National and International Context

14

THE EXTERNAL INFLUENCES ON DECISIONS IN ORGANISATIONS

Introduction

Decisions in organisations are affected by many internal factors, such as the policies of the organisation, its management structure and the range of its resources. However, no organisation operates in isolation, and the changing nature of the external environment will influence the nature of decisions in all types of organisation.

One of the most likely resource decision areas to be influenced by external factors is that of decisions relating to people. When a firm is recruiting, selecting or promoting employees, it must take account of the policies and activities of the Race Relations Board and the Equal Opportunities Commission. Similarly, when an organisation is planning its training programmes, it will be influenced by changes in the education system.

A second example where external factors influence a firm's decisions is in investment decisions. If, for example, a firm is considering the feasibility of building a new factory, there are obvious external influences which it will take into account, such as the level of interest rates or the size and nature of any government incentive schemes. Slightly less obvious is the strike record of the local workforce. Investors, particularly overseas investors, have been deterred from expanding into areas where the workforce in general has a reputation for militant action.

Possibly the most obvious area where decisions are influenced by external factors is in marketing. Factors such as changes in the structure of the population, the increasing earning power of young people, the growth of single-parent families, the growth in the employment of women, the increased willingness to buy on credit will have a marked influence on decisions in both public and private organisations.

The following are examples of some of the major changes in social value which have occurred during the past twenty years and which have had and are having an influence on organisations:

——— Changing social values ———

Women as employees

Between 1990 and the turn of the century the number of men in the labour force is projected to remain static at 16 million; but the number of women is projected to increase by 700 000 to 12 million employees.

The relative increase in the number of women in employment has meant that there has been increased demand for certain types of products, such as convenience foods and microwave ovens; and the increased demand for such services as nurseries and creches.

In addition, the growth in the women's rights movement has led to legislation on sex discrimination and the establishment of the Equal Opportunities Commission.

Industrial training and education

The growth in youth unemployment and the relative decline in the British economy has led to changes in education and training policies. Industrial training is controlled by the Department of Employment. In 1991 a new framework of training was set up. The four principles on which the policy was based were:

1   All training should contribute to business success and economic growth.

2 Employers and individuals should share a greater burden of the costs.
3 Standards of competence relevant to the workplace should be established.
4 Responsibility for the delivery of training should be localised through Training and Enterprise Councils.

Democracy and participation

Several factors have led to increased participation of employees in their own organisations. Firstly, management education has improved people's knowledge about motivation techniques, and it is understood by many managers that the motivation of employees increases when they are involved in decisions and participate in policy formulation. Secondly, improvements in the presentation of information and communication skills has made employees more aware of their rights and more knowledgeable about their working environment. Thirdly, in some firms, the employees have been encouraged to become shareholders and in effect have become part-owners of the organisation for which they work.

Unemployment

A major feature of society is unemployment. It is estimated that the total number (including children and other dependents) who are affected by unemployment in the UK exceeds 12 million. Although the welfare state provides benefits for the poor and needy, the gap in material terms between those in employment and the unemployed is growing and has contributed to modern social trends, such as increase in the juvenile crime rate, increasing urban decay, a growth in the black economy and increased illness from stress and deprivation.

Attitudes to money and debt

A significant change in values which is fostered by the modern economy is people's attitudes to savings and debt. In contrast with the nineteenth century when thrift was considered a virtue, modern consumers are encouraged to purchase goods and services on credit. High levels of inflation, the development of credit cards, and the increased competition in the financial markets between commercial banks and building societies have led to an encouragement to many to borrow and spend rather than to save.

The organisations which are most directly affected by changes in social values are central and local government – because it is the changes in social values which largely determine the policies of the political parties. Changes in attitudes to health, education, social security as well as changes in demography, unemployment and urban and rural life contribute to the formulation of policies and the decision-making process in central and local government.

One of the major dilemmas which face governments is the evaluation of their decisions. Poor decisions in the private sector can result in poor profitability or even liquidation of the business. Poor decisions in the public sector, if they are discerned, could mean that the party which made them might not be re-elected; even so, there is no direct measure of performance such as profitability. Nevertheless, public organisations do have to make resource decisions which involve considerable sums of money. In order to assess whether the decisions have been sound, the technique of social cost benefit has been developed.

——— Social costs and benefits ———

Many of the goods and services which we enjoy are provided by the State. For instance, almost everyone derives some benefit from Britain's defence policy, the motorway system, National Parks, the Education Service and the National Health Service. Although it is relatively easy to determine the actual cost of these public goods and services, it is difficult to assess whether the costs are efficiently controlled and even more difficult to assess their effectiveness.

Managers in the public sector cannot easily be rewarded for their good decisions nor punished for their bad ones. As a consequence, a technique has been evolved which enables politicians and public servants to evaluate the effectiveness and efficiency of public organisations. For example, the technique is cost-benefit analysis (CBA). CBA helps to improve the public decision-making process.

Problems in cost-benefit analysis

Which costs and which beneficiaries should be included? In many instances, the beneficiaries of public services are easy to identify.

For instance, the number of hospital beds occupied or the number of university places taken up is easy to calculate. Less easy to identify are the beneficiaries of urban renewal or of anti-pollution measures.

How are the benefits to be valued?   The results of a public strategy are often difficult to quantify. For example, what is the value of improved relations with Sweden and Norway which resulted from British measures to reduce acid rainfall? Similarly, what value can be put on the estimated lives saved by the introduction of the compulsory wearing of seat belts in motor vehicles? What is the social cost of allowing larger and noisier aircraft to land near residential areas?

The problem of time.   The cash flows of public projects can be very difficult to predict. Many projects, such as the Channel Tunnel or the Severn Barrage, give very long-term benefits. Consequently it is difficult to assess the total benefits and to select an appropriate rate of interest for assessing the costs.

—————————— **Exercises** ——————————

Comprehension

1   Give examples of external factors which can influence a firm's decisions.

2   List the social consequences of high unemployment.

3   Describe the changes which have taken place in industrial training.

4   Give examples of 'social costs'.

5   What is meant by 'increased participation of employees'?

Research

1   Examine the consequences of women becoming a larger proportion of the working population.

2   Assess the impact of changing social values on business organisations.

3   Analyse the problems of cost-benefit analysis.

Project

Analyse TV advertising and compile a list of products which illustrate the effect of increased earning power of young people.

15

THE INFLUENCE OF MAJOR INSTITUTIONS ON ORGANISATIONS

— Central government departments —

The implementation and administration of the Government's policies is carried out by a wide variety of institutions which, as we have seen, are similar in many respects to private organisations, and which are themselves affected by the policies they implement. For example, the central government departments have to comply with employment legislation and the requirements of the Health and Safety at Work Act. In addition, they are far more likely to be directly affected by changing levels of public expenditure than organisations in private enterprise.

Separation of power

The framework in which government departments operate provides some clue to their nature. The power of the State is in three separate divisions.

1 The Legislature. Legislation is the primary element in state activity. The policies of elected governments are translated into laws which prescribe the activities of organisations and citizens, and help to resolve disputes between parties. The function of Parliament (the

Legislature) is to approve or reject the proposals which will make policy legal. Members of the House of Commons and the House of Lords may debate and amend, reject or enact the legislative proposals of the Government; but the two Houses do not formulate policy.

2 The Executive.   Policy is formulated by the Government (the Executive), assisted by civil servants in the central government departments. The Cabinet, which is the focal point of the Executive, does not make laws but puts Bills before Parliament for approval. Once the policies of a government become law, they are implemented by the central government departments.

3 The Judiciary.   The administration of justice is separate from the administration of public policy. Judges (the Judiciary) interpret the laws passed by Parliament, and the courts provide the framework for the enforcement of legal rules.

The three 'powers' in the State are not entirely separate. The Government is very active in the legislative process, and the development of quasi-judicial bodies such as Administrative Tribunals is an example of the Executive's infringement of the autonomy of Judiciary. The central government departments are not part of the Legislature or the Judiciary; they play a vital role in the Executive's administration of policy.

Characteristics of central government departments

Impartiality.   Although civil servants are the secretariat of the Government and work very closely with politicians, it is a tradition that the advice which they give to ministers is as objective and impartial as possible. Civil servants should not allow their own judgment to be affected by political considerations: it is the elected politician's role to inject political philosophy into policy formulation. The characteristic of impartiality means that civil servants can assist and advise any type of government, regardless of its politics.

Anonymity.   The Cabinet has ultimate responsibility for government policy. Civil servants give advice, but policy decisions are collectively made by ministers. It is a custom that civil servants will not be individually identified with particular proposals: they remain anonymous.

Continuity. An important feature of government departments is that they provide continuity in the system of government, and in the administration of policies. It would be wrong to assume that the impartial and anonymous nature of Civil Service advice reduces its value. Government departments bring knowledge, experience and continuity to the policy-making process.

Methodology. The factors which determine the Government's policies are varied: the political philosophy of ministers, and the knowledge and experience of administrators, are extremely important. Equally important is the reaction of interested groups. The Civil Service has evolved a system of consultation with advisory bodies and pressure groups which is an indispensable part of public policy formulation.

Functions of central government departments

The characteristics of the Civil Service provide an indication of the functions of government departments. The following brief summary of the functions of central government departments illustrates this relationship:

Policy formulation

The translation of political ideas into practical proposals is a process which requires considerable skill. An important function of government departments is to assist ministers in this process. Civil servants provide facts and ideas; they help ministers to assess alternative strategies; they provide a system of consultation with advisory bodies; they evaluate previous strategies; and they help to translate policy into legislation by drafting government Bills.

Policy Implementation

The implementation of policy requires that the *internal* management of central government resources must be efficient. There are approximately three-quarters of a million civil servants in government depart-ments, and the management of such a large number of employees, as well as the management of resources of government departments, requires skills which are similar to those required of the management of any large organisation. Civil Service administrators have to possess organisational skills and knowledge in planning, budgeting, recruiting, purchasing, accounting, and so on.

The task of most civil servants, however, is to implement and control public policy. This is achieved in two main ways:

1 Provision of services. Some government services, such as those relating to employment and social security, are provided *directly* to the public. For example, local offices such as Job Centres are found in every major town. Specialist services, such as the Information and Advisory Service of the Ministry of Agriculture, are provided on a regional or even a national rather than a local basis.

Much of the machinery of government is highly centralised, but it would be impossible to administer all government services directly from central government. Consequently, many government services are *decentralised*, or delegated to outside bodies. The Government still retains some control over standards of provision, and the amount of resources to be employed. Local authorities, for example, provide commercial services, and semi-autonomous bodies such as the BBC provide a diverse range of commercial and non-commercial services.

2 Regulation. A major function of government departments is to ensure that public policy is operated correctly, and they use the following techniques of regulation to control the activities of individuals and organisations:

(a) Inspection. For example, the provision of education and the health and safety of employees is examined by inspectors.
(b) Rules and regulations. Government departments provide rules and regulations on how certain functions should be performed (for example, Building Regulations).
(c) Registration and licensing. Certain acts, ranging from birth to the purchase of a car, have to be registered, and some activities cannot be carried out until the operator has a licence – for example, if a person wants to drive a car on the public highway, or if an organisation wants to offer credit facilities.

(d) *Public inquiries.*   Central government departments carry out public inquiries into a wide range of matters which affect the public interest, such as accidents, disasters and planning decisions.

(e) *Financial controls.*   The operations of many delegated services are regulated by the imposition of strict cash controls, and by district audit investigations.

Delegated legislation

The functions outlined above are supported by subordinate or delegated legislation, which is the power to make subordinate laws. The formulation of policy and its approval by the Legislature forms a major part of the work of the Government and Parliament. However, it is impossible in modern times for Parliament to make laws which cover every detail of complex technical operations, such as aviation or architectural design. The problem has been solved by delegating the power to government departments and to local authorities to make their own subordinate laws. These laws have to be made within the constraints of statutes passed by Parliament; and they take the form either of a regulation or statutory instrument published by a government department, or a by-law passed by a local authority.

Government departments and business

The number of government departments which exists at any one time varies according to the nature of the Cabinet which is formed by the Prime Minister. Since World War II there have been many amalgamations and creations of government departments to ensure that the State is able to meet the ever-changing economic and social needs of society.

The Treasury

It is a department which has existed since the seventeenth century, and, because its origins are so distant, there are no statutes governing its structure and powers. The powers of most other departments have been created by statute rather than custom. Through custom the Treasury has become the 'Ministry of Finance': it controls national finances as well as the internal machinery of government.

The main function of the Treasury are to:

(a)   Forecast movements in the economy, and to assist the Government in planning its economic strategy.

(b)   Administer fiscal policy by implementing the Government's policies on taxation and public expenditure.

(c)   Help other departments in the administration of economic policies with particular reference to prices and incomes, monopolies and mergers, capital investment, and employer/employee relationships.

(d)   Control the expenditure of government departments by such techniques as planning-programming-budgeting-systems (PPBS), and Programme Analysis and Review (PAR). The Treasury co-ordinates the control of public expenditure through the Public Expenditure Survey Committee (PESC), a top-level finance committee which has representatives from each department and is chaired by an official from the Treasury.

Quasi-governmental bodies (QUA(N)GOs)

Government departments exist primarily to implement and influence the policies of the Executive. But there are governmental functions which are so specialised or so technical that central government departments have neither the resources nor the expertise to administer them. As a result, quasi-autonomous bodies have been established to provide specialised services. There is no coherent principle which accounts for the establishment of these bodies, and the following list of functions illustrates the diversity of services which they provide:

1   Basic services.   Public corporations have been established to provide essential services such as broadcasting.

2   Employment and training services.   In 1991 a network of 82 Training and Enterprise Councils (TECs) was set up. The priorities which the TECs are required to deal with are:

(a)   Encourage employers to invest in training.

(b)   Motivate people to develop relevant skills which the economy needs.

(c)   Improve the flexibility of training provision.

3 **Regulation.** The growth of delegated legislation has meant that the activities of some individuals and organisations are regulated by quasi-autonomous bodies. For example, the licences for those who want to practise chiropody are issued by the Board for the Professions supplementary to Medicine; the licences of those who wish to operate airline routes, both public and private, are issued by the Air Transport Licensing Board.

4 **Research.** The Government sponsors research into the environment, technology, science and the social sciences through research councils. The purpose of the councils is to vet applications for research funds, and to promote research into fields of public interest.

The Bank of England

The Bank of England is one of the most important semi-autonomous governmental organisations. The Bank, which has had a long relationship with the Government, was nationalised in 1946. It performs a two-way role: it acts like a government department, and in cooperation with the Treasury helps to control the Government's economic policy; and it is the City's representative in government. The Bank of England has close links with commercial banks, the Stock Exchange and other commercial organisations; and it is able to represent their views when policy is formulated.

The Bank of England has two main functions:

1 **Monetary Policy**
(a) The Bank liaises with the Treasury on economic forecasts, and advises the Government on the supply of money.
(b) It controls short-term and long-term government loans.
(c) It controls the level of interest rates through the Minimum Lending Rate (MLR) and advises the Government on the need for adjustment.
(d) The Bank manages the gold and foreign currency reserves, and helps to regulate the price of sterling.

2 **Banker**
(a) The Bank of England is the banker to the Government, to the commercial banks and to other central banks.
(b) It manages and controls the issue of bank notes in the UK.
(c) The Bank issues loan stock, and manages the Public Sector Borrowing Rate (PSBR).

Local government

Local authorities provide specific public services within a statutory framework: they are obliged by law to provide certain services, and can spend money only on those activities which have been authorised by Acts of Parliament. Any expenditure outside this statutory authority is *ultra vires*, and those who sanction such spending are likely to be surcharged by the District Auditor.

The reasons for local rather than central provisions are:

(a)   Those who have local knowledge and experience are more able to organise services which suit local variations.

(b)   Central government is a series of large organisations, and, because of its size, it has problems in internal and external communication. The decentralisation of many public services helps to improve the administration of the services; and gives the clients the opportunity to communicate directly with the providers.

(c)   Local government councillors have powers of discretion on expenditure within the cash limits set by central government, and this devolved local power can be scrutinised more directly by the electorate. Such direct inspection increases democratic participation in the provision of public services.

The main services provided by local authorities are:

1   Education and recreation.   Local authorities administer almost all the public money which is spent on education, which forms the largest single item of local government's *revenue expenditure* budget. In addition, local authorities provide finance for museums, art galleries and libraries, as well as recreational facilities such as parks, gardens and leisure centres.

2   Environment and conservation.   The nature of the environment is influenced by the decisions of local councillors. Local councils control most private building, and design their own schemes for housing and urban development. Municipal housing accounts for almost sixty per cent of *capital expenditure* by local government. In addition, local authorities are responsible for such environmental services as slum clearance, drainage and refuse collection.

3 Communications. Where it is necessary, local authorities subsidise public bus services; they are responsible for the maintenance of roads (except motorways), and administer traffic control systems.

4 Guardianship. Protection of the public is an important duty of local government. Almost ten per cent of revenue expenditure is spent on the Police, the Fire Service and the administration of justice. Local authorities are directly involved in consumer protection: they employ Trading Standards Officers and Environmental Health Officers. 'Protection' in a wider sense is also part of local government services: they provide the Social Services, and take care of the homeless and orphans.

Exercises

Comprehension

1 Describe the three divisions of state power.

2 List the characteristics of central government departments.

3 What is meant by 'policy formulation'.

4 Give examples of delegated legislation.

5 What are the main functions of the Treasury?

Research

1 Use examples to explain how government policies are implemented.

2 Assess the role of the Bank of England.

3 Do you think that government is becoming too centralised in Britain? Explain your answer.

Project

Identify the Local Authorities in your locality and find the annual cost of the various services which they provide.

16

THE INFLUENCE OF MAJOR INTERNATIONAL AGENCIES

— Institutions in international trade —

The European Community (EC)

The European Community was established in 1957 by France, Germany, Italy, Belgium, Netherlands and Luxembourg. The United Kingdom 'became a member in 1973. The objectives of the EC are:

1 The development of a full customs union, with free trade between member states in agricultural and industrial products, and common tariffs on goods imported into the Community. The variable nature of agricultural production has led to the development of a common agricultural policy (CAP) to control the price and distribution of produce within the Community.

2 To develop a common market for labour and capital, so that resources can move, without restriction, throughout the Community.

3 The long-term integration of social and economic policies. The aim is to eliminate differences in approach to monopolies and mergers, to prices and incomes policy, and to fiscal and monetary policy.

4 To unite member states in a common political union. The establishment of the European Parliament is the first step in this long-term aim.

In 1991 the members of the EC developed these aims further and agreed a treaty at Maastricht. One part of the treaty covered economic and monetary union (EMU). The other part dealt with political union. The main agreements were:

1   The introduction of a single European currency. The UK reserved the right not to participate and to retain sterling.
2   The right of EC citizens to live anywhere in the Community and to participate in local and European elections.
3   Increased powers to the Commission to make proposals on health and education.
4   Improved information and consultation over working conditions for all employees.

The executive body of the Community is the *European Commission*. The Commission administers the policies of the *Council of Ministers*, which is made up of representatives from member states. The decisions of the Council and the Commission are enforced by the *European Court of Justice*.

The International Monetary Fund (IMF)

The United Kingdom is a founder member of the IMF, which was established in 1944. The IMF's functions are to:

1   Ensure that world trade expands in a balanced way. The surpluses of foreign earnings by one country will create deficits in other countries. The IMF helps to bring about equilibrium in trading nations' Balance of Payments in the long term.
2   Promote harmony in international monetary relations, by discouraging erratic movements in exchange rates, and by promoting communication between members states.
3   Stabilise exchange rates by providing short-term credit for those trading countries which run into Balance of Payments difficulties.

There are over 100 member countries, and each pays a contribution (25% in gold, and 75% in its own currency) to the Fund, the amount depending on the country's GNP. Members can use the Fund to exchange their own currency for other currencies, so that a trading state can draw foreign currency to solve short-term Balance of Payments problems.

The General Agreement on Tariffs and Trade (GATT)

The United Kingdom subscribes, along with 82 other contracting members, to the General Agreement on Tariffs and Trade which came into existence in 1948. The aims of the Agreement are to:

1   Eliminate quotas (limits on imports).
2   Regulate trading disputes between member states.
3   Reduce tariffs (taxes) on imported goods.

The attainment of these three aims rests on four basic principles: *(a)* signatories should treat each other on an equal basis, and should not restrict trade concessions to favoured countries; *(b)* all existing trade agreements should be observed; *(c)* all limits (quotas) on trade should be prohibited; and *(d)* special trade concessions should be made for developing countries.

———————— Foreign exchange ————————

Exchange rates

The price of a particular currency, which is expressed in other currencies, is its exchange rate. The price, like most prices, is determined by the supply of and demand for a particular currency. Since the market for foreign exchange is worldwide and since, with modern telecommunications, the market information of the buyers and sellers is very sophisticated, the foreign exchange market is almost a perfect market.

ERM

The exchange rate mechanism (ERM) was set up in 1979 by nine members of the EC. The UK joined the operation in 1991; Greece and Portugal have never participated. The members agree to keep the exchange value of their currency within agreed limits against a central rate. The purpose of ERM is to bring about stability in the European currencies and to reduce inflationary pressure.

──────────── Multi-nationals ────────────

A multi-national company is an organisation which extends over many countries. Because of their size and their international character, multi-nationals are generally well known. For instance, most people will be familiar with multi-national companies such as Coca-Cola, Nestle, Shell, IBM and Ford.

A characteristic of the largest multi-national corporations is that they operate predominantly either in the motor car industry or in the oil industry. For instance, General Motors and the Standard Oil (ESSO) company of New Jersey are two of the largest companies in the world.

A third characteristic of multi-national firms is that most of them are based in the United States. Fourteen out of the top twenty largest companies in the world are based in the USA. The major European multi-nationals are: Shell, Unilever and Philips; and in Japan they are: Toyota, Mitsubishi and Hitachi.

The influence of multi-nationals

The immense size and wealth of these large business corporations means that they have a world-wide influence on business activity. These influences are:

1 Political power. Few governments would knowingly offend the policy-makers in a multi-national corporation. The withdrawal of Coca-Cola and IBM from South Africa in 1986 was regarded as a major blow to the South African economy.

2 Foreign exchange. The international nature of the operations of multi-nationals means that they are heavily involved in the exchange rate market.

3 Levels of employment. The diverse range of most multi-nationals means that they are large employers and therefore they can often influence employment markets. Shell, for instance, owns over 500 subsidiary organisations.

4 Tariff barriers. Multi-national corporations are able to by-pass tariff barriers by giving business franchise to foreign governments or foreign firms. Similarly, some multi-national organisations, such as the

Japanese car manufacturers, make joint arrangements with home producers so that import controls are avoided.

Exercises

Comprehension

1 What is the role of the International Monetary Fund?

2 List the aims of GATT.

3 Give examples of foreign multi-national corporations which operate in Britain.

4 List the main objectives of the EC.

5 Find the current rates of exchange of major currencies.

Research

1 Explain how the Exchange Rate Mechanism (ERM) operates.

2 Assess the implications for the UK of the Maastricht Treaty 1991.

3 'The world-wide influence of multi-national corporations is not beneficial'. Do you agree with this statement? Explain your answer.

Project

Analyse newspaper reports regarding GATT talks and from them summarise the present position of GATT.

17

THE INFLUENCE OF GOVERNMENT POLICIES ON ORGANISATIONS

—————— Investment and wealth ——————

The wealth of a country is determined by the nature of its resources, and by how efficiently resources are allocated. Investment is the key to the growth of wealth in a country, as in individual organisations. Capital expenditure enables organisations to expand and so increase production, but more importantly, it helps them to improve productivity by acquiring modern and more efficient plant and equipment. If organisations are not willing to invest in improved methods of allocating resources, then the amount of wealth which is created will decrease.

As we have seen, however, the investment decisions of organisations are influenced by many external factors. The interdependent nature of business means that organisations can never act in isolation: the investment decisions of one organisation will affect the level of activity in other organisations. For example, a decision by a steel company to invest in a large new plant which will employ over 1000 new employees will affect firms in the construction industry, the commercial service industries such as telecommunications and electricity, the social service sector such as housing and education, the local employment service, and local authority planning officers. Once the plant has been constructed, then the income which the extra workforce will receive will be spent in the locality, bringing increased revenue to organisations in the region, and eventually to organisations in the whole country. Investment by one firm thus creates extra wealth throughout the economy.

The circular flow of income

All spending, either by organisations or by people, is someone's income. There is a balance between the level of expenditure in the economy and the level of income.

The amount of money which is available for investment is determined by the level of spending on finished goods and services. If organisations and people spend *all* of their income on the immediate 'consumption' of wealth, then there will be no finance or 'ploughback' available for capital expenditure. Investment can take place only when people and organisations save some of their income.

National Income

The circular flow of a nation's income and expenditure (see Figure 17.1) can be counted during a period (usually one year) to give a measurement of a country's wealth. The measurement of the National Income is important for three reasons:

Business Activity
Creates wealth and provides earnings: wages, salaries, profits, interest, rent

Earnings give **Income**
The general public either *spends* money on finished goods and services (consumption), or *saves* money through institutions. Organisations use these savings to purchase capital assets (investment)

Expenditure
Becomes demand for finished goods and services (consumption), or investment in capital assets and other resources which generate business activity

Fig. 17.1 The circular flow of income

1 It provides information on how income and spending are distributed; and highlights the relationship between variables such as savings and investment.

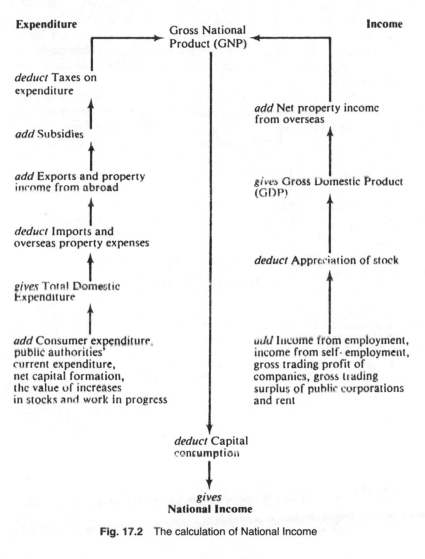

Fig. 17.2   The calculation of National Income

2 It provides a means of comparing the growth or decrease in the standard of living in a country over a number of years.

3 It enables the wealth of different countries to be compared.

The wealth of a country provides housing, food and material goods; in addition, it gives the Government the resources to improve the welfare of the people by providing services such as education and health. Consequently, governments take a keen interest in the National Income and its component variables; and they try to ensure that wealth is created by business.

Increases in wealth occur only when investment and increases in productivity take place. Although the Government can attempt to stimulate the level of investment, an important factor which influences investment decisions is the level of confidence of businessmen: if organisations are confident that they will obtain a 'reasonable' return on their capital expenditure then they will invest. The confidence of businessmen is greatly influenced by the activities of other organisations, and by the Government's economic policy. But no government in a free country can control the overall level of business activity, although it can influence it.

The aims of government economic policy

In an attempt to improve the material well-being of the people, successive British governments have had the following aims in economic policy:

1 **To promote economic growth.**   A major aim of British governments has been to make the economy grow. Increases in living standards provide material benefits such as houses, roads and durable goods; and bring about improvements in health, education and other welfare benefits. Therefore it is not surprising that all governments would like to see real increases in the National Income. However, increases in wealth occur only when there is an increase in the production of goods and commercial services. Hospitals, schools, museums and libraries improve the well-being of people, and they are signs of economic growth; but most public expenditure does not directly create wealth. Economic growth requires private capital investment, which is influenced by many factors, including the Government's economic strategies.

2 To improve people's welfare. An aim of economic policy is to reduce or even eliminate deprivation, and to improve the welfare of all citizens. This aim requires both an increase in prosperity, and a redistribution of wealth from the rich to the more needy, such as the homeless, pensioners, the disabled and the sick. The system of income tax, which is used by all British governments, is progressive: it falls more heavily on the higher income earners. The intention in using progressive taxation is to redistribute wealth.

3 To curb inflation. The stability of business activity depends on money retaining its value. Changing money values create distortions in the distribution of wealth, and seriously suppress business confidence. All governments want to reduce inflation, but although many strategies have been tried, no successful formula for permanently reducing inflation has yet been devised.

4 To reduce unemployment. Unemployment is measured by dividing the number who are registered as unemployed by the total working population, and multiplying by 100. This gives the percentage who are unemployed. A certain proportion of the working population will always be unemployed at any one time; the Government's concern increases once this proportion exceeds 1.5%.

5 To stimulate exports. The UK is a trading nation and requires gold and foreign currency in order to purchase food and raw materials from overseas. Gold and foreign currency has to be earned by selling British goods and services overseas; and the Government's aim is to ensure that overseas earnings are sufficient to pay for imports.

These five aims of economic policy have been pursued by all British governments regardless of their political philosophy: the difference between governments has been on *how* to achieve the five aims. A major problem is that the strategies which are used can be contradictory. For example, the encouragement of investment to relieve unemployment might increase the rate of inflation. The management of the economy is a complex technical process, and there are no obvious solutions. Economic policies affect all types of organisation, and require the cooperation of the many sectors of business if they are to succeed.

Monetary policy

The Government can control the supply of money which is circulating in the economy. Many economists and politicians argue that close control of the supply of money is the key to controlling the rate of inflation: if people have more money (either wages or credit) to spend, then unless productivity improves, prices will rise. Some economists go even further and argue that there is a consistent relationship between the quantity of money in the economy and the monetary value of the National Income.

Whatever the merits of the monetarists' views, it is important to understand that there is a relationship between the level of business activity and the supply of money, and that the Government can control the quantity of money in the economy. This control has a direct effect on business: the supply of money affects a firm's working capital and long-term capital, and generally influences industry's attitude to investment.

The supply of money

In the UK the total supply of sterling is defined as:

- M0   Notes and coins in banks etc., and held by businesses and the general public.
- M1   Notes and coins plus deposits which can be withdrawn without notice (sight deposits).
- M2   M1 plus deposits of up to £100 000 with a maturity of one month or less.
- £M3   Notes and coins plus all sterling bank accounts.
- M3   £M3 plus deposits of people resident in the UK which are held in foreign currencies.

Changes in the supply of money

A remarkable feature of the banking system is that it creates money by what is known as *credit creation*. Any deposit in a bank will generate credit, and the following example illustrates the process:

Bankers know from experience that it is rare for depositors to demand more than 8% of total deposits at any one time. Let us assume that Bank *ABC* plays very safe and maintains a reserve ratio of 20%, and on receipt of a deposit from Mr Y of £100, lends £80 to other people and to businesses.

The £80 will be spent on goods and services, and will thus become someone's income. The recipients will deposit this income in a bank which, like Bank ABC, retains 20% for withdrawals and lends 80% i.e. £64. This process repeats itself so that from the initial deposit of £100 by Mr Y, the banking system can generate £500, while maintaining a 20% reserve ratio. The lower the reserve ratio, the more credit is generated, because more money is allowed into the system.

The Government can control the supply of money by:

1   Open market operations.   The Government, through the Bank of England, can issue gilt-edged stock which will be purchased by institutions and by the general public in the open market. The purchase of stock will cause a fall in the level of bank deposits, and so reduce the amount of credit which the banks can create. Conversely, the Government can buy back loan stock, and this will release money which will be deposited in the banking system, and will generate more money. The Bank of England may also issue Treasury Bills on the open market to alter the position of the reserve assets of commercial banks.

2   Special deposits.   The Government can control the amount of money created by having the Bank of England call in special deposits from the commercial banks. By calling in these cash deposits, which are part of the banks' cash reserves, the Bank of England can effectively reduce the amount of money which the banks can lend.

3   Changing the Minimum Lending Rate.   MLR is the rate of interest to which the rates of interest of bank deposits, and other lending rates, are directly linked: the commercial banks pay 2% less than MLR to most of their depositors, and charge more than the MLR to their borrowers. MLR is in fact the minimum rate of interest at which the Bank of England will provide money to the commercial banks. By changing the MLR, the Bank of England, in effect, changes interest rates throughout the economy, and directly influences the cost of all borrowing.

Although the Government can control the supply of money, the monetarists do not maintain that there is a precise relationship between the money supply and the creation of real wealth, or that the control of money will enable the Government to control all the variables in the economy. The reason why monetary policy is advocated is that it is felt that when governments produce money without considering the state of the market, they are causing distortions in the allocation of resources, and that these distortions lead to inflation, unemployment and low investment.

Fiscal policy

Unemployment was the most crucial economic problem in the 1920s and 1930s. During that period, J. M. Keynes devised a theory which helped governments, after World War II, to resolve some of the problems of mass unemployment. A simple explanation of Keynesian theory is that there is a relationship between the level of demand for goods and services, and the level of resource utilisation (employment of factors). Keynes said that governments are in a position to influence the level of demand in the economy because public expenditure is a large part of total (aggregate) demand. If total demand is falling, causing unemployment to increase, then the government can spend more than it received in revenue and stimulate business activity. Equally the level of demand can be influenced by taxation policies. For example, increases or decreases in income tax will reduce or increase personal expenditure (and personal savings), and influence total demand in the economy.

The Budget

As a result of Keynesian theory, the Budget has become a major form of strategy in economic policy. The Budget has two functions:

1　It is a statement of how the Chancellor intends to raise revenue to meet planned public expenditure.
2　It is an instrument which will enable the Government to try to achieve a balance between demand in the economy and resource utilisation.

If economic forecasts show that demand will exceed the capacity of resource allocation, then high rates of inflation become more likely; the Government can curb excess demand by increasing taxation and/or reducing public expenditure to give a *Budget surplus*. Conversely, if forecasts show that total demand will be lower than productive capacity, then unemployment is almost certain to increase; and in this instance, the Government can reduce taxation and/or increase public expenditure to give a *Budget deficit*.

There are many factors which the Government will consider when deciding on budget strategy. Unfortunately, as we have seen, some of the aims of government economic policy require conflicting strategies. Thus, when inflation is increasing and high unemployment occurs at the same time, a budget surplus will aggravate the problem of unemployment. Conversely, a budget deficit will make the problem of inflation worse.

Revenue policies and their effect on business

Changes in personal taxation. There are two main ways in which the Government can alter the level of personal taxation: it can change the rates, or it can alter the allowances. Changes in personal income will have a direct effect on business: if taxation is increased, people will buy fewer goods and save less, firms will require fewer productive resources, and the level of business activity will decline. On the other hand, if direct taxation is reduced, not only does this stimulate demand, but it could also stimulate productivity by encouraging people to work harder.

Corporation tax. For purposes of taxation, the Government distinguishes between a company and its shareholders: companies pay corporation tax on profits, while shareholders pay income tax on dividends received. This distinction can cause distortions in the distribution of dividends, since it might encourage companies to retain profits rather than distribute them. In addition, a high level of corporation tax could affect growth in the economy because companies would have less finance for private capital investment.

Value-added tax (VAT). Increases in indirect taxation generally reduce the turnover of businesses. The most common indirect tax – VAT – is levied on all goods and services, apart from those which are either zero-rated or exempt. Examples of goods which are zero-rated are food, coal, gas and electricity; those services which are exempt are postal services, insurance, education and health. The effect of VAT is to increase the price of all other goods and services; and increases in price generally lead to reductions in demand.

Expenditure policies and their effect on business

Despite fluctuations, public expenditure accounts for almost half of the economic activity in the UK. Naturally, this level of expenditure has repercussions throughout the whole economy.

Transfer payments. A major element in the growth of government expenditure has been the growth in transfer payments. A transfer payment occurs when money which is contributed by taxpayers is transferred to other sections of the community. For example, subsidies on council rents, unemployment benefit, sickness benefit, child benefit and retirement pensions are all transfer payments. Although most transfer payments are made for social reasons, there are certain firms which receive direct assistance from the government in the form of subsidies – for example, some of those engaged in house-building and agriculture, and those firms in the regions which are eligible for investment grants and other incentive payments. These industrial subsidies in effect re-allocate the costs of production from the firms to the taxpayer, and in doing so interfere with market forces.

Wages and salaries. Public organisations are labour intensive and wages and salaries form a large part of total government expenditure. Wage inflation in the 1970s led to large increases in public expenditure so that it reached a level which many thought was extravagant. Consequently, when the Conservatives gained power in 1979, they took action to reduce the number of civil servants and curtail local authority spending. The resultant savings in public expenditure were passed on to taxpayers in an attempt to encourage them to work harder (but see Chapter 6). In addition to controlling expenditure levels, the Government, as an extremely important employer, can influence the pattern of income distribution; and interfere in labour markets.

Current expenditure. Public organisations are similar to private organisations in that they have to acquire resources on a day-to-day basis in order to function. Different public services require different items: schools want books, the armed forces require fuel, hospitals need food, and all public offices use stationery and office equipment. In addition, all public organisations use commercial services such as electricity, transport, telephones, post and insurance. These items, and many thousands more, come under the heading of 'current expenditure', and they have to be acquired from many different types of organisation. The Government is an important customer to many private organisations; so that changes in public expenditure can also have a direct effect on the private sector.

Capital formation includes public expenditure on new fixed assets, the purchase of land and buildings, and the stocks of government trading enterprises. It includes the construction of schools, hospitals, roads and bridges, as well as the purchase of aircraft, ships, and transport and communication facilities. Public capital investment thus has a direct effect on such industries as construction, shipbuilding and aerospace. Changes in the level of expenditure will also leak into other sectors of the economy and affect private capital investment.

Table 17.1 Public expenditure by programme

Programme	% of total
Social security	28.6
Health and Welfare	12.6
Defence and Overseas Aid	10.5
Education	12.2
	63.9
Employment services	4.5
Law and Order	4.7
Roads	3.6
Environmental services	3.4
Housing	3.9
Others	16.0
	100.0%

It is interesting to reflect that only three items – roads, housing and environmental services – contribute directly to the creation of wealth. On the whole, public programmes tend to be consumers, rather than producers, of affluence.

Investment incentives

The Government can encourage the purchase of capital assets by allowing depreciation to be treated as an expense on the Profit and Loss Account. In addition to this type of non-specific allowance, however, governments have attempted to stimulate private investment by various kinds of incentive, such as cash grants and low-cost loans to encourage businesses to invest in areas of high unemployment.

Employment policy

The Government can attempt to solve the problem of unemployment by influencing total demand in the economy. However, unemployment tends to occur in specific locations rather than be distributed evenly throughout the country.

The main types of unemployment are:

1 Casual unemployment. People who are changing jobs, and people with seasonal jobs (for example, those employed in tourism and agriculture), can be temporarily unemployed during part of the year.

2 Structural unemployment. The changing nature of business means that some employees become redundant because their type of industry, and its associated skills, are no longer needed (for example, the decline in shipbuilding has reduced the demand for labour on Tyneside and on the Clyde; changes in coal production have resulted in miners becoming redundant in Wales and South Yorkshire). So structural unemployment is high in those regions where basic industries have changed or declined. It also occurs in industries where improved methods of operation are introduced (for example, the introduction of containerisation reduced the demand for dock workers).

3 Cyclical unemployment. Booms and slumps are a common feature of industrialised market economies. During a slump (now more usually called a recession) business activity is low, the general demand for labour is also low, and so unemployment increases.

The demand for labour is directly associated with the level of economic activity. If governments can stimulate business investment by increasing public expenditure or through other fiscal or monetary measures, then unemployment will be reduced. However, in addition to these main policies, British governments have tried specific measures to increase employment:

(a) Retraining. In 1991 a new training framework was established. Government policy regarding training is carried out by the Department of Employment. The aspect of the policy which is directed at unemployment is Employment Training (ET). This is a training scheme for unemployed adults which provides a combination of directed and practical training.

(b) Jobcentres. These centres provide a free service for bringing together employers who need workers and people looking for jobs.

(c) Jobshare/Jobclubs. These two programmes aim to improve employment by encouraging employers to provide part-time jobs or by assisting unemployed people to find work by offering advice and help.

International trade policy

Imports

Overseas *visible trade* (the import and export of goods) in the UK amounts to almost one-third of the Gross National Product. This proportion of GNP gives some idea of the importance of overseas trade to British business.

Britain is dependent on imported goods for three main reasons:

1 Natural resources. 'Nature's gifts' are not distributed evenly throughout the world. The UK has oil and coal, but lacks raw materials such as timber, furs, copper, aluminium, rubber, lead and zinc, all of which have to be purchased from countries overseas.

2 Climatic conditions. The ability to grow food depends on climatic conditions and the amount of suitable land. Britain is able to produce only half of its own foodstuffs, the rest – such as dairy products, cereals, sugar, coffee and tea – have to be imported.

3 Surplus demand. In spite of Britain's ability to produce manufactured goods, UK producers cannot meet the total demand in the home markets. In order to satisfy demand, therefore, the United Kingdom imports cars, watches, footwear, clothes and many other kinds of finished goods.

In addition to these imported goods there are items of *invisible trade*, such as the British Government's expenditure on armed forces in Europe and on embassies around the world, and the expenditure of British tourists who travel overseas.

Exports

The United Kingdom's visible and invisible imports have to be paid for out of gold and foreign currency reserves – either the currency of the exporting country or in some other acceptable currency, such as US dollars or Deutschmarks. The only way in which Britain can earn this foreign currency is to export visible goods and invisible services. The United Kingdom's main visible exports are manufactured goods, chemicals, fuel and machinery. However, these visible exports do not earn enough foreign currency, and invisible earnings in banking, insurance, tourism and shipping help to make up the balance.

——— The Balance of Payments ———

Fig. 17.3 shows the items on the Balance of Payments. The goods and services which are acquired from overseas are recorded as debit items; and the goods and services purchased by foreign countries are recorded as credit transactions.

The Balance of Payments is similar to a balance sheet in financial accounts in that it always balances, and the 'balancing item' shows whether a surplus or deficit in foreign earnings has occurred. A surplus means that the United Kingdom's gold and foreign currency reserves have increased; a deficit means that the reserves have decreased.

Deficits on the Balance of Payments have been a recurrent problem in the British economy, and many technical measures have been used to try to redress the balance. As far as business is concerned, the most direct measures have been import controls, encouragement to exporters, and the manipulation of exchange rates.

Import controls

Since most of the United Kingdom's imports are essential raw materials and vital foodstuffs, it is unwise to restrict, on a general basis, the import of goods, either by *tariffs* (taxes on imports) or by *quotas* (limits on the amount of imports). Both of these measures would tend to increase the price of vital supplies, and would therefore add to inflation while also reducing consumer choice. The control of specific items, such as cars from Japan, could assist the home producer, but it might lead to retaliation on

Current Account

Visible trade items:

(*a*) *Imports*
Food, Beverages, Tobacco
Basic materials

(*b*) *Exports*
Fuels
Manufactures

Imports *less* exports *gives* the *Balance of Trade*.

Invisible trade items:

(*a*) *Government Transfers and Services*
Military services
Diplomatic services
Economic grants
Payments to international organisations

(*b*) *Interest, Profits and Dividends*

(*c*) *Commercial Services*
Banking
Insurance
Shipping

(*d*) *Tourism*

Capital Account (long-term transactions)
(*a*) Private long-term investment
(*b*) Long-term government loans
(*c*) Transactions with overseas monetary authorities (e.g. IMF)

Balancing Item Shows a surplus or credit on the Balance of Payments.

Fig. 17.3   The main components of the UK Balance of Payments

British exports by the country concerned. Therefore, import controls are opposed by GATT and by many economists as a means of improving the Balance of Payments' position. However, the United Kingdom is a member of the EC, and the Community's policy is to have completely free trade within the Community, and to have 'common' barriers to imports. Thus the EC's policy is to have free trade in food between the member states, and to use tariffs to discourage the import of food from non-member states, such as Australia and New Zealand.

Encouraging exports

The Export Credits Guarantee Department (ECGD) of the Department of Trade assists exporters by providing insurance cover against the risk of default by a foreign buyer. In addition, exporters are given encouragement by such schemes as honours awards, overseas trade exhibitions and free information on the nature of overseas markets. Many people feel that, although these 'incentives' and services help the exporter, the real solution is for British business to improve the quality, reliability and availability of products; and to sell them at competitive prices.

Exchange controls

The price of sterling (its exchange rate with other currencies) will affect the price of imports and exports. If the exchange rate is low, then imports are more expensive and exports become comparatively cheaper. If the exchange rate is high, then imports are cheaper and exports become more expensive. One way to restrict imports is to impose a low rate of exchange (*devaluation*). Until 1972, the exchange rate between sterling and the dollar was fixed, and any changes in the rate required direct government decisions. Since 1972, however, the price of the pound has been determined by the supply and demand for sterling. Nevertheless, the Bank of England can influence the exchange rate by selling sterling when the Government wants the rate to go down, and by using foreign currency reserves to buy sterling when the Government wants the exchange rate to increase.

In 1991 the UK joined the European Exchange Rate Mechanism (ERM), and consequently sterling has to keep within 6% of a central rate which is fixed by the member states. Membership of ERM restricts the flexibility of the Bank of England in the currency exchange markets.

Movements in the price of sterling will affect all those businesses which import and export goods and services, and will have repercussions throughout the economy. Government intervention normally occurs when stability is required, because instability in the exchange rate creates uncertainty and can lead to a decline in overseas trade and in business activity generally.

Regional policy

The aim of regional policy is to assist directly those parts of the United Kingdom which have suffered from economic decline. The main thrust of any government's regional policy is to attract new businesses into the declining areas; but, since economic decline also creates high levels of unemployment, regional policy is also a means of tackling unemployment.

The reasons for regional decline

Foreign competition. Many traditional British industries have experienced fierce competition from the newly industrialised countries (NICs). British shipbuilders, coal producers and textile manufacturers have not been able to compete successfully with overseas competition; and this has led to economic decline in the North, in Wales and in Scotland.

The attraction of the South East. Many new industries have not been attracted to those areas which are in decline. Motor car production, aircraft production, as well as high technology industries, have tended to locate their business operations in the more affluent South East of England.

The growth of the tertiary sector. Although three-quarters of industry can be located almost anywhere, the service industries have to be located where the markets are most dynamic. Since the South East is richer than most other regions, the service industries such as finance, distribution and hotels and catering have tended to expand outside the regions which are in decline.

Assisted Areas

Special assistance is available to firms which operate in certain areas of the country. This assistance encourages firms to expand and to modernise. The schemes include:

1   Selective assistance to specified businesses.
2   Regional enterprise grants to encourage expansion and development.
3   Consultancy initiatives.

In addition the Government has set up Enterprise Zones which over a ten-year period provide the following benefits to a business:

1 Exemptions from taxes on property.
2 Capital allowances for investment.
3 Simplified planning procedures for new buildings.
4 Reduction in the requirements for information by the Government.

Exercises

Comprehension

1 Give two reasons why National Income is measured.

2 List the main aims of government economic policy.

3 How is the supply of money measured?

4 Briefly explain what is meant by 'fiscal policy'.

5 Define 'capital formation'.

Research

1 Using examples, explain how wealth is created.

2 Why should the Government want to control the supply of money?

3 Explain how the expenditure policies of a government can affect business organisations.

Project

Assume various minimum reserve ratios and then calculate how much credit can be created against each ratio.

18

THE INTERRELATIONSHIP —— BETWEEN —— ORGANISATIONS AND THE STATE

An interesting aspect of cost-benefit analysis is that, although it is used in the public sector, it highlights the important fact that the aims and activities of organisations are not independent. Private organisations create hidden costs and benefits for other firms and for society in general. No organisation acts in isolation.

Everyone in a modern industrial society is a consumer, and most of the adult population are producers. No one could exist entirely on his own efforts – even those who produce food require services and goods produced by others, such as housing, clothing and education, as well as additional types of food. The more economically advanced society becomes, the more interdependent people and organisations become, so that if one sector such as electricity fails to function, then most businesses also fail to maintain output.

The activity of one business completes or complements the activity of other businesses. The extent of complementary activity or interdependence can be illustrated by several examples:

1   The need for raw materials and producer goods.   One of the best examples of interdependence is the need that most organisations have for the products of other firms. Farmers need fertilisers and farm machinery; the health service needs hospitals, pharmaceuticals, complex medical equipment, as well as everyday items such as beds and linen. All organisations require basic supplies such as fuel, stationery, water and waste disposal.

2   The need for social services.   Firms are dependent on one another for raw materials and producer goods. This is a fairly obvious form of interdependence. Less obvious but equally necessary is the need for educated and healthy people. All organisations depend on the education service to provide literate and numerate people, and they also depend on the health service either to prevent illness or to help sick or injured employees to return to work as soon as possible.

3   Strike action.   Strikes, particularly in basic industries such as fuel and power or transport, can soon disrupt the whole of the economy. In a rail strike, for instance, people cannot easily get to work, many goods are not distributed, and letters and parcels are not delivered.

4   The need for imports.   The United Kingdom is heavily dependent on other countries to provide food and raw materials. Some 80% of all goods imported in the UK fall into this category. If supply of these products is restricted by war, political unrest, climatic catastrophe or any other factor, then organisations will be affected. A good example is the 1979 revolution in Iran, which reduced total world oil supplies by only five per cent, but caused severe problems for business and governments in the industrial world.

5   Levels of employment.   Mass production requires mass consumption. All goods and services which are produced have to be bought, otherwise the producing organisation will go out of business. When people become unemployed, their income falls and with it their purchasing power. Unemployment caused by the failure of one firm will often lead in this way to the failure of other firms.

6   Level of public expenditure.   Demand for goods and services is, as we have seen, the basis for all organisational activity. The Government, through its expenditure policies on defence, housing and social services, represents the most important customer for many firms and thus, by controlling public expenditure, can influence the level of business activity. Cuts in public expenditure frequently lead to unemployment in many other organisations, as well as those directly affected.

7 Inflation. Harold Wilson, when Prime Minister, said that one man's wage increase was another man's price increase. This comment illustrates the relationship between costs and prices. All wages and salaries are part of an organisation's costs, and they will be taken into account when prices are determined. Increases in wages will often lead to increased costs which will lead to increased prices: wages and prices are interdependent, though the extent to which this is so is often disputed.

— The constraints on organisations —

Most organisations would prefer to operate in an environment where policy decisions could be made without any influence from internal and external agencies. However, such influence is an integral and necessary part of a free society. Democracy implies that participation will take place by people in their capacity as customers, employees and voters. Their influence may be seen by organisations as a restriction or constraint; so that, in a democracy, government ministers and company directors will try to ensure that their organisation adapts to the influence of pressure while still making autonomous policy decisions.

Internal constraints

1 Shortage of resources – finance. All organisations have to allocate resources in order to produce, and the most immediate as well as long-term problems which they face are the shortage of finance or shortages in manpower and equipment. Government departments have the perennial problem of working to cash limits; and private firms frequently have to deal with cash-flow problems and the deterioration of equipment. The major task all managers face is to get the most out of existing resources. Policy decisions are frequently restricted by resource limitations.

2 Employees' attitudes – the informal organisation. Individuals have hopes and aspirations which they will retain and show when employed by an organisation. Since the successful implementation of any policy will depend upon the cooperation of the workforce, it is unrealistic for policy-makers to ignore employees' hopes and aspirations. For example, it would be unwise to re-locate an organisation from the South East to the North East unless key members of the organisation were prepared to move. Similarly, it would be unwise to introduce a new electronic data-processing system into a business unless existing operators were prepared to retrain or become redundant. For instance, severe industrial relations problems have occurred in the newspaper industry because of the introduction of electronic typesetting.

3 Bureaucracy – the formal organisation. Organisations can become so large that their inflexibility can restrict policy decisions. Rigid and well-defined organisational structures exist in both the public and private sectors, and although bureaucracy simply means that the organisation is centrally organised, most people are familiar with the 'red tape' which is a characteristic of bureaucratic institutions. The difficulty which policy decision-makers face is that they have to recognise the limitations of central control and the problems in communication that this can cause: policy rules must be specified in great detail in an attempt to cover every case. For example, the rules which govern the administration of social security are rigid and the civil servant who implements the policy will stick to the 'rule book'. The officials do not themselves make allowances for exceptional cases even when the rules seem unfair, but such cases can usually be referred to higher authority.

External constraints

1 Changes in demand. The ever-changing nature of markets and of needs is the main external risk which an organisation faces. The political demand for a service can change overnight when an election takes place and an organisation can find that it is no longer required. For example, the Price Commission was abolished almost as soon as the Conservatives took office in 1979. In commercial organisations, demand for the product or service can change for a variety of reasons, such as changes in fashion (shorter term), or changes in demography or levels of income (longer term). Any such change can be a major constraint on an organisation's policy decisions.

2 Changes in alternative products or services. New inventions and new ideas are constantly being developed and create the need for organisations to consider new marketing strategies and new product ideas. For example, electronic data-processing is replacing manual processing, plastic drainpipes have largely replaced metal ones, nuclear submarines have replaced aircraft carriers.

3 Legal constraints. The Government, through Parliament, imposes many legal restrictions and requirements on organisations. Policies relating to employees are influenced by legislation in health and safety, employment protection and discrimination. Marketing policies are constrained by restrictive practice laws and consumer protection.

4 Government constraints. The Civil Service is concerned with the conduct of the whole range of government activities: from the formulation and implementation of the Government's policies to the routine administration of departments. Civil servants are directly responsible to their respective minister and are required to carry out their functions with impartiality. The general activity of a government will have indirect consequences on an organisation. The complex and interdependent nature of the British economy, where many firms rely on public expenditure for orders, means that the level of public expenditure will influence many organisations in the private sector. This is particularly true of the construction industry and of those companies engaged in the production of arms; but it is also true of many firms which are indirectly dependent on government spending, such as sub-contractors in the aircraft or ship building industries.

There are more direct restrictions which can be imposed by the Government in the form of taxes, overseas trade regulations and credit restrictions. When a company decides on its policies it will closely examine the influence of government controls.

5 Pressure groups. As we have seen, the whole nature of policy formulation in government is influenced by pressure groups. Although pressure groups have some constraining power on private organisations, their influence is much less on them than it is on public organisations.

Pressure groups fall into two broad categories:

(a) Permanent pressure groups. The groups which are well established are generally the most influential. Many permanent pressure groups have become integrated into the State's policy-formulation process. For example, the British Medical Association has representatives on many NHS advisory bodies; similarly the vice-

chancellors of universities have a strong voice in the allocation of funds through the University Grants Committee. Less effective, but equally well established, are groups such as the RSPCA, NSPCC, RAC, AA and the Consumers' Association. All of these organisations exist not only to provide a direct service to their members, but also to serve their members' interests by bringing pressure to bear on other organisations.

(b) *Temporary pressure groups.*   Pressure groups are often formed to change a specific policy; once the change has been made, then the need for that pressure no longer exists and the group is disbanded. Such groups as those concerned with the siting of London's third airport, or with the reform of the law on abortion, are in this category.

Forms of pressure

Pressure groups can use the following techniques in their attempt to influence policy:

1 Membership of the decision-making body.   This is the most effective form of pressure. Trade union-sponsored Members of Parliament or worker-directors are examples of this technique.

2 Use of the media.   Articles in newspapers or documentaries on television can influence organisations. For example, pressure from the *Sunday Times* was a major factor in obtaining compensation for the victims of the drug thalidomide which caused problems for unborn children.

3 Demonstrations and marches.   On many Sundays, pressure groups hold rallies in major cities in the hope of bringing pressure on organisations. These groups range from conservationists to the Gay Liberation Front. Marches are a very common form of action by pressure groups and some such as the Jarrow marches against unemployment in the 1930s, or the Aldermaston marches for nuclear disarmament in the 1950s, have become part of British history.

4 Strikes.   Trade unions can bring pressure to bear on the Government and on individual organisations by industrial action. Almost all strikes are directed against a particular organisation and are undertaken either to remedy a grievance or to try to improve wages and conditions.

However, withdrawal of labour in key industries such as energy or transport can cause such widespread inconvenience, or even chaos, that governments have reconsidered their policies, especially those in relation to prices and incomes.

5 Lobby Members of Parliament. A common pressure-group technique is to try to influence Members of Parliament, either directly in the Lobby of the House of Commons or through Petitions and letters. This form of pressure is not as effective as many other forms, but it is recognised and traditional method of democratic action.

Pressure groups do not simply use one technique. They will adopt a variety of the above methods with the intention of changing policy decisions. This constraint on business, with the other external constraints, exists because of the interdependent nature of business activity. Everyone has an interest in public and private business, and in a democracy people can try to influence any business's policy decisions.

—————— Exercises ——————

Comprehension

1 Define 'producer good'.

2 List the internal constraints which exist in organisations.

3 In what ways can a pressure group exert pressure on decision-makers?

4 Give examples of how firms are dependent on one another.

5 Define 'bureaucracy'.

Research

1 Do you consider that changes in demand for a firm's product or service is the main external constraint it will face?

2 Explain why strike action by employees is less common in the 1990s than in the 1970s.

3 What consideration do you think a firm should give to the attitudes of employees when making decisions? Explain your answer.

Project

Select one national pressure group and, from reports in the media, compile a list of the actions which it has undertaken.

— PART FIVE —

The Organisation and Change

19

THE MAJOR —— CAUSES OF —— CHANGE

—————— Causes of change ——————

The causes of change are very complex: economic, social and political influences combine to create a dynamic framework for business operations. Organisations have to try to survive in an environment which is constantly influenced by changes in technology, changes in competition, changes in politics and economics. As a result, organisations are always changing: they are constantly redefining their goals and policies, developing new products and services, acquiring new resources, appointing new people and introducing new systems and techniques of management. In order to survive, organisations have to be dynamic.

The stimulus for change comes from various sources.

Economic change

Economic influences and government policy. The Government's influence on the economy is very great. The reason for this is that public expenditure through central and local government accounts for about half of the total national expenditure. Any government's fiscal policy, i.e. the control of taxation, government borrowing and public expenditure has a direct effect on all organisations. Consequently, any changes in a government's strategy or political philosophy will cause a change in the business environment.

Many government activities, such as regional policy or taxation policy, have a direct influence on organisations; but most of the Government's influence is on the general level of business activity. For example, the level of confidence which managers have about investment and the actual cost of the investment through interest rates is largely a reflection of the success or failure of the Government's economic strategy. Another example is the general level of demand in the economy. The volume of people's spending is influenced directly by levels of taxation, interest rates and spending on roads, schools and hospitals, and similar governmental decisions.

As already indicated, the economic policy of any government is never consistent. Even though the influence of the Government is massive, it does not have absolute control over other events. Changes in international relations, changes in attitudes of the electorate, changes in technology and many other variables combine to create shifts in a government's strategy. Governments have to take a broader view than businesses on social and political matters. Consequently, the economic framework for business decisions is never constant.

Changes in the composition and nature of the market. Business organisations have not only to cope with changes in demand and changes in products, they also have to beware of changes in their competitors. Their main rivals could become more efficient and then be able to reduce prices or improve the quality of their products. Equally, the competitors could undertake a more vigorous marketing strategy and capture a larger proportion of the market.

It is important to bear in mind that the changes in the market which a firm faces are not confined to a local region. Most products have a national and international market; and the rise of the newly industrialised countries (NICs) and the competitive strength of Japan is one of the most significant economic changes in recent years and has led to the decline or limited growth in many British industries, including shipbuilding and motor car production.

The changing nature of demand is best illustrated by the notion of a product's life-cycle. The life of different products varies considerably. For example, most pop records have a very short life, which is measured in weeks rather than years. On the other hand, some products (such as Pears' Soap) have been on the market since Victorian times. Different brands within products have different life-cycles – different models of cars, for instance, have lives which vary from five years to twenty years. The important point to remember is that very few successful products remain successful indefinitely. The changing nature of demand is a permanent feature of business activity.

Technological change

Advances in technology occur in all kinds of human activity, and business organisations in particular have to be alert to technical change in products and changes in business processes and systems.

The search for efficiency stimulates change. The development of Jumbo jets and High Speed trains are examples of innovations which improve the competitiveness of the producer and, at the same time, improve the transport service.

Many people believe that the development of microelectronics will cause an industrial and social revolution which will be as far-reaching as the changes brought about in the eighteenth and nineteenth centuries by the invention of mechanical power. Although no one can be sure of the long-term effects, microelectronic technology will cause significant economic and social changes during the next decade, and this process has already begun.

Microelectronic equipment consists of large numbers of highly complex electronic control circuits, which are packed into a very small space. The circuits use very little power, they are very reliable, and they can be manufactured in large quantities at low cost. The significant growth has been in the power of a single silicon chip: the number of component parts of an electronic circuit which could be placed on a chip of silicon only one quarter of an inch square has grown astronomically since 1960, as Table 19.1 shows.

The table also illustrates how rapid modern technological change can be.

The growth in the power of the silicon chip has had a very significant impact on computers; however, this is only a small part of the impact which microelectronics has had on all types of organisations, and on all kinds of market. One of the most important developments in microelectronics has been the development of the *microprocessor*, a micro-

Table 19.1 Miniaturisation in the microelectronics industry, 1960–1985 (number of parts per square quarter-inch of silicon chip)

Year	No. of parts
1960	10
1970	700
1976	10000
1977	30000
1981	100000
1985	250000

circuit which can be programmed to carry out many different functions. Any product or process which involves elements of measurement is being affected by either the microprocessor or microelectronic instruments. The Advisory Council on Applied Research and Development identified the following industries which are being significantly affected by microelectronic developments: energy, food processing, agriculture, transport, telecommunications, car production and domestic equipment. The Department of Trade and Industry goes even further, and says that it is difficult to point to any sector of business which is *not* affected.

Examples of the effects of developments in microelectronics can be found in products, production methods and information systems.

Products

Domestic appliances. Many domestic appliances use electronic controls (for example, there are timing devices in washing machines, dishwashers, cookers and toasters). The microchip not only increases their reliability, but also makes them easier to control and use.

Motor cars. Developments in microelectronics mean that the electric system in cars is more reliable, and that electronic devices such as 'trip computers' are becoming standard features in modern cars. In addition, garage mechanics are able to carry out electronic diagnostic maintenance, which is quicker and easier than previous methods of diagnosis.

Lighting and ventilation systems. The heating and lighting of homes and places of work is made safer and cheaper by microelectronic control systems, because the fire warning devices and thermostats are more sensitive and more reliable than previous systems.

Automatic vending machines. The silicon chip has improved the reliability of vending machines; consequently, retailing and other commercial service facilities are being affected by the changes in technology. Food, cash and many different kinds of products are now readily available, on a 24-hour basis, from automatic machines.

Replacement of existing products. Some products have changed dramatically in style, and in character, as a result of the application of microelectronics. For electronic calculators, digital watches and electronic tills have replaced mechanical products, because they can perform more functions, are more reliable, and often cost less.

New products. Microelectronics has led to the invention of new products. This is particularly true of 'leisure' markets, where electronic toys, electronic keyboards and TV video games are replacing the more traditional leisure games and toys.

Personal computers, and Prestel. The management of domestic affairs is gradually changing. Personal home computers, and the British Telecom's Prestel service, enable people to acquire and make use of a wealth of information. For example, they can determine which investment or savings scheme to join, keep accurate financial records, and obtain up-to-date market prices. The purchase of goods by electronic mail order is now possible; and learning packages have been compiled in all kinds of subjects, so that studying at home is becoming easier and more effective.

- Production methods and processes -

Assembly-line operations. The production of those products which are manufactured by mass-production techniques, such as cars, television sets and durable household goods, is affected by the changes in microelectronic technology. For instance, many functions which have involved manual/mechanical operations – counting, sorting, inspecting, testing, weighing – have become electronically controlled. In addition, electronic 'robots' are taking over many jobs previously undertaken by semi-skilled workers.

Clerical operations. Another range of semi-skilled occupations affected by the advances in electronics are clerical operations. For example, cash dispensers are replacing counter occupations in commercial banks, and word processors are replacing some secretarial functions.

The handling of materials. Automatic warehousing and electronic materials-handling is increasing, and the storage and retrieval of stores and equipment is being made fully automatic in many firms. Electronic stock control reduces the opportunities for pilfering; and gives immediate information on the stock level of each item, and when re-orders are due.

Automatic transport. Automatic pilot systems have been devised which rely far less on human control than the traditional mechanical systems. Electronic traffic control in air, road and rail transport means that transport systems are more efficient and much safer.

———— Information systems ————

In Chapter 5, it was noted that money is the lifeblood of organisations: if organisations do not receive a flow of cash they go out of business. Information plays a similar role. The flow of facts, figures and words through an organisation's administration is its nervous system.

The nature and flow of information determines how 'sensitive' an organisation is to customers, employees, changes in the market, levels of sales, and so on. The functions of *information processing* are receiving, sorting, analysing, filing, retrieving and communicating. The purpose in performing these functions is to *plan*, *record* and *control* the activities of the organisation.

For many organisations, the greatest impact of technological change has been in the processing of its information. During the last thirty years, there has been a constant increase in the cost of administration. In 1950, for example, office costs formed 20% of total costs in most businesses. They now account for 50% of total costs. Consequently, information processing is an area where the application of electronics is having a substantial economic effect on all types of business organisation.

The advantages of electronic information processing are:

1 Speed. Information on almost any aspect of an organisation's system can be sorted, analysed and retrieved almost instantly.

2 Accuracy. Employees' mistakes are the main cause of errors in information. There is far less human involvement in electronic information processing, consequently errors are reduced. For example, in word processing, standard letters are typed only once and then stored for future use.

3 Reliability. Microelectronic equipment is more reliable than humans and mechanical equipment. People at work become tired and distracted and often make mistakes, while mechanical equipment has many moving parts, any one of which can fail causing the machine to break down.

4 Flexibility. Electronic information-processing means that the analysis of information is both accurate and sophisticated. Microprocessors can be programmed to perform many operations which previously would have been too complicated or taken too long.

5 Improved quality. The finished copy of written communication is greatly improved by word processing. In addition, the content can be improved. For example, financial and other statistical information is easily up-dated in reports. Information becomes less historical, and therefore is more useful.

The 'information revolution' is not confined to the internal systems of organisations. Developments such as British Telecom's Prestel service mean that customers and clients have access to up-to-date information on prices, transport timetables, entertainment guides and all kinds of other market information. The growth in external information makes consumers and organisations more knowledgeable about market conditions, and therefore markets tend to become more perfect and competition increases.

——— The organisation's response ———

The microelectronic revolution has wide-ranging implications for all kinds of products, production methods and information systems, and it has made technological change even more dynamic than ever. In order to survive during a period of rapid change, businesses have had to become more aware of how technological changes affect their organisation systems, as well as the effect on products and services. In many organisations, the Research and Development function is expanding. R&D not only concentrates on designing and developing products within existing conventional processes, but also includes an analysis of the radical changes which are taking place in other products and production systems with a view to incorporating these innovations into the organisation's existing strategy.

——— Demographic change ———

The distribution of age groups within the population structure, the geographical location of the population and the total population are never constant and cause many changes which affect organisations. The importance of analysing shifts in the nature of the population have been recognised by governments for many years, and data relating to changes in the population is collected systematically by various government departments.

——— Sources of UK population data ———

1 The census of population

Population statistics are collected by the Office of Population and Census Surveys. To carry out a complete count (census) of every person in the country is complicated and expensive. Consequently, the census is only fully conducted once every ten years, when, on a given night, account is taken of every person in the United Kingdom. There is a statutory obligation on every household to provide the following information:

(a) The type of housing, the number of rooms, toilets, etc.
(b) The number of people in the house.
(c) Each person's age, sex, marital status, occupation, educational attainment and country of birth.

2 Vital statistics

In addition to the main census, other information – on births, deaths and marriages – is constantly being obtained by the Registrar General's Office. These statistics are known as 'vital statistics', and provide up-to-date details of the population structure. The population picture is made complete by the information on immigration and emigration which is collected by the Home Office.

—— Change in the UK population ——

The organisations which are responsible for planning in the economy are concerned about *relative* changes in the population rather than the absolute statistics. Consequently, the information which is provided by the Registrar General on births, deaths, and marriages, is quoted in *rates of change*:

1 Birth rate: fertility

During the past 70 years, birth rates have declined greatly. In the early part of the century, the average number of children for each married woman was six, compared with the modern level of two. However, this trend has not been constant, and Table 19.2 illustrates how birth rates have fluctuated during the twentieth century.

Table 19.2 Population change: actual and projected

Year	Thousands
1951	50290
1961	52807
1971	55928
1981	56352
1991	57561
2001	59174
2011	60033
2021	60379

2   Death rate: mortality

Discoveries in medicine and improved hygiene caused life expectancy to increase during the first half of the twentieth century. In recent years, however, there has been a tendency for mortality, at some adult ages, to become worse rather than better – for example, the death of men in their fifties due to heart disease. Even so, the expectation of life has improved as the century has progressed. For example, if we compare the chances of survival in the 1930s with the 1980s, during these 50 years the chances improved for babies by 13%; for men and women up to the age of 60 by 25%; for men up to 77 by 7%; and for women up to 77 by 20%. Improvements have not taken place for those over 90 years of age.

The most significant feature of the United Kingdom death rate is that, for many age groups, people have a 25% better chance of reaching a given age than they did 50 years ago.

3   Migration rate: mobility

Traditionally, emigration has exceeded immigration in the United Kingdom. However, during the early 1960s there was a substantial inflow of immigrants from the Commonwealth. This inflow of people was reduced by legislation, which restricted entry into the United Kingdom; and the traditional trend was soon re-established. For example, during the decade 1964 to 1974, 2.8 million people left and 2.3 million came to the United Kingdom to live.

——— Total population changes ———

These rates of change in births, deaths, and migration determine the total population.

Optimum population

Much discussion has taken place on what would constitute an optimum or ideal population for the United Kingdom. However, there is no consensus either on what would form an optimum population, or on how it could be achieved. Obviously, changes in the structure of the population affect the provision of public services, such as education, housing and health; and all governments hope for stability in the birth rate. But there is little that democratic governments can do to control birth rates directly.

Recent changes in the population structure

	1941	1961	1981
Total Population:	48m	53m	56m

The total population in the United Kingdom has been increasing since World War II. A sharp decline in the birth rate during the 1970s interrupted the trend; but the projections for the rest of the century show a continuing, if slower, growth.

An implication of net growth of the population is that there is an increase in demand for all types of product and services; this is particularly true of the need for housing. During the thirty years 1951 to 1981, the total number of dwellings in the United Kingdom will have increased from 12m to almost 19m; and the size and standard of accommodation has also improved. Thus the problems which a growth in population can cause, such as overcrowding and homelessness, have been greatly relieved since World War II.

The increased demand for food is another important implication of population growth. The United Kingdom produces only half of its requirements for food, and so increases in the population not only require home producers to become more efficient, but also put pressure on the Balance of Payments to pay for imported food.

Under-sixteens

Children between the ages of five and 16 years must, by law, attend school. Therefore any variation in the number of those under 16 years has significant implications for the education service. The figures given below show how the number of children who require education has fluctuated since 1941.

	1941	1961	1981
% of the pop. under 16 years	21%	25%	22%
Actual number	10.1m	13.1m	12.3m

It is these fluctuations which cause problems: when the school population is increasing, then there is pressure to build more schools, to purchase more educational equipment, and to train more teachers. However, when the school population declines – as it did in the United Kingdom during the 1970s because of the falling birth rate – then some of these expensive resources become redundant.

A second major difficulty occurs when a large proportion of people aged 16 years leave school and are unable to find employment. For example, the children born in the 'bulge' in the birth rate which occurred in the early 1960s became part of the working population during the late 1970s. Many of them could not find jobs, and the Government, in an attempt to solve the problem, set up Youth Opportunity Programmes, paid youth employment subsidies to employers, and in 1983 introduced the Youth Training Scheme.

Retired people – men over 65 years, women over 60 years

	1941	1961	1981
% of the pop. who are retired	12%	15%	18%
Actual number retired	5.7m	7.7m	9.8m

Children and retired people are part of the *dependent population* – that is, they have to be supported by the working population. The statistics show how the proportion of elderly people has steadily increased since World War II. The main implications of this growth are for the social services and the National Health Service.

The expenditure on the social services has increased dramatically since the 1940s; and the increase in the numbers of elderly people has been a major factor in this increased spending. For example, half of the Government's expenditure on social security is spent on the elderly. In addition to this support, retired people often need hospital treatment or visits from GPs; as the proportion of elderly people grows, so does the need for more geriatric treatment and other forms of health service.

The working population

The working population includes all those who are in employment, those registered as unemployed, and the self-employed. Fig. 19.1 shows the composition of the labour force from 1951 to 1991.

Since World War II, there has been a gradual increase in the working population from approximately 20m to around 26m in the 1980s. The most significant change in the composition of the United Kingdom's labour force has been the increase in working married women.

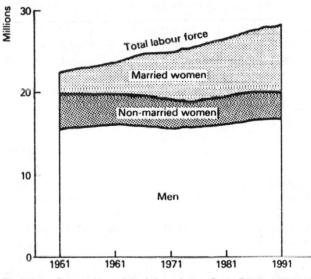

Fig. 19.1 Composition of the labour force, Great Britain 1951–1991
(source: *Social Trends*)

The change in the composition of the working population has implications for all types of consumer markets. For example, working women have more money to spend on clothes and cosmetics; and, because their time at home is limited, they will tend to buy convenience food rather than fresh foods. There are also social implications. For example, the Equal Pay Act, 1970, and the Sex Discrimination Act, 1975, illustrate how the Government has had to formulate social and economic policy to meet the increased political power of female employees.

– Demographic change and attitudes –

Changes in the structure of the population cannot be separated from changes in people's attitudes and beliefs. People's opinions about such things as marriage, material needs or politics can influence the nature of the population structure. Two examples of recent changes in attitudes which have social, political, and economic implications are attitudes to marriage and family life, and attitudes to rural and urban living.

Example 1   Attitudes to marriage and family life: birth rates

The pressure to liberate women from certain roles in society has led to changes in the economic power of working women. Legislation has helped to enforce these changes: the Equal Pay Act, 1970, prevents discrimination against women in the terms and conditions of employment; the Sex Discrimination Act, 1975, set up the Equal Opportunities Commission to ensure that discrimination in employment does not occur. These changes in the law have themselves altered the economic status of women and, in turn, have affected attitudes to family life and to child rearing. In addition to legal changes, improved techniques in contraception, as well as a greater understanding of family planning, have led to changes in attitudes concerning the size of families. These legal, social and economic changes certainly influenced a dramatic fall in the birth rate during the 1970s, a fall which will have long-term consequences for employment and social policy, and immediate consequences for education policy.

Example 2   Attitudes to rural and urban living: migration

Far fewer people now choose to live in the centres of cities and inner urban areas. Richer members of society have been able to find homes outside these areas. As a result, city centres have the problems of decaying and derelict homes, poor schools and high crime rates. Many of these problems are related to 'problem immigration', because a large proportion of poor immigrants settle in the urban areas where accommodation is cheapest.

Associated with urban decline are the problems of overcrowding and poverty; the slums of the inner cities create homelessness, poverty and destitution. In addition to urban decay are the problems of traffic congestion and pollution, which make planning and redevelopment imperative.

Successive governments have tried to solve these problems. For example, the provision of employment assistance and the social services helps the disadvantaged in the inner cities. The Inner Urban Areas Act, 1978, designated the city areas which required the most help, and provided finance to improve premises and transport facilities. The long-term aim of the Government is to attract business back into the inner city areas.

These two examples illustrate the important point that population changes and changes in attitudes are linked; and that both have a direct and indirect effect on public and private organisations.

Social change

There are many forms of social change. These include physical changes, such as shifts in the structure of the population and changes in housing and welfare facilities; and changes in attitudes. Most forms of social change are interrelated to economic change. An obvious relationship is between increases in economic wealth and general improvements in the standard of living. The extent of the interrelationship between social and economic change means that many business organisations are affected by changes in society. The following are some of the most influential forms of social change:

1 The nature and structure of the family

The nature of family life is constantly changing and some of the changes have been far reaching and fundamental to organisations. For instance, if we compare the late twentieth with the late nineteenth century, the significant changes are that families have fewer children, fewer people live near to their parents and grandparents, more marriages end in divorce and there are far more working mothers and working wives.

All these changes have some impact on the economy and on business. Fewer children means that fewer schools and teachers are needed. An increase in nuclear families means that more old people have to be cared for by the State. Divorce creates single parents who prefer part-time employment to a full-time commitment. An increase in the number of working women means that there is greater demand for convenience foods and domestic appliances.

2 Work and leisure

The pattern of people's working lives has changes and this had led to an increase in the time available for leisure pursuits. The shorter working week has increased the demand for entertainment inside and outside the home. For instance, in the home there has been a growth in hobbies such as gardening and DIY as well as in entertainment through television and other electronic equipment. Outside the home there has been a growth in such services as local leisure centres, restaurants and sports facilities. Similarly, longer holiday periods have created an ever-increasing demand for travel and tourism.

3 Education and training

During the 1980s there have been significant changes in attitudes to education and training. This is partly due to the growth in unemployment as well as to changes in technology. The Government considers that education should be more relevant to the needs of industry and commerce. The Department of Employment now plans the provision for technical education and controls the provision of vocational training schemes through Training and Enterprise Councils.

4 Environmental and urban decline

There is greater political awareness of the effect which industry and commerce have on the environment and on scarce natural resources and people are less tolerant of the decline in their surroundings. The measures which have been taken to control the use of the environment range from local government planning and building controls to legislation against noise and atmospheric pollution. In some instances, such as Liverpool, the Government has used direct measures to halt urban decay and improve the amenities and living conditions in the inner cities.

Political and legal change

The policies of political parties result from a combination of sources such as basic philosophy, party pressure groups, reaction to economic and technological developments and changes in attitudes and opinions in society. An underlying range of principles distinguishes the different parties. For instance, the Labour Party supports central planning and public ownership in contrast to the Conservative Party which prefers privatisation. However, in spite of these principles, the policies of the parties are constantly being revised.

Since the policies of political parties are subject to change, then the details of government legislation and regulations, which generally are based on policies, can be unpredictable. Frequently, business organisations have to respond to the changing details of law and regulations. The following list gives examples of some of the major changes in legislation which have taken place in recent years, and it shows that political and legal change is a significant feature of the business environment:

1 Consumer legislation

The Trade Descriptions Act, 1968
The Fair Trading Act, 1973
The Consumer Credit Act, 1974

2 Employment legislation

Contracts of Employment Act, 1972
Health and Safety at Work Act, 1974
Employment Protection Act, 1975
Sex Discrimination Act, 1975
Race Relations Act, 1976
The Employment Act, 1982

3 Company legislation

Companies Act, 1985
Company Securities (Insider Dealing) Act, 1985
Business Names Act, 1985

4 Annual Budget

Affects levels of taxation

The legislation listed above affects almost every company, regardless of the nature of its business. In addition, there are many different regulations which affect specific businesses. For example, public health regulations affect the hotel and catering industry, transport regulations affect firms involved in distribution.

Central government is not the sole source of laws and regulations. Local authorities also enact their own by-laws, and the EC has become an important source of control and therefore an important cause of change. In addition, those firms which deal in foreign trade have to comply with the changing nature of international trade agreements.

─────────── Exercises ───────────

Comprehension

1 List the main sources of change in modern society.

2 Give examples of the 'information revolution'.

3 What are 'vital statistics'?

4 Define 'working population'.

5 Give examples of the features of urban decline.

Research

1 Examine the effects of technological change on business activity.

2 Explain how social changes influence business activity.

3 Why do you think that there is so much legislation relating to business activity?

Project

Obtain the most recent copy of *Social Trends* (HMSO), and compile a report of examples of change which are relevant to business organisations.

20

THE IMPACT OF ——— CHANGE ON ——— ORGANISATIONS

As we have seen, there are many types of dynamic change which affect business organisations: economic, technological, social and political. All organisations must assume that change is inevitable; consequently, businesses have to ensure that they are capable of meeting rapid change.

The two main functions which organisations are required to develop in response to change are sound planning and a willingness to adjust.

Planning

Before an organisation can plan successfully, it has to identify its aims and objectives and to anticipate and analyse trends in technology, customer demand, politics and economics. This type of information then enables firms to develop plans in relation to manpower and investment needs.

In addition to the common need to anticipate diverse change, the nature of business of some firms makes it imperative that they concentrate on new products and new ideas. Those firms which are engaged in industries such as defence, pharmacy, chemicals and electronics have to devote a lot of resources to research into new products and the development of possible products.

Adjustment

The function of planning is not easy. Many of the decisions which an organisation takes in connection with its plans will be based on estimates and guesswork rather than hard evidence. However, adjustment to change is even more difficult for a firm to attain. Flexibility within an organisation requires a human response, and many people fear change and are not willing to respond.

Yet change has an effect on almost all forms of employment. Many middle-management tasks are now performed by computers; equally, craft-based occupations in many industries have been replaced by computer-aided machines and robots. The adjustments which some people have to make in response to change can be great. At worst, it can mean redundancy and unemployment, and in almost all instances it requires the provision of training programmes.

— Economic implications of change —

Increased productivity

Developments in technology generally lead to increased efficiency and growth. It is estimated that the invention of electronic memory devices has increased productivity in offices by 50%. Not only has the quantity of information increased, but the quality has also improved. Business information is now more accurate and more up to date than ever before.

Improved information from external sources such as Prestel creates greater market efficiency. As customers and clients become better informed about prices and market opportunities then competition increases, and this stimulates business efficiency.

De-skilling of occupations

The increase in information means that employees have to improve their skills in sifting, absorbing and using large quantities of data. However, for many occupations, the electronic revolution has reduced the skills which are needed, not increased them. For example, secretarial and clerical functions are being replaced by word processors; Post Office employees are by-passed by the electronic transmission of documents; and the skills of print workers are now carried out by electronic typesetters.

Creation of new jobs

The electronic revolution has created new jobs in the electronics industry, and in those industries which have been able to adapt to the new technology. However, the major change is in the service industries. As wealth has increased, the leisure and social service industries – travel, sport, welfare, hotel and catering – have been employing an increasing proportion of the working population.

Rapid advances in technology tend to alter the *nature* of employment rather than reduce it. The main implication of technological change is that it changes the nature of many occupations, and requires people and organisations to be both adaptable and flexible.

—— Social implications of change ——

Education and training

Technological change, particularly the information revolution, has implications for education.

1 Computer-assisted learning. Programs are being devised to cover many different types of subject. These learning programs, unlike normal television, require participation by the student and make learning without a teacher much easier and more effective.

2 Social skills. The skills needed in many occupations are changing. Greater emphasis is needed on the development of skills which electronic devices cannot replace, such as social skills, and on interpersonal relationship (see Chapter 6).

3 Continuing education. The need for adaptability and flexibility in people means that many more will continue or return to education and training after leaving school and college.

Leisure

As material wants are satisfied by increased wealth, people are demanding non-material services: there is increased emphasis on physical and mental welfare, and on entertainment such as sport and travel. The growth in travel agencies, leisure centres and keepfit clubs illustrates this change of emphasis in life-styles.

Attitudes to work

Technological change causes a shift in the nature of occupations and also tends to make organisations more remote from employees. It often creates a series of sub-routine tasks which neither stimulate the employee nor sustain his/her interest. These factors, as well as the satiation of many people's material needs, have caused changes in employees' attitudes to work.

The changes in attitudes which are outlined below are not uniform throughout society, and do not apply to everyone. They are examples of change in different sectors of society, and in some instances conflict with one another. This is not surprising. It would be unrealistic to believe that attitudes change throughout society in a consistent pattern.

1   **Decline in craft skills careers.**   Many traditional craft skills, in engineering, and printing for example, are becoming redundant. As a result, many young people do not want to spend many years on low pay as apprentices to master craftsmen. Career opportunities are not as clear as they used to be, and consequently many feel that it is pointless to spend time becoming a specialist in a discipline which might be overtaken by technology.

2   **Unemployment.**   An increasing number of people, unable to find employment, are becoming unemployed for long periods. The number of long-term unemployed (those unemployed for over one year) increased more than five-fold from 1976 to 1986. Some use this as evidence to support the opinion that unemployment is becoming more socially acceptable. The inability to find work does not appear to carry the social stigma that it did during the inter-war years.

3   **Shorter working week.**   Increased early retirement, and the demand for a shorter working week, illustrates how more and more people regard life outside the working environment as more important than being at work. Although many employees take advantage of shorter working hours to work more overtime, there is a shift away from the work 'ethic' to more leisure activities. Work is becoming less important in people's lives.

4 Flexibility in work. Many employees do not want to be restricted by rigid timekeeping and other working rules. Consequently, some organisations have introduced flexible working hours which gives the employees some responsibility for the decision on when they attend work.

Exercises

Comprehension

1 Briefly explain what is meant by 'change' in the business environment.

2 List the ways in which organisations respond to change.

3 Briefly outline the economic implications of change.

4 Give examples of de-skilling in occupations.

5 What is meant by 'flexible working'?

Research

1 Do you think that constant change in organisations is inevitable? Explain your answer.

2 Examine how attitudes to work have changed in recent years, and assess their impact on business organisations.

3 Why do you think that the service industries have expanded so much in recent years?

Project

Prepare your own action plan of how you intend to respond to change. Your plan should include all aspects of your life.

21

COMMUNICATION AND —— THE RESPONSE —— TO CHANGE

—————— Conflict and change ——————

The social and economic effects of change, such as unemployment and direct action, create tension and stress. In a democratic society, change makes conflict inevitable: the interests of individuals and of organisations will not always coincide. For example, the interests of organisations can conflict with the following groups:

Customers and clients

Most producers want high profits which, in effect, means that they would like to charge high prices. Customers and clients on the other hand want low prices. Equally, producers want to produce at low cost, which often means poor quality products or services. But customers and clients want high quality goods and services. In a free economy, market forces generally resolve this problem: firms have to adapt to the changing needs of consumers. Sometimes, though, in the 'conflict' between consumer and producer, the producer uses unfair methods; in this instance, legislation exists to protect the consumer (see Chapter 13).

Competitors

Market competition is recognised as a desirable form of conflict. The main problem for an organisation occurs when a competitor introduces a new product, or becomes more efficient because of the introduction of new production methods or systems. The law does not generally resolve the conflict between organisations. It is assumed, in a free economy, that those businesses which are unable to respond to change and become inefficient should go out of business. Consequently there are thousands of liquidations and bankruptcies every year: these are cases where organisations have lost in the 'conflict of competition'.

Society

The policies of organisations, and of governments, sometimes conflict with the interests of sections of the community. The existence of *pressure groups* illustrates how conflicting interests are managed in a democratic society. When individuals or groups feel that their interests are threatened, they attempt to persuade decision-makers to take account of their sectional views. For example, cuts in education expenditure have caused the Teachers' Union to campaign against the Government; the decision of British Coal to open a new mine in Leicestershire generated a campaign against the decision by local residents.

Technological change often spoils the environment with noise, fumes and visual pollution, and this frequently causes conflict between organisations and pressure groups. An *injunction*, which is an order requiring some person to refrain from breaking the law, is sometimes used to prevent organisations from carrying out actions which might be detrimental to sectional interests.

Another legal form of conflict resolution is a *Public Inquiry*, which is a technique used by Parliament for giving objectors to a scheme a fair hearing before a decision is made. For example, an Inquiry was held into the siting of the third London airport.

Employees

The most frequent form of conflict which occurs in business is the conflict between employers and employees. Technological change has both economic and social effects which make conflict an inevitable feature of organisations. Some of the main features of employer/employee conflict are:

1 It affects all levels. Traditionally, automation has mainly replaced unskilled and semi-skilled workers. But the developments in microelectronics are creating devices and systems which replace jobs in management and in highly-skilled occupations, such as those in inspection and control.

2 Resentment. The relative importance of jobs changes as technology develops. Skilled craftsmen, such as watchmakers, find that years of training and experience count for very little. The electronic revolution has de-skilled many occupations – print workers, secretaries, postal workers. Such de-skilling can reduce an employee's sense of personal value, and cause dissatisfaction and resentment.

3 Trade union reaction. Some trade unions react against change, especially if they find that their membership is declining as their members' occupations are automated. The threat of unemployment, and the lack of security, can create great conflict between employers and employees. There are many instances where trade unions, in resistance to change, have refused initially to cooperate with the employers – for example, print workers in the Times Newspapers dispute; the dock workers' refusal to cooperate with containerisation; and the Post Office workers' rejection of electronic sorting equipment.

Employers can attempt to resolve the inevitable conflict which change brings by:

1 Communication. Ignorance breeds rumour and fear. By constantly informing employees of decisions which will affect them, organisations can reduce the fear and hostility which insecurity and ignorance create.

2 Retraining. Organisations can examine the different needs of employees and provide facilities which enable people to learn new skills and new techniques. Skills in team work and cooperation, as well as improved understanding of the nature of an organisation's operations, are necessary in a changing environment.

3 Participation. It is generally agreed that participation improves employee cooperation (see Chapter 6).

There are two main types of employee participation. Firstly, there is share participation (part-ownership of the company). The European Commission recommends that private organisations should encourage employees to become part-owners of the enterprise for which they work, so that they can readily identify with the firm's success. Secondly, there is participation in the working environment. Structured work groups are formed, and the groups' responsibilities are increased. Emphasis is placed on common tasks and on job rotation. This form of participation makes the individual's role more flexible, and the employee becomes more adaptable, and more responsive to change.

4 Negotiation. The conflict between employers and employees is often resolved through collective agreements. However, in Britain, unlike other countries in the EEC, negotiation and collective bargaining are mainly concerned with salaries and conditions of employment. The European Commission recommends that collective agreements ought to be much wider, and cover such aspects of change as investment plans, location, takeovers and mergers, as well as plant closures.

Communication, participation and negotiation do not resolve all the problems which change creates. When conflict is not resolved by these measures, the parties seek independent *arbitration* and employees can resort to an *Industrial Tribunal*.

Communication

Communication between people is common to all jobs and is one of the most important activities in any organisation. Organisations are able to improve their efficiency by controlling operations, coordinating functions and motivating employees through communication. Communication techniques give business organisations the means to inform and persuade people to respond positively to change.

All forms of communication have four basic elements:

1 The message. People communicate in order to pass on a message. The variety in the content of business messages is enormous: messages range from simple signs, such as 'Enquiries', through verbal requests or instructions, to complex financial or technical reports.

2 A source – the transmittor. All messages arise from a source. Communication can only take place when a message is transmitted. Communication is not taking place if facts, opinions and ideas are never expressed.

3   A medium – transmission.   There are many formal methods which a person can choose to transmit information in business – letters, memos, reports, etc. Equally important are the informal methods, such as facial expression, posture and other forms of 'body language'.

4   A receiver.   Communication only becomes complete when the message is received. People in business receive orders, instructions, reports, etc., which often require them to perform some action. However, it is not realistic to assume that a receiver will always respond to a message or, if a response does occur, that it will be performed in the way the transmittor intended. Messages can be misunderstood, and are frequently misinterpreted.

Communication within the organisation

The purpose of internal communication

It is important for business efficiency that internal messages are understood. The purpose of most formal internal communication is to initiate action, and the performance and efficiency of an employee will be influenced by the effectiveness of internal communication. Messages are transmitted for a variety of reasons, the following being some of the most important:

1   Informing – presenting fact.   A lot of business communication occurs because people have to be kept informed. Managers have to be given information on all aspects of an organisation to enable them to control the organisation's activities. Employees have to be informed of changes which will directly affect their working environment, such as changes in safety procedures or the introduction of new technology. They will also have to be informed of changes in the conditions of employment, such as wage rates, fringe benefits and pension schemes.

2   Commanding – giving instructions.   If an employer wants full cooperation from an employee, it is unwise to issue direct commands. Cooperation has to be encouraged rather than commanded. Nevertheless, when tasks are delegated, orders and instructions have to be issued. If the transmittor – who is generally the supervisor – wants cooperation, then instructions have to be communicated in a considerate manner.

3 Negotiating – presenting a case. Differences in opinion are common in all human activity. A person's responsibilities, experience, knowledge, attitude and personality will colour his opinions and make conflict an inevitable part of an organisation's activities. Sectional interests, for example, create conflict and make negotiation a common form of business communication: departmental heads have to argue a case for more resources, trade union leaders have to negotiate for increased wages, government ministers have to persuade their Cabinet colleagues to approve changes in policy.

4 Reporting – presenting findings. Reports can be routine daily statements on such things as sales, absenteeism, costs and so on; or they can be used to present the findings of an investigation, such as an auditing or market research exercise. In many instances, a report will include recommendations or suggested solutions.

5 Coordinating – organising people. In order to coordinate activity it is necessary to keep people and departments fully informed about plans and policies. For example, if an organisation is planning to hold an exhibition, then all the departments involved should be given details of what is expected from them in terms of time, personnel and equipment. Communication is used to clarify responsibilities and improve coordination.

6 Cooperating – improving teamwork. Coordination between different sector of an organisation will be effective only if the sectors cooperate. Cooperation is improved when participants in a joint exercise agree with the goals and objectives. To achieve agreement, most organisations have developed systems of committees where different members of a team can learn about corporate goals and strategies, and at the same time contribute to the plans. Communication improves planning and teamwork.

7 Motivating and influencing attitudes. Committees can help departmental managers to become more committed to an organisation's plans, but the success of any exercise is ultimately dependent on the participants. Communication can be used to increase the involvement of people in an organisation's activities. Managers, by talking to employees and by taking notice of their needs, can attempt to encourage and motivate them and so improve their performance.

It is likely that communication will take place for more than one reason: a supervisor could be instructing a subordinate and at the same time motivating him. Whatever the reason for messages, organisations will be more efficient if communication is effective. The effectiveness of communication can be improved in the first instance by selecting the most appropriate route and the most appropriate method.

— The routes of internal messages —

1 Downwards. The formal information in an organisation generally flows from the higher to the lower level. Commands, instructions, decisions, plans and delegated tasks are passed down the line management system through supervisors and managers to subordinates.

2 Upwards. Apart from reporting, it is rare for formal information to flow from a lower level to a higher level. Some organisations, however, have developed formal systems such as staff development interviews and joint consultative committees to encourage the upward flow of ideas and opinions.

3 Horizontal. The need for coordination between different depart ments means that communication between people at the same level in an organisation's hierarchy is common. This is particularly true of departmental heads who frequently meet in committees in all organisations.

4 Multi-direction. Informal communication such as gossip and rumour flows in all directions. A grapevine flourishes on misunderstanding, and concentrates on sensational and often distorted interpretations of a message. Where formal methods of communication are not effective, then generally informal methods are strong and often lead to misinterpretation and inefficiency.

The flow of information and the extent of rumour and gossip provide some guide to the effectiveness of an organisation's communication. Organisations can improve their efficiency by analysing the flow and attempting to make formal methods more effective. The formal organisational chart is important in this respect because it shows employees where formal messages *should* be sent. Financial reports go to the accounts manager and the chief executive. Production plans go from the production manager down the line to the factory operatives. Absenteeism is reported to the supervisor.

Communication is made more effective if it is transmitted to the appropriate person. In addition, it is important to select the most suitable method. The selection will depend on:

(a) The content of the message. Is it confidential?
(b) How quickly the message has to be sent. Can the telephone be used?
(c) To whom the message is to be sent. Is there more than one appropriate receiver? If there is, then copies will be required.
(d) Is a permanent record of the message required? If it is, then oral methods cannot be used.

The methods which can be selected are:

Oral

1 Spoken instructions. Face-to-face contact between supervisor and subordinate is the most common method of communicating instructions. If the organisation is authoritarian, like the armed forces, then the communication is almost always downwards through the line of command.

2 Interviews are very common when employees are selected. They also take place when a person is considered for promotion or is being disciplined. Interviews give the interviewee the opportunity to ask questions and to state a point of view. They thus provide a means of upward communication.

3 Committee meetings. Committees exist in all types of organisation. The range of committee work generally is very wide and includes library committees in colleges, finance committees in commercial organisations, and Select Committees in the House of Commons. Committee work in business can be a major part of a manager's and administrator's work and provides the best opportunity for inter-departmental (horizontal) communication.

4 Telephones have the advantage of speed and availability. The existence of the telephone encourages communication and facilitates coordination and cooperation.

5 Casual conversation is predominant in the informal structure of an organisation. It is important for the formal structure in that it gives managers the opportunity to try out ideas and plans in an informal environment.

Body language

Messages can be passed without the use of spoken language: a nod, wink, shrug, frown or glance can convey its own special meaning. The attitudes of people are frequently indicated by gestures, facial expressions and bearing rather than by the spoken word. The ability to observe these 'body signs' is an important part of communication: it is a social skill.

Written

1 Letters are not usually used as an internal method of communication. They are used to inform people about employment matters such as appointment or promotion, and they are therefore common in the personnel departments. But other departments will tend to use memos and standard forms rather than personal letters.

2 Memoranda. Internal memos provide a written record of communication between people in an organisation. It is common for several copies to be made so that those involved in a decision or activity can be kept informed. The content of memos is varied: they are often used to initiate action or to summarise an agreed course of action.

3 Manuals. The established practices of an organisation are sometimes written in manuals or similar instruction documents. Manuals provide a reference for employees, and the information in them can range from broad policy decisions to detailed instructions on routine tasks.

4 Reports. Reporting is a common activity in organisations. There are technical reports, financial reports, research reports, personnel reports, marketing reports and so on. It is usual for most reports to present a collection of facts, to describe alternative solutions to a problem, to state conclusions and to submit recommendations.

5 **Minutes** are formal written records of meetings. They record what has been agreed and summarise the main point of any discussion.

6 **Notice boards/circulars.** Organisations sometimes use impersonal methods to communicate general information. Notices on safety and welfare are often transmitted by circulars or notice boards.

The developments in microelectronics has meant that many organisations now transmit information using computer terminals or fax machines. The various types of written information which are listed above still exist but are sent electronically instead of manually.

– Feedback – response to a message –

Messages which are received will normally create a response in the recipient. The response may not be what the transmittor intended, in that it could be a frown or a shrug, but any response to a message is called 'feedback'. Feedback indicates whether the message has been understood and accepted. A recipient can respond with informal gestures or he can choose some of the methods of communication which are listed above, such as conversation, letter, report, etc.

One-way communication: authoritarian-style leadership

One-way communication takes place when the transmittor does not expect, and does not get, a response from the receiver (Fig. 21.1). This type of communication is prevalent in organisations which are authoritarian in the way they deal with employees. In an authoritarian system managers issue commands, supervisors order subordinates to perform tasks, and foremen give direct instructions to operatives.

Transmittor ⟶ Designs the ⟶ Selects the ⟶ *Receiver*
message   medium

Fig. 21.1   One-way communication

In one-way communication, there is no guarantee that the message has been received, and consequently inefficient action through misunderstanding can occur.

Two-way communication: democratic-style leadership

Those organisations which want to avoid misunderstanding and to make communication more effective will encourage feedback. By examining the response to a message, a manager can assess whether the message has been understood, and at the same time he can gauge the extent of an employee's motivation (Fig. 21.2). The desire for feedback – that is, consultation – will in itself help to encourage an employee. This type of participative or people-centred management is found when there is democratic-style leadership.

Fig. 21.2 Two-way communication

Organisations are traditionally authoritarian in the way they communicate with employees. However, people-centred management is growing, and feedback and participation are being encouraged.

_____ The problems of internal _____ communication

Feedback helps the transmittor to learn whether the message has been understood. But the communication process is complicated: messages and responses are not always what they seem and feedback is no guarantee of effective communication. At each stage of transmission, the message or response can be distorted (Fig. 21.3).

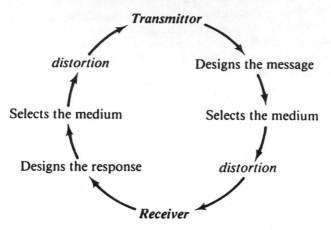

Fig. 21.3 Distortion in communication

Some common causes of distortion or breakdown in communication are:

Perception.   Differences in perception are a major cause of distortion. People are different and it is common for messages to be perceived in different ways. We all interpret messages according to our experience, motives and state of mind. For example, suspicion, anger, frustration, shyness and confusion can distort our ability to communicate and to respond to messages.

Language problems.   Careless use of language is a common cause of misunderstanding. Technical language, jargon and abbreviations, as well as ambiguity, can confuse the receiver. A common example is the use of legal jargon in government publications. Further problems can arise in communicating with those for whom English is not the first language.

Vague purpose.   Communication can be ineffective when the transmittor has not clearly thought out why, or for whom, the message is being transmitted – for example, issuing a command when consultation is necessary, or sending a report on education standards to the housing department in a local authority.

Inappropriate medium. Messages can be delayed by selecting an inappropriate medium – written messages are obviously slower than oral messages. In addition, selection of the wrong medium can cause other problems: for example using casual conversation, which could be overheard, to pass on confidential information.

Failure to communicate. A breakdown in communication sometimes occurs because an employee informs some, but not all, appropriate recipients. This often happens when the chain of command is by-passed and a subordinate ignores his immediate superior and sends messages directly to a higher authority.

Status, social distance. There are occasions when communication becomes distorted because of the different status of the participants. For example, when a managing director is discussing a problem with a new recruit or an operative, there can be a degree of stiffness and formality which impairs the discussion.

Red tape, bureaucracy. Communication often breaks down in large organisations because of the number of employees involved. Messages in highly centralised organisations can be impersonal, inflexible and ineffective because bureaucracy creates 'red tape': many internal messages are not specifically designed for the individuals who will receive them.

Location. Geographical distance between participants can cause distortions in communication. It is more difficult to communicate with people overseas, for example, and with salesmen or with government inspectors who spend much of their time out of the office.

Distraction of the receiver. Communication can be made ineffective when the receiver does not give his full attention to the message. An employee might be distracted by family problems, ill health, or even noise, which affect his ability to interpret a message.

Hostility between the participants. A poor relationship between two people will tend to distort their communication. An employee who has not been promoted, or a supervisor who feels let down by a subordinate, will generally find it difficult to communicate effectively while the feeling of grievance persists.

Stress or frustration. The work in organisations can cause tension and stress in people. Repetitive and boring work, or the failure to have good work recognised, will tend to cause frustration and strain which will affect an employee's performance and distort his ability to communicate. Conflict in organisations is often a result of misunderstanding caused by stress.

The grapevine. The grapevine, or informal methods of communication, can establish opinions which formal communication is unable to change. Rumour thrives on distorted and sensational interpretations of information, and it can distort an employee's ability to perceive the true situation.

— Improvements in communication —

The efficiency of an organisation depends on the effectiveness of internal communication. Because people are different, communication between employees will always be a problem. The twelve sources of misunderstanding which are outlined above illustrate the extent of the difficulties in creating effective communication. Organisations can meet this problem in the following ways:

Improve communication skills

Courses have been designed which will help to improve an employee's understanding of communication. The two parts of such courses are:

1 Social skills. Awareness of other people is an essential requirement for effective communication. If employees are more sensitive to the different attitudes and motivations of others, then relationships will improve and the distorting effect of different perceptions will be reduced.

2 Technical knowledge. An employee can learn to improve his technical ability to communicate by understanding (a) the different roles in organisations and who should receive a particular message; (b) the most appropriate medium for a particular message (letter, memo, telephone, etc.); (c) when messages should be communicated; and (d) the need for feedback, and the need to recognise signs in body language (nods, frowns, winks, etc.).

Decentralisation

Red tape and long lines of communications are common in highly centralised organisations. Government departments are notorious for their bureaucratic, formal methods of communication. However, it is unavoidable that the central government should have an elaborate system of rules and regulations: the Government has to have a standard approach to the provision of services to ensure fairness and equity. It is a mistake to believe that bureaucracies are necessarily inefficient – all organisations exhibit some characteristics of bureaucracy. The problem is that centralisation can lead to ineffective communication and poor control.

Large organisations can attempt to overcome this by decentralisation – that is, by greater delegation. In decentralisation, the organisation is divided into several autonomous units and each unit is responsible for its own performance.

Motivation and participation

Organisations can use the grapevine as a source of feedback rather than as a source of rumour and misunderstanding. The formal organisation can also use informal relationships to induce greater commitment from employees. The theories of McGregor, Maslow and Herzberg (see Chapter 6) can help organisations to improve their internal communication. Communication can be made more effective by praising effort and encouraging employees to perform better, by recognising work which is well done, and by giving people more responsibility for their own tasks.

The problems of hostility, stress and frustration can be reduced by increased employee participation. For example:

1 Job enlargement means that the employee carries out a series of different tasks where the level of difficulty and responsibility remains the same (horizontal move in the hierarchy). For example, a shop assistant could move from one department to another. The different working environments relieve monotony, boredom and frustration, and improve communication.

2 Job enrichment. In job enrichment, the employee is given a greater variety of tasks which differ in difficulty and the level of responsibility (vertical move in the hierarchy). For example, office workers could be given a range of jobs from dealing with the incoming post to helping the personnel department recruit a new colleague. The increased responsibility provided by job enrichment gives greater job satisfaction and reduces stress and hostility.

3 Job rotation. There are several problems which are associated with job enlargement and job enrichment: the employees might not have the skill and knowledge to transfer from one job to another, the trade unions might object, the employee could demand more pay for increased responsibility, and so on. These problems can be avoided by job rotation, where employees learn several minor skills which form a complete process. A team is formed and the team members can rotate the jobs democratically.

Job rotation occurs in all types of employment. For example, Volvo and Saab apply the technique to the production of cars; the Halifax Building Society rotates a team in its Head Office.

Job rotation increases individual responsibility, reduces boredom and improves understanding. It also increases employee cooperation and breaks down barriers to effective communication.

___ The external communications ___ of companies

The image of an organisation is determined to a large extent by its external communication – whether with shareholders, suppliers, customers or the general public. Depending on the intended recipient, a business can use several different methods of communication.

Annual reports and accounts

Every company is required to send a directors' report to its shareholders each year, and the Companies Act 1948–85 require the following information to be included:

1 The Profit and Loss Account. Companies must disclose items of expenditure and income as well as any appropriations from profits. The intention is that the directors should provide a 'true and fair view' of the financial position of the company, and any material item which is unusual and significant, or arises from a change in the basis of accounting, should be disclosed.

2   The Balance Sheet.   The published Balance Sheet must show the share capital and the reserves, any liabilities and provisions such as loans and taxation, and the fixed and current assets. Since the valuation of assets and the quantification of liabilities relies on the judgment of the directors, then the Balance Sheet should be read in conjunction with additional notes made by the directors and the auditors.

3   Source and Application of Funds Statement.   All companies with a turnover in excess of £25000 per annum are required to produce a funds flow statement which should show the sources from which money has come into the company and the way the money has been used in the operations of the business.

4   Report of the Auditors.   Since the directors use their judgment when calculating such items as the value of assets and liabilities, depreciation charges and the value of stock, then the auditors' report must contain explanation of the methods which have been used. Very often, the auditors' report contains far more detail than the other financial statements.

In addition to financial matters, the directors' report is required to highlight details of other types of information, such as political and charitable donations, the earnings of individual directors where they exceed £60000 a year, and the value of exports.

Non-financial reports

The concern which is currently expressed about the social costs and social responsibilities of private organisations has led to an increased demand for information other than financial to be publicly disclosed. The following list illustrates some of the items of 'non-financial' information which companies could produce: *(a)* an outline of social objectives; *(b)* an environmental report; *(c)* a statement on the company's commitment to racial and sex equality; *(d)* a declaration on industrial relations policy; *(e)* an analysis of productivity per employee.

Advertising and other communication with customers and clients

The public image of a company is influenced by its advertising and its relationship with customers/clients. Companies have a wide choice of advertising media: television, posters, newspapers, direct mail, exhibitions and displays. Advertising agencies will advise companies on the best media to use.

Dealing with customer complaints and enquiries requires a degree of sensitivity and understanding which is characteristic of good internal communication. Prompt and sympathetic replies to complaints, as well as accurate invoices and statements, not only promote sales but also enhance a company's image.

Reports to journalists

The image of a company depends on its formal public reports and its communication with customers. In addition, communication with the press, radio and television has become an important aspect of public relations. The methods of communication include special reports, briefing groups and question and answer sessions, all of which are designed to improve public understanding of business as well as to increase a firm's prestige.

—— Government communication ——

Government ministers and local authority councillors communicate with the press, radio and television even more than private enterprise does: government policy requires public understanding if it is to succeed. The problem which faces the Government is that there are many different messages required and many different recipients. The many different messages arise from changes in policies which can affect such diverse groups as pensioners, school leavers, tax payers, the disabled, the unemployed, other governments, and so on.

The main methods of communication which the Government uses are:

1 Green and White Papers. Changes in legislation must be approved by Parliament. The Government sometimes publishes its ideas about proposed changes in policy in a *Green Paper*. This is a discussion document which provides feedback to ministers and civil servants; analysis of the reaction to its proposals helps the Government to formulate policy in a more realistic light. A *White Paper* is a formal government report which will generally deal with one specific issue, such as unemployment or education. Some are published on a routine basis, such as the White Paper on Public Expenditure which is published annually. Others are issued only when changes in policy are to be reported.

2 Popular media. As with commercial organisations, the Government uses television, posters and newspapers to inform – either the total electorate or special groups, such as tax payers. Apart from election material, the content of government communication is mainly either social (for example, health warnings) or it seeks to explain and give details of changes in policies.

3 Official publications. Government policy is so extensive and complicated, and affects so many different groups, that the Government issues many hundreds of different explanatory leaflets on changes in policy. In addition, the Central Statistical Office and the government departments provide a statistical information service. The information which they publish covers all aspects of business activity: population, labour, production, prices, finance, exports and so on.

───────── Exercises ─────────

Comprehension

1 How can employers attempt to resolve conflict?

2 List the basic elements of effective communication.

3 Give examples of oral communication in business.

4 Define 'body language'.

5 What is the 'grapevine' in an organisation?

Research

1 Why is conflict inevitable in a changing environment?

2 Explain why it is essential for organisations to try to ensure that internal communication is effective, and assess the methods

organisations can use to make internal communication more effective.

3 Analyse the main methods the Government uses to communicate with the general public.

Project

Select one national company and collect examples of its methods of external communication.

APPENDIX ONE: —— POPULATION —— STATISTICS

Table A1.1 Population changes and projections 1901 to 2021

United Kingdom   Thousands
Average annual change

	Population at start of period	Live births	Deaths	Net natural change	Net civilian migration and other adjustments	Overall annual change
Census enumerated						
1901–11	38 237	1091	624	467	− 82	385
1911–21	42 082	975	689	286	− 92	194
1921–51	44 027	824	555	268	− 67	201
1931–51	46 038	785	598	188	+ 25	213
Mid-year estimates						
1951–61	50 290	839	593	246	+ 6	252
1961–66	52 807	988	633	355	+ 12	367
1966–71	54 643	937	644	293	− 40	253
1971–76	55 907	766	670	96	37	60
1976–81	56 206	705	662	43	− 8	35
1981–82	56 352	722	669	53	− 99	− 46
1982–83	56 306	722	660	62	− 21	41
1983–84	56 347	718	652	66	+ 47	112
1984–85	56 460	745	659	86	+ 72	158

Table A1.1 *continued*

United Kingdom Thousands
Average annual change

	Population at start of period	Live births	Deaths	Net natural change	Net civilian migration and other adjustments	Overall annual change
Projections (1985-based)						
1987–91	56891	804	647	157	− 17	140
1991–96	57452	834	645	190	− 17	172
1996–2001	58312	795	648	146	− 17	129
2001–06	58957	732	654	78	− 17	61
2006–11	59259	713	663	50	− 17	33
2011–16	59422	736	677	59	− 17	41
2016–21	59629	763	694	69	− 17	52

Source: *Social Trends*, 1987

Table A1.2   Sex and age structure of the population

United Kingdom Millions

	0–4	5–14	15–29	30–44	45–59	60–64	65–74	75–84	85+	All ages
Census enumerated										
1901	4.4	8.0	10.8	7.5	4.6	1.1	1.3	0.5		38.2
1911	4.5	8.4	11.2	8.9	5.6	1.2	1.6	0.6		42.1
1921	3.9	8.4	11.2	9.3	7.0	1.5	1.9	0.7		44.0
1931	3.5	7.6	11.8	9.7	8.0	1.9	2.5	1.0		46.1
Mid-year estimates										
1941	3.4	6.8	9.2	10.3	8.5	2.3	3.2	1.3		44.9
1951	4.3	7.0	10.2	11.2	9.6	2.4	3.7	1.8		50.3
1961	4.3	8.1	10.3	10.5	10.6	2.8	4.0	1.9	0.3	52.8
1971	4.5	8.9	11.8	9.8	10.2	3.2	4.8	2.2	0.5	55.9
1976	3.7	9.2	12.4	10.0	9.8	3.1	5.1	2.3	0.5	56.2
1981	3.5	8.1	12.8	11.0	9.5	2.9	5.2	2.7	0.6	56.4
1983	3.6	7.6	13.1	11.1	9.4	3.2	5.0	2.8	0.6	56.3
1984	3.6	7.4	13.3	11.2	9.3	3.3	4.8	2.9	0.7	56.5

Table A1.2 *continued*

	0–4	5–14	15–29	30–44	45–59	60–64	65–74	75–84	85+	All ages
1985										
Males	1.9	3.7	6.8	5.7	4.6	1.5	2.2	1.0	0.2	27.6
Females	1.8	3.5	6.6	5.6	4.7	1.7	2.8	1.9	0.5	29.0
Total	3.6	7.3	13.4	11.3	9.3	3.1	4.9	2.9	0.7	56.6
Projections (1985-based)										
1987		10.7	13.5	11.6	9.2	8.0		3.8		56.9
1991		11.0	12.9	12.1	9.5	7.9		4.0		57.5
1996		11.7	11.6	12.6	10.5	7.7		4.2		58.3
2001		12.0	10.8	13.2	11.0	7.6		4.4		59.0
2006		11.7	11.0	12.6	11.6	7.9		4.5		59.3
2011		11.1	11.7	11.3	12.1	8.8		4.5		59.4
2015		10.8	12.0	10.6	12.6	9.1		4.5		59.6

United Kingdom — Millions

Source: *Social Trends*, 1987

APPENDIX TWO: — SUPPLY AND — DEMAND ANALYSIS

— Demand —

(i)   Changes in demand caused by changes in price
In Fig. A2.1, when the price falls from P_1 to P_2 more people buy the product, and Q_1 increases to Q_2. However, as shown in Fig. A2.2, when

Quantity demanded increases

Fig. A2.1   Extension along an existing demand line

the price of a product increases, then fewer people buy the product and the market contracts.

Fig. A2.2 Contraction along an existing demand line

(ii) Elasticity of demand
Elasticity of demand measures the response of demand to changes in price. Demand is *inelastic* when a change in price causes only a small response in demand (Fig. A2.3). When the proportionate change in demand is greater than the price change, then demand is *elastic* (Fig. A2.4).

(iii) Shifts in demand (changes in demand caused by changes in the market)
Changes in demand which occur even when the price remains constant are called *shifts* in demand. Shifts occur primarily because of changes in fashion, income, the price of other goods, advertising and the introduction of new products. When a shift occurs (as in Figs. A2.5 and A2.6), the whole relationship between price and demand changes, and a new demand line is formed.

— **285** —

Fig. A2.3 Inelastic demand line

Fig. A2.4 Elastic demand line

Fig. A2.5 Shift (increase) in demand

Fig. A2.6 Shift (decrease) in demand

Supply

(i) Changes in supply caused by changes in price

If we assume that costs remain constant then, since profits equal price less costs, a price increase leads to an increase in profits; in the longer term, profits attract more firms into an industry and supply increases (Fig. A2.7). Conversely, a fall in price squeezes profits, firms have to leave the industry and supply decreases (Fig. A2.8).

(ii) Shifts in supply

Even when the price remains constant, producers can change the amount they produce. The factors which cause a shift in supply are primarily related to efficiency. For example, improvements in production brought about by capital investment can cause an increase (shift) in supply (Fig. A2.9). Conversely, inefficient management and industrial disputes can lead to a reduction (shift) in supply (Fig. A2.10).

Fig. A2.7 Extension along an existing supply line

Fig. A2.8 Contraction along an existing supply line

Fig. A2.9 Shift (increase) in supply

Fig. A2.10 Shift (decrease) in supply

— Interaction of supply and demand —

Figs A2.11–15 provide examples of the market acting as a mechanism. Fig. A2.11 shows how price – in a competitive market – will stabilise at the point where supply equals demand (point of equilibrium). Disturbance of the equilibrium is brought about either by shifts in supply (e.g. new technology, strikes) or by shifts in demand (e.g. changes in income, fashion).

Example 1: Reduction in supply

Figs. A2.12 and A2.13 illustrate how a reduction (shift) in supply causes the price to rise, and as a result demand contracts until a new equilibrium point is reached at P_3Q_2.

Example 2: Reduction in demand

Similarly, Figs. A2.14 and A2.15 show a reduction (shift) in demand causing the price to fall, and as a result supply contracts until a new equilibrium point is reached at P_3Q_2.

Fig. A2.11 Equilibrium of supply and demand

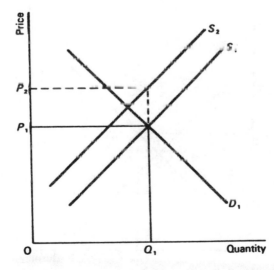

Fig. A2.12 Reduction in supply: in the short run, customers continue to buy the product and the price is forced up to P_2

Fig. A2.13 Reduction in supply: in the long run, P is considered too high by many buyers and demand contracts to a new equilibrium at P_3Q_2

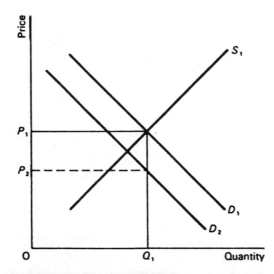

Fig. A2.14 Reduction in demand: in the short run, suppliers are unable to adjust to the shift in demand and the price falls to P_2

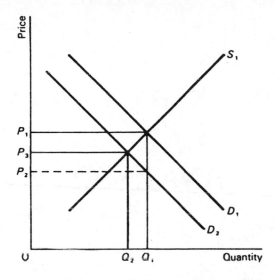

Fig. A2.15   Reduction in demand: in the long run, P_2 forces many suppliers out of business and supply contracts to a new equilibrium at P_3Q_2

APPENDIX THREE: —— BREAK-EVEN —— ANALYSIS

Consider two companies which manufacture identical products which are sold for £3.00 each. The fixed costs of both firms are £100000; and the variable cost per unit for Company A is £0.50, and for Company B is £1.00. The production capacity of both firms is 60000 units.

From this information, the following tables and diagrams can be constructed:

Company A

Output	Fixed costs (£)	Variable costs (£)	Total costs (£)	Average costs (£)	Average revenue (£)	Total revenue (£)	Profit/ Loss (£)
1000	100000	500	100500	100.50	3.00	3000	−97500
10000	100000	5000	105000	10.50	3.00	30000	−75000
20000	100000	10000	110000	5.50	3.00	60000	−50000
30000	100000	15000	115000	3.83	3.00	90000	−25000
40000	100000	20000	120000	3.00	3.00	120000	0
50000	100000	25000	125000	2.50	3.00	150000	+25000
60000	100000	30000	130000	2.16	3.00	180000	+50000

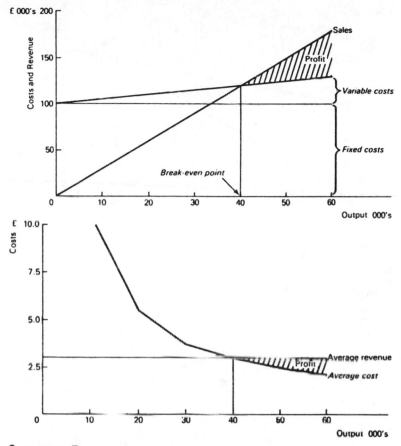

Company B

Output	Fixed costs (£)	Variable costs (£)	Total costs (£)	Average costs (£)	Average revenue (£)	Total revenue (£)	Profit/ Loss (£)
1 000	100 000	1 000	101 000	101.00	3.00	3 000	−98 000
10 000	100 000	10 000	110 000	11.00	3.00	30 000	−80 000
20 000	100 000	20 000	120 000	6.00	3.00	60 000	−60 000
30 000	100 000	30 000	130 000	4.33	3.00	90 000	−40 000
40 000	100 000	40 000	140 000	3.50	3.00	120 000	−20 000
50 000	100 000	50 000	150 000	3.00	3.00	150 000	0
60 000	100 000	60 000	160 000	2.67	3.00	180 000	+20 000

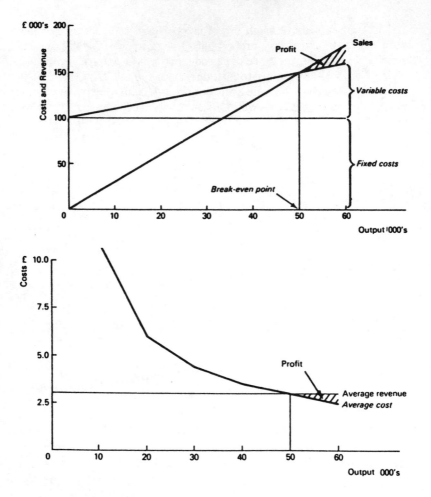

The diagrams illustrate three fairly obvious but important features of break-even analysis:

(a) A constant price is the average revenue.
(b) Average costs fall as the fixed costs become a smaller proportion of total costs.
(c) The break-even point always occurs when average costs equal average revenue.

These examples, although useful in showing the basic relationship between costs and profit, are simplified illustrations of real business activity. In practice, the price of a product or service is rarely constant; and, although it is reasonable to assume that average costs will fall initially – because fixed costs become a smaller proportion of total costs – in the long run, variable unit costs will increase as the diseconomies of scale set in.

APPENDIX FOUR:
– FINANCIAL RECORDS –
AND ANALYSIS

_____ Profit and Loss Account, _____ and Balance Sheet

Profit and Loss Account for *XYZ* Ltd

for the year ending (date)

Trading Account

		£	£
Income from sales			232000
Costs:	Raw materials	122000	
	Wages (direct)	68000	
	Fuel and Power	6000	196000
Gross Profit on Trading			£36000
Gross Profit (b/d)		36000	
Income from other sources		5000	41000
Expenses not incurred in manufacturing:			
	Debenture interest	800	
	Directors' fees	8000	

	£	£
Depreciation:		
Plant and Machinery	5600	
Motor Vehicle	600	
Wages and Salaries	12000	
Rent and Rates	1500	
Hire of equipment	1500	
Light and Heat	1000	
Advertising	1200	
Post and Telephone	750	
Other expenses	2050	35000
Net Profit before taxation		£6000

Appropriation Account

Net Profit (b/d)		6000
Taxation (40%)		2400
Net Profit after tax		£3600
Net Profit after tax	3600	
Balance from previous year	13500	17100
Deduct appropriations:		
Dividends proposed (gross)	3000	
Transfers to reserve	1100	4100
Balance on the Profit and Loss Account		£13000

Balance Sheet of XYZ Ltd as at (date)

	£	£
Fixed Assets:		
Premises at cost		10000
Plant and Machinery at cost	34200	
less depreciation	16800	17400
Motor Vehicle at cost	5000	
less depreciation	2400	2600
Long-term Capital		30000

	£	£
Current assets:		
Stock in trade	46 200	
Trade debtors	32 100	
Balance at Bank	1 000	
	79 300	
deduct Current Liabilities:		
Trade Creditors	52 300	
Working Capital	27 000	
deduct Reserve for future taxation	2 000	25 000
Net Worth of the Company		£55 000
Financed by:		
Issued Shared Capital:		
Ordinary Shares (20 000 at £1 each)		20 000
Preference Shares 5% (10 000 at £1 each)		10 000
Profit and Loss Account		13 000
General Reserve		4 000
Loan:		
10% Debentures		8 000
		£55 000

───── Ratio Analysis of *XYZ* Ltd ─────

Test of Liquidity

(i) Current ratio

Current Assets : Current Liabilities

79 300 : 52 300

1.5 : 1.0

(ii) Acid Test ratio

Current Assets *less* Stock : Current Liabilities

79 300 – 46 200 : 52 300

0.7 : 1.0

(iii) *Average period of collection of trade debts*
Debtors : Annual Sales
32 100 : 232 000
Period = 1:7 (almost 8 weeks)

Test of Profitability
(i) Rate of return on capital
Net Profit : Capital employed
6 000 : 30 000 + 27 000
6 000 : 57 000
0.105 : 1.0 (or 10.5%)

(ii) Profit to Sales
Net Profit : Sales
6 000 : 232 000
0.025 : 1.0 (or 2.5%)

Gross Profit : Sales
36 000 : 232 000
0.155 : 1.0 (or 15.5%)

Capital Gearing (ignoring reserves)
Ordinary shares : Preference shares + Debentures
20 000 : 10 000 + 8 000
20 000 : 18 000
1.1 : 1.0

—————— Depreciation ——————

The purpose of depreciation is to reduce the cost of fixed assets to a scrap or realisable value. If we examine the final accounts of *XYZ* Ltd, it can be seen that the amount of money used to reduce the cost of the motor vehicle, in addition to being deducted from the initial capital outlay in the Balance Sheet (£5000–£2400), is treated as a legitimate expense in the Profit and Loss Account (£600). The method used by *XYZ* Ltd is the *Reducing Balance Method*.

This method recognises that the value of an asset is higher during the first few years of ownership. The depreciation charge is a fixed percentage which is charged on an annual basis; consequently, each year the actual cost of depreciation falls. For example:

Motor Vehicle cost	£5000

Annual depreciation charge is
fixed at 20%.

Year 1 (20% of 5000) charge	1000
Balance	4000
Year 2 (20% of 4000) charge	800
Balance	3200
Year 3 (20% of 3200) charge	600
Balance	2600
and so on . . .	

In the *XYZ* Ltd Profit and Loss Account, the depreciation charge is £600 and the Balance Sheet shows the vehicle to be worth £2600, so it is three years old.

An alternative method which *XYZ* Ltd could have used is the *Straight Line Method* of depreciation. The scrap value of the vehicle is estimated and deducted from its initial cost. The remainder is written off over the expected life of the asset on a constant (fixed instalment) basis. For example:

Motor Vehicle cost £5000
Estimated life is 5 years
Estimated scrap value in five years time is £750

The annual depreciation charge will be:

$$\frac{5000 - 750}{5} = \frac{4250}{5} = £850$$

£850 will be charged to the Profit and Loss Account each year, and will be deducted from the cost of the motor vehicle each year until after five years it is completely 'written off'.

APPENDIX FIVE: INVESTMENT APPRAISAL TECHNIQUES

Pay-back method

The pay-back period is the length of time it takes for the earnings on an investment to cover the cost of the investment. The investment project with the shortest pay-back period is considered to be the most attractive. The technique has the advantage that it is fairly easy to understand, and it enables firms to assess future cash flows because it takes account of the cash received. It is particularly useful in period of rapid technological change when capital equipment can quickly become obsolete, and therefore the project which brings the quickest return is the most attractive.

The technique's main disadvantage is that, because it does not pay attention to any cash flows which occur after the pay-back period, it does not measure the long-term profitability of an investment project.

Example

A firm has to make a decision between two investment programmes each cost £3000. It is estimated that programme A will yield a constant, but relatively low return of £750 per annum for five years. Programme B will provide a relatively high initial return which will diminish as follows:

	Programme B	Programme A
Year 1	£1450	£ 750
2	950	750
3	600	750
4	300	750
5	100	750
Total return	£3400	£3750

As the graph shows, the pay-back period for A is four years and for B three years. The decision is to invest in B even though after four and a half years, A provides a better return.

—— Average rate of return method ——

The average rate of return is the ratio of net profit to capital cost. There are alternative methods of calculating the profit and the capital costs. For example, the capital could simply be the initial sum invested or it could include capital outlays over a period of time. Similarly, the returns could be an estimate of only the first year's profits, or they could be an average estimated yield over the assumed life of the project.

Example

A firm has to make a decision between two investment programmes. The initial cost of both programmes is £2000, and their estimated life is five years. It is predicted that the repairs and maintenance costs will be a constant £200 per annum. The average annual costs and the estimated returns on each programmme are:

Year	1	2	3	4	5	Total
Average capital cost	£400	400	400	400	400	£2000
Repairs and maintenance	£200	200	200	200	200	£1000
Estimated annual cost	£600	600	600	600	600	£3000
Estimated yield, programme A	£600	600	700	1000	1000	£3900
Estimated yield, programme B	£900	800	700	600	600	£3600

Average rate of return

	Year 1	Year 5
Programme A	100% (600:600)	130% (3900:3000)
Programme B	150% (900:600)	120% (3600:3000)

Programme B is likely to be preferred to programme A, even though in the long run A provides a better average rate of return. This is because it is more probable that predictions of events in the near future (short term) are more reliable than long-term estimates; and programme B looks a safer prospect in the short term.

The average rate of return method is considered to be more satisfactory than the pay-back method because it pays attention to cash flows. However, it does not take account of the incidence of the cash flows: the method becomes more effective when the timing of the cash flows is taken into account, and when care has been taken in the selection of which years to assess.

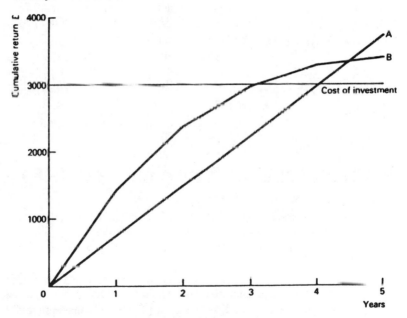

──────── Net present value ────────

The pay-back method and the average rate of return method do not recognise that cash in hand is worth more than cash received in future periods. Discounted cash flow techniques (DCF) do recognise this fact, and by using discount tables cash flows can be discounted at a rate which reflects the cost of capital.

Example

An investment project costs £3000, and it is estimated that it will yield an annual rate of return for five years.

Year	Net cash flow (£)	Discount factor (10%) from tables	Present value of cash flow
0	−3000	1.0000	−3000
1	+ 800	0.9091	+ 727.3
2	+ 800	0.8264	+ 661.1

Year	Net cash flow (£)	Discount factor (10%) from tables	Present value of cash flow
3	+ 800	0.7513	+ 601.0
4	+ 800	0.6830	+ 546.4
5	+ 800	0.6209	+ 496.7
	Net present value of yield (net) £		+ 32.5

− Internal rate of return method (IRR) −

IRR is the rate of interest which, when used to discount the cash flows of a proposed investment, reduces the net present value (npv) to 0. The discount rate is found by trial and error. Using the example above, we know that a discount rate of 10% gives a npv of +32.5. The IRR must be somewhere near to 10%. In the following example a rate of 12% gives a npv of −116.2. We can assume that the rate which gives a npv of zero is nearer to 10% than to 12%, and, as the example shows, a discount factor of 10.4% gives a npv of 0.

Year	Net cash flow (£)	Discount factor (12%)	Present value of cash flow (12%)	Discount factor (10.4%)	Present value of cash flow (10.4%)
0	−3000	1.0000	−3000	1.0000	−3000
1	+ 800	0.8929	+ 714.3	0.9058	+ 724.6
2	+ 800	0.7972	+ 637.8	0.8205	+ 656.4
3	+ 800	0.7118	+ 569.4	0.7432	+ 594.6
4	+ 800	0.6355	+ 508.4	0.6732	+ 538.6
5	+ 800	0.5674	+ 453.9	0.6098	+ 487.8
		npv	=−116.2	npv	= 0*

* figures do not add up exactly to zero because of rounding.

If the cost of the capital (plus a premium for risk since the cash flows are estimates) is higher than the IRR – in this example 10.4% – then the proposed investment should be rejected.

GLOSSARY

ACAS The Advisory Conciliation and Arbitration Service established by the Employment Protection Act, 1975 to act as an independent body which investigates industrial relations problems and helps to solve disputes between employers and employees.

Acid Test Ratio The ratio of current assets (less stock) and current liabilities.

Arbitration To submit a decision to an independent judge/referee.

Articles of Association The internal rules of a company dealing with the rights of members.

Audit An independent judgement/evaluation of records, especially financial records.

Authority The right to use power in an organisation.

Balance of Payments A financial summary, for one country, of all of the transactions which have taken place in international trade.

Balance of Trade A financial summary, for one country, of the transactions in goods (visible imports and exports) which have taken place in international trade.

Balance Sheet A statement of the financial position of a company at a certain date.

Bankrupt A person whose business has failed because outstanding debts cannot be paid.

Below-the-Line Advertising Sales promotion methods which are additional to advertising such as free gifts and discount schemes.

Body Language Messages conveyed by a person's bearing, gestures and facial expressions.

Branding   The use of trademarks, labels and packaging to enable customers to identify particular products.

Break-even Point   When total costs equals total sales revenue.

Budget   A financial plan based on future revenue and future spending.

Budget Deficit   Where actual expenditure exceeds planned expenditure or expected revenue.

Budget Surplus   Where actual expenditure is less than planned expenditure or expected revenue.

Business Plan   A plan which identifies the nature of a business and its main competitors and gives a financial assessment of future business activity.

Capital   The long-term funds and assets owned by, or loaned to, a business which are used in the operation of the business.

Capital Gains Tax   A tax on the profit gained from the sale of an asset.

Capital Gearing   The ratio of a company's debts (long-term borrowing) to the equity owned by shareholders.

Capital Expenditure   Where a company purchases an asset which will be used over a long period of time.

Capital Market   The market which deals with long-term loans (over 91 days).

Cash Flow   A statement showing balances of the anticipated flow of cash in and out of a business in a given period.

CBI   Confederation of British Industry: an organisation which represents employers which was formed under a Royal Charter in 1965.

Census of Population   A count of every person in the country.

Civil Service   The organisation which administers central government departments.

Collective Bargaining   Negotiations between employers and employees on pay and conditions of employment.

Conciliation   Persuading people in conflict to agree.

Conglomerate Companies   A company which deals in a wide range of different products.

Contract   Rules and conditions in agreements between people and/or organisations.

Contract of Employment   A contract between employer and employee which gives details of the conditions and terms under which a job is to be performed.

Corporation Tax   A tax levied on company profits.

CBA   Cost-benefit analysis: the evaluation of the costs and benefits of a project.

Cost-Plus Pricing   The average cost of a product or service plus a profit margin.

Current Asset   An asset which is either in cash or can be converted into cash within 12 months of the date of the Balance Sheet.

Current Liabilities   A debt which has to be paid within 12 months of the date of the Balance Sheet.

Data Protection   Regulations which govern how organisations can use information on individuals which is recorded and processed electronically.

Debentures   Long-term loans to companies which bear a fixed rate of interest and are redeemed at the end of a stated period.

Debt Factoring   An arrangement whereby a factoring house buys and then pays a firm's trade debts as they occur. The factoring house charges for this service.

Delegate, To   To give instructions, tasks or objectives to an individual in an organisation.

Demography   The distribution of age groups within the population structure.

Depreciation   An accounting technique which organisations use to provide for the future purchase of capital assets.

Desk Research   The collection of marketing information from published sources such as journals, magazines and company reports.

Direct Taxation   Taxes which are directly levied on income or capital.

Distribution   The methods used by organisations to get products to the customers.

Economies of Scale   Reductions in unit costs which result from increases in production or business activity.

EEC   European Economic Community, established in 1957 to develop economic, social and political integration amongst member states.

Exchange Rate   The price at which one currency can be exchanged for another.

External Economies   The benefits to an organisation of a particular geographical location.

Factors of Production   The essential elements needed for production to take place: raw materials/natural resources, equipment and people.

Forecasting   A semi-scientific prediction of future events, e.g. sales forecast.

Finance Lease   The user has the option to purchase at the end of the leasing period.

Fixed Assets   Assets which are not for sale but which a firm intends to use in the operation of its business.

Fixed Costs   Costs an organisation always has to pay, even when production and sales are not taking place, e.g. rent.

Formal Organisation   The organisation structure which has been designed by senior management.

Fringe Benefits   Alternative financial rewards such as pension schemes, sick pay, subsidised meals, company cars and private health care.

GATT   General Agreement on Tariffs and Trade, established in 1948 to promote agreement in international trading regulations.

GNP   Gross National Product: the total market value of the goods and services produced by a country in one year.

Goodwill   The reputation of a business and its trade connections.

Hire Purchase   A finance company pays for goods which a business obtains through a normal supplier, and the ownership remains with the finance company until the end of the payment period.

IMF   International Monetary Fund, established in 1944 to promote harmony in international monetary relations.

Indirect Taxation   Taxes which are levied on expenditure.

Induction   The practice of introducing a new employee to a job in an organisation.

Industrial Tribunal   A quasi-legal hearing to settle disputes between employers and employees.

Inflation   A constant increase in prices. The rate of the UK's inflation is measured by the Retail Price Index.

Informal Organisation   Social groups in organisations which can create pressure on the formal organisation because their beliefs, objectives and aspirations conflict with the organisation's objectives.

Inheritance Tax   A tax on the transfer of personal wealth.

Insolvency   The inability to pay debts when they are due.

Investment   The expenditure by a business on assets such as equipment and buildings which can be used in the future production of goods or services.

Invisible Exports/Imports   Services, such as insurance, banking and tourism, which are sold to foreign clients.

Job Description   A broad statement of the purpose, scope, duties and responsibilities of a particular job.

Job Specification   A detailed statement of the physical and mental qualities which a person would need to do a job.

Law of Diminishing Returns   The law states that as more and more resources are allocated to a fixed asset, then eventually output reduces or diminishes.

Level of Unemployment   The percentage of the working population who are out of work.

Limited Liability   The personal liability of the shareholder is limited to the amount invested in the company.

Line Management   An organisation where control is from the top and instructions are passed downwards.

Liquidation   When a business ceases to trade.

Liquidity   The cash in a business plus the business's ability to pay short-term debts.

Market Research   Investigation into the nature of a particular market, and into the attitudes and disposition of customers and clients in that market.

Marketing Mix   A combination of marketing functions such as sales promotion, advertising, pricing and distribution policy.

Memorandum of Association Defines the constitution and powers of a company and the scope of its activities.

Merger When two organisations agree to amalgamate.

MLR Minimum Lending Rate: the rate of interest, set by the Bank of England, to which the rates of interest of bank deposits and other lending rates are directly linked.

Monetary Policy Government control of the supply of money which is circulating in the economy.

Money Supply The total stock of money in the UK.

Money Market The market for short-term loans.

Monopoly A market dominated by one organisation.

Multi-national Corporations A private 'holding' company with shares in many overseas subsidiary companies.

National Income The value of the flow of goods and services in a country in one year.

Operating Lease Separates the use of equipment from ownership: the leasing company hires the equipment to a user. Ownership remains with the leasing company.

Opportunity Cost Having committed expenditure, it is the lost opportunity of spending money on alternative schemes.

Partnership An incorporated association of members governed by the Partnership Act, 1890.

Patent A monopoly right granted to the inventor of a product.

Policy A definition of what people in organisations must or must not do.

Preference Shares Shares which give their owners preference over ordinary shareholders in the payment of dividends.

Pressure Group Formal and informal groups of people who get together in order to influence the policies of organisations and of government.

Price Discrimination Different prices for the same product or service such as off-peak pricing practised by British Rail.

Primary Production Business activity which is mainly concerned with natural resources such as farming or mining.

Private Limited Company A company which restricts the issue of its shares to private individuals.

Privatisation Where control and ownership of an organisation is transferred from the public sector to the private sector.

Producer Goods Goods which are produced for other producers such as machinery.

Product Differentiation The use of packaging and labels to help customers to differentiate between products.

Productivity A measure of output in relation to costs.

Product Liability The responsibility an organisation has for injuries caused to a person by any defective products which they have manufactured.

Product Life-cycle   The growth and decline in the sales of a product.

Profit   The difference between the revenue earned and the expenditure incurred by a business in a given period of time.

Profit and Loss Account   A summary of the financial transactions which have taken place in an organisation during a specific period of time.

PSBR   Public Sector Borrowing Requirement: the difference between planned government income and expenditure.

Public Corporations   Organisations created by Parliament and owned by the State.

Public Limited Company   A company which issues shares on the Stock Exchange which are then sold to the public.

QUANGOs   Quasi-autonomous governmental organisations such as Industrial Tribunals.

Quota   A limit on the volume/amount of goods which can be imported into a country.

R&D   The research into, and the development of, new and existing products.

Redundancy   When a job is no longer required by an organisation.

Responsibility   Tasks and duties given to an individual in an organisation.

Revenue Expenditure   Where a company spends money but does not obtain a permanent asset.

RPI   Retail Price Index: a standard measure of the price of goods and services during a given period.

Secondary Production   Business activity which is mainly concerned with manufacturing, processing or assembly work.

Share Capital   The amount of money introduced into a company by shareholders.

Sole Traders   Businesses which are owned by a private person who uses his own money to run the business.

Source and Application of Funds   A statement which shows the sources from which money has come into a business and the way the money has been used in the operations of the business.

Stock   Raw materials, finished products or savings owned by a business.

Strategic Plan   A review of the aims of an organisation and identification of the main action to be taken to achieve them.

Takeover   Where one firm, without necessarily having the consent of the other firm, acquires sufficient shares to have a controlling interest.

Tariff   A tax imposed on imports.

TEC   Training and Enterprise Council. 82 were established in 1990/91 to foster economic growth and to contribute to the regeneration of local communities.

Tertiary Production   Business activity which is mainly concerned with providing a service such as transport, insurance and finance.

Theory X   Work-centred management.

Theory Y   People-centred management.

Tort   Wrongdoing such as injury to a person or an infringement of their rights.

Trade Mark   A sign used in connection with goods and services which helps customers to identify a particular business organisation.

Turnover   The total revenue derived from sales.

Unit Costs   Total costs divided by the number of units produced.

VAT   Value Added Tax, a tax imposed on products and services at every stage of production.

Variable Costs   Costs which vary with output or other business activities, e.g. raw material costs.

Vicarious Liability   Responsibility for the wrongdoing of others.

Visible Exports/Imports   Goods (not services) in international trade transactions.

Vital Statistics   Information on births, deaths and marriages collected by the Registrar General's Office.

Working Capital   Money which is available for day-to-day operations in a business.

Working Population   The total number of people who are eligible for work, i.e. all those who are in employment, those registered as unemployed, and the self-employed.

INDEX

OTHER TITLES AVAILABLE
IN TEACH YOURSELF

☐	0 340 50540 0	**Setting up a Business** Vera Hughes and David Weller	£5.99
☐	0 340 36513 7	**Basic Accounting** J. Randall Stott	£4.99
☐	0 340 55643 9	**Book-keeping** A. G. Piper	£5.99
☐	0 340 55843 1	**VAT: A Practical Handbook** David Lee	£5.99
☐	0 340 57399 6	**Business Writing** Mary Dunston Turner and Robert Louis Abrahamson	£5.99

All these books are available at your local bookshop or newsagent, or can be ordered direct from the publisher. Just tick the titles you want and fill in the form below.

Prices and availability subject to change without notice.

HODDER AND STOUGHTON LTD, Cash Sales Department, Bookpoint, 73c Milton Park, Abingdon, Oxon OX14 4TD, UK. If you have a credit card you may order by telephoning 01235 831700.

Please send cheque or postal order for the value of the book, and add the following for postage and packing:

UK including BFPO – £1.00 for one book, plus 50p for the second book, and 30p for each additional book ordered up to a £3.00 maximum.

OVERSEAS, INCLUDING EIRE – £2.00 for the first book, plus £1.00 for the second book, and 50p for each additional book ordered.
OR Please debit this amount from my Access/Visa Card (delete as appropriate).

CARD NUMBER ☐☐☐☐ ☐☐☐☐ ☐☐☐☐ ☐☐☐☐ ☐☐☐☐

AMOUNT £ ....

EXPIRY DATE ....

SIGNED ....

NAME ....

ADDRESS ....

....